Thinking Outside the Book

Thinking Outside the Book

Essays for Innovative Librarians

Edited by CAROL SMALLWOOD

Foreword by JOY M. GREINER

McFarland & Company, Inc., Publishers

Jefferson, North Carolina, and London

ALSO BY CAROL SMALLWOOD AND FROM MCFARLAND

Free or Low Cost Health Information:
Sources for Printed Materials on 512 Topics (1998)

Recycling Tips for Teachers and Libraries (1995)

Helpful Hints for the School Library:
Ideas for Organization, Time Management
and Bulletin Boards, with a Resource Guide (1993)

Free Resource Builder for
Librarians and Teachers, 2d ed. (1992)

Reference Puzzles and Word Games for Grades 7–12 (1991)

Library Puzzles and Word Games for Grades 7–12 (1990)

Current Issues Resource Builder: Free and
Inexpensive Materials for Librarians and Teachers (1989)

Health Resource Builder: Free and
Inexpensive Materials for Librarians and Teachers (1988)

COMPILED BY CAROL SMALLWOOD, BRIAN P. HUDSON,
ANN MARLOW RIEDLING AND JENNIFER K. ROTOLE

Internet Sources on Each U.S. State: Selected Sites
for Classroom and Library (2005)

LIBRARY OF CONGRESS CATALOGUING-IN-PUBLICATION DATA

Thinking outside the book : essays for innovative librarians /
edited by Carol Smallwood ; foreword by Joy M. Greiner.
p.   cm.
Includes bibliographical references and index.

ISBN 978-0-7864-3575-3
softcover : 50# alkaline paper ∞

1. Library science.   2. Library science — Technological innovations.
3. Librarians— Effect of technological innovations on.   4. Libraries
and community.   5. Public services (Libraries)   I. Smallwood, Carol, 1939–
Z665.T4965   2008   020 — dc22   2008018493

British Library cataloguing data are available

Cover art ©2008 Images.com

Manufactured in the United States of America

McFarland & Company, Inc., Publishers
Box 611, Jefferson, North Carolina 28640
www.mcfarlandpub.com

This collection is for
the innovative librarians
who shared their experiences

Table of Contents

PART 4: THE INTERNET

PART 5: VISION IMPAIRED

PART 6: HOSTING LIBRARY EVENTS

PART 7: THE CURRICULUM

PART 8: GRANTS

PART 9: PRESENTATIONS

PART 10: WORKING WITH YOUTH

PART 11: PUBLIC RELATIONS

PART 12: LIBRARY INSTRUCTION

PART 13: REVIEWING

PART 14: GOING DIGITAL

PART 15: WORKING WITH THE COMMUNITY

PART 16: THE WRITING WORLD

PART 17: MANAGEMENT

PART 18: DISTANCE EDUCATION

PART 19: LIBRARIANS HELPING ABROAD

PART 20: CONTINUING TO LEARN

Foreword

JOY M. GREINER

Thinking Outside the Book: Essays for Innovative Librarians delivers a resounding blow to the stereotypical librarian image. Editor Carol Smallwood has collected and organized an encyclopedia of progressive librarianship. The book is organized by subject which allows the person seeking information on a specific topic to readily access appropriate articles.

The contributors describe "what works" based on their experiences. Topics include preparing and delivering effective presentations, writing a successful grant proposal, the librarian as author or book reviewer, the changing dynamics of librarian and customer interaction, an innovative approach to library instruction, and services to special groups.

Thinking Outside the Book is a valuable resource for professional librarians and for students preparing for a career in information agencies of all types. The experiences described by librarians in the field provide excellent examples for faculty and students in schools of library and information science.

"Grant Writing" by Loriene Roy and Sara Albert offers practical guidelines for the librarian seeking funding from a variety of agencies. The authors give succinct and practical suggestions and provide specific guidelines for constructing the grant proposal. For example, the authors advise that librarians should read the grant application more than once, take time to know the rules for the particular agency and the specific grant, and find samples of funded grants to use for reference. Applicants are also admonished to carefully review the grant before they submit it.

In her essay, "Community Partnerships," Elizabeth M. Timmins describes innovative community partnerships implemented by enthusiastic librarians. She advocates that librarians participate in political activities such as State Legislative Day and talk with local representatives. She reports that city council members and a school district representative serving on the library board is a win-win situation.

Ruth A. Barefoot recommends in "Customers in the Driver's Seat" that librarians change places with customers, moving out of the seat of power and letting the customers take charge. Barefoot explains that the four principles in the San José Public Library are customers first, teach customers, reinvent environments, and enable staff. Barefoot cautions that this service model "has taken years to develop so don't try this overnight."

Margaret Lincoln's "The Traveling Museum Exhibition: A Resource for Learning" is a moving account of a traveling exhibition in Battle Creek, Michigan, from the U.S. Holocaust Memorial Museum. Lincoln secured a grant from the W.K. Kellogg Foundation to bring the exhibition on Oskar Schindler to the Temple Beth El in Battle Creek in 2002. Then, in 2005, the Art Center in Battle Creek was selected for another exhibition, Life in the Shadows: Hidden Children and the Holocaust. The educational and cultural activities that resulted from these exhibits are monuments to the human spirit.

Librarians interact with legislators and members of the city council. Funding agency representatives know their names and their organizations. They publish and review publications. Technology is their friend and a tool for teaching and communicating. Librarians are indeed visible beyond the circulation desk.

Preface

Thinking Outside the Book: Essays for Innovative Librarians is for public, school, special, and academic librarians seeking insider tips from innovative colleagues in the trenches. In these days of change, librarians must include innovation and creativity in their toolbox in order to further their careers and their profession. As Steve Jobs, cofounder of Apple Computers and Pixar Animation Studios, has noted, "Innovation distinguishes between a leader and a follower."

The 71 contributors to this book are located across the United States and represent public, research, music, law, business, university, or state libraries; media centers; and talking book centers. Most have several years of experience; many have doctorates; and several teach. They are in administration, are technology and Web specialists, hold offices, are volunteers, and work with youth. Many have been published, received awards, written successful grants, and founded organizations. Some have been librarians abroad as Fulbright scholars. All have track records of thinking outside the box and were eager to share.

If you are looking for ways to get your library noticed, increase its use, improve your collection, or widen your flexibility, let these successful professionals help you transform wannabe wishes into showcase models of success. Just a few of the topics include: traveling exhibitions, blogs, hosting authors, innovative community partnerships, multimedia story time, oral and written histories, and music in the library. Essays on the partnership of librarians and educators, using cybertorials, preserving local culture, and dealing with teen library employees inspire innovative solutions.

The 79 essays are topically arranged into twenty sections, covering a wide range of subjects important to today's librarian. While the essays are necessarily concise the spectrum of topics they cover is broad, and the contributors' insight and experience is meant to benefit librarians on every level, from the novice to the long-time professional.

Carol Smallwood, Editor

The Amplified Library

Grabbing Users by the Ears

ERIKA BENNETT *and* JAINA LEWIS

Libraries are often viewed as quiet places where peaceful people can enjoy silent activities. To the average library user, libraries and popular music may seem like unlikely companions, perhaps even opposing forces. We want to change the music-to-libraries relationship.

In our opinion, music can amplify libraries.

Music has recently taken a central and ubiquitous presence in people's lives. One in five Americans owns a portable MP3 player. College students say they love their iPods more than beer. In light of this wave of noise, libraries must check their service foundations and the durability of their music bearings.

We, the librarians behind the Amplified Library blog (www.amplifiedlibrary.blogspot. com), would like to recommend some tools to help library services pipe up in the world. Our blog focuses on creative ways to put a little more rock and roll into your library collection and programming, and it is written in a casual, conversational manner. The site is updated each weekday with the latest in music news, music publications, and event ideas. The following includes some of our best ideas to date regarding collection, reference tools, events, and services.

Collection: Energize Your Music Bins

Users

Surveys can be a great feedback tool. However, sometimes informal methods appeal more to the antiestablishment crowd (that is, teens and music lovers). As an experiment, place a whiteboard with the question, "What do you listen to?" by the CD racks. You can gather the results daily for a statistical breakdown.

Sometimes casual polls can offer valuable results because of their flexibility. Take a look at teen patrons' T-shirts. They just might reveal what bands and genres are held dear. (Note: Be wary when conducting this experiment. The 16-year-old in the Hall and Oates shirt is probably wearing it as a joke.)

Music Publications

Music trends may be fickle, but there are respectable gauges to measure the breadth of your popular music collection such as:

- Top 20 or 100 lists, like "The Rolling Stones's 500 Greatest Albums of All Time," can be easily found through your favorite search engine. Note the biases; search widely.
- Billboard Research Services publishes a number of reference lists for different years and genres.
- Magazines like *MOJO* offer compilation CDs that provide a great launching point for genre period ordering.
- Conduct research on the Rock's Backpages. Website at www.rocksbackpages.com. It offers "the ultimate library of rock music writing and journalism."
- Local record stores can offer discounts comparable with large media vendors. Explore the possibility of having a local expert help you select music.

Regional Events

Some cities are lucky enough to have radio stations that highlight local and independent music. Alternatively, local event calendars will reveal which acts are hot. Newspapers and regional magazines should have concert reviews and traveling show calendars. These will offer clues on what albums to keep handy. Consider buying an extra copy or two to coincide with big happenings, like you would with books and author events.

Rock and Roll Reference: Be a Rock Star Reference Librarian

Librarians aspire to be knowledge generalists. They set aside their personal opinions and provide objective, excellent informational services. Why would we approach music any differently? In order to provide proper rock-and-roll reference services, we cannot stress this enough: Keep up-to-date.

Your knowledge of early 90s Sting may come in handy somewhere down the line, but people ask about new music. Questions that begin "I heard this song on the radio..." or "When does the new album by _____ come out?" are common.

Some great sources for music news include:

- Music magazines. Examples include *Rolling Stone, Spin, Vibe, Billboard, Paste,* and UK magazines *NME, Mojo, Magnet,* and *Q.*
- Newspapers. Music reviews in newspapers. Don't forget regional reviews in free publications like the *Onion* and upcoming concert listings for your town.
- Podcasts. The National Public Radio pop culture podcast is great. MTV also offers several as well. Major music magazines like *Paste* have also started producing their own music review podcasts.
- TV. MTV's *Total Request Live* (a.k.a. TRL), et al. Pay attention to what patrons might be watching. Chances are that what they are watching is related to what they are listening to as well. What songs were featured on popular television shows this week? What is on the soundtrack for the newest hit movie?
- Teens. Consider having teen volunteers on hand afternoons and weekends.

- Web Sites. These include, among others, Allmusic.com, which lists biographies, full discographies, full member lists, and influences of different bands, and Pitchfork.com, which has reviews of new indie albums.
- Web 2.0 alerts. Keep up with new online services. For instance, Pandora.com offers an automatic listener's advisory. Patrons can create a custom radio station that gives users tracks from their favorite artists, interspersed with artists who sound similar.

Events: Outreach Creatively

Here is the place to walk your talk. Host music events at your library. Some ideas include:

- Listening parties for new music. Set up some couches, pop some popcorn, and dust off those turntables (or laptops) and treat your patrons to something they've come to only expect from their local record stores.
- Rock shows. Besides just attracting a new demographic, the library has the advantage of being a vice-free, all-age venue. The library can also strengthen its ties to the local community by showcasing local acts and music by its patrons.
- A musical lecture series. Enlighten not only your patrons, but also your staff. How about a songwriting workshop? Or a panel discussion on music censorship? The possibilities for lectures concerning music are endless. (If a lecture series seems too stuffy, consider showing MTV's *TRL*, the Grammy Awards or music-themed movies.)

Services: Put Your Patrons on the VIP List

Consider offering new services that not only appeal to a changing demographic but also showcase your commitment to popular music. Here are some ideas:

- Install listening stations. If bookstores can do it, why can't a library? This is a great way for patrons to preview music before checking it out.
- Consider offering iPods for checkout. Libraries like the South Huntington Public Library in New York have paved the way. IPods can be preloaded with music from the library's collection or even with audio books.
- Teens and young people communicate and find new music on social networking sites like MySpace.com and Facebook.com. Make a profile for your library so patrons can stay connected and receive updates on new acquisitions, events, and other important library news.
- Set aside a certain percentage of your acquisitions budget for patron requests. This is perhaps the best service you can offer.
- Promote! Promote! Promote! If you make big "loud" changes in your library, let people know. Consider advertising on local radio stations, making visits to high schools, or even putting up flyers around town. Pass out bookmarks shaped like guitars or library calendars that look like records. Do whatever it takes to let your public know that you rock.

An Embarrassment of Riches at an Academic Library

Let Patience, Alertness, a Positive Attitude, and a Little Luck Work for You

ANNE MARIE CANDIDO

It is a tribute to the flexibility of the library profession that it can often take advantage of — and sometimes even cater to — individual talents of librarians and library professionals. My experience working in an academic library has now evolved to such an extent over the 18 I have worked at the University of Arkansas Libraries that I thought perhaps my own story might be interesting enough to be included in a book such as this. I am sure that mine is only one of many good examples of how one's background and talents can actually shape a job in a library rather than be made to fit into a preexisting job description. As the library field becomes more complex and requires continual new focus, library directors and administrators are becoming increasingly flexible in their thinking about the nature of positions and the qualifications of applicants — even in academic and research libraries. Those of you just starting out in the library field should be encouraged by this trend, which is reflected in my own experiences described below — particularly if you are beginning your career doing work that you feel is not ideally suited to your talents.

A Manuscripts Processor

I begin at the beginning, when I was first hired in 1988 as a temporary manuscripts processor in Special Collections. I had a PhD in English by that time but no library degree, and I was looking for an interesting job at the university after teaching temporarily in the English Department and being an editor for the University of Arkansas Press for approximately two years. And so I was assigned to be the processor of a manuscript collection donated by John Williams, a prize-winning American writer. I was delighted to have such a position related to a literary figure that ideally required some literary knowledge. But after only three months, a permanent position came open in the library for an assistant to the director, which was conventionally regarded at the university as a high-level secretarial position, although, oddly enough, it was originally advertised as requiring a library degree. I did not have a library degree, but the director was willing to entertain the idea of hiring someone without this degree if the person had some academic experience and could write and edit letters, memoranda, reports, and other documents well enough for the demands of the position. Before I knew it, I was offered the job.

A Writer/Editor

Although I had the single title of assistant to the director, my primary duties evolved to become much more varied than I expected. I began editing brochures and handouts produced by reference librarians, overseeing the processing of dissertations, and performing administrative tasks involving personnel matters and public relations. Eventually my responsibilities included editing and proofing professional papers written by librarians who asked for this service to be sure that their work was written and organized as clearly as possible before they submitted it for publication or for acceptance at library conferences.

It was not long before I was unofficially considered the "library editor," and I was asked to produce a house style sheet for library personnel to consult when writing material for distribution to students, faculty, or any other readership outside the library. I soon joined a group of campus editors, who shared editing tips and their writing and editing experiences within other colleges and units. It was then that I began to feel that I was participating in the mission of the university and was gratified to know that I was being of some service to the profession and to the university besides being "just" an assistant to one or two people.

A Bibliographer

As a result of a literary interest that the director and I shared, I began to enter data into a Pro-Cite database for a bibliographic project the director was working on, and I became intimately acquainted with the project. When it became clear that the director did not have the time to devote to the project, he asked me to be a cobibliographer with him in the project, which consisted of compiling a bibliographic list of all the publications of New Directions Publishers. New Directions was the original and primary publisher of American writers such as Ezra Pound, William Carlos Williams, Thomas Merton, and Tennessee Williams, as well as many 20th-century European writers. Once again, I felt that this assignment went beyond the conventional borders of an "assistant to the director," and I felt fortunate that the director was interested in broadening my duties to this degree.

A Public Relations Coordinator

One other aspect of my job duties that was certainly atypical of my position had to do with public relations. As it happened, the director and I shared another interest: opera and American literature. And so I found myself designing a series of showings of recordings of opera and American short stories on film in the libraries' viewing room. The showings were free and open to the public, and I arranged for speakers to comment on them and to open discussion about each opera or short story. After the director retired in 1998, an interim director was appointed, and she extended my duties so that I served as chair of the library's Art Advisory Committee, which identified suitable artists to display their works in the library on a rotating basis.

A Subject Selector, Instructor, and Humanities Coordinator

A new, permanent dean was hired in 2000, and she saw my responsibilities in yet a different light. Even though I retained my duties as her "assistant," my duties as library editor to some degree, and many duties in public relations, the dean, knowing that I had graduate degrees in literature, asked if I would also be willing to be the book selector for literature as well as library liaison to the English Department. Subject selectors were just then being created in our library. I readily accepted this new assignment, and I even began to work at the reference desk for a few hours a week to get a sense of the needs students had in various fields, but especially in literature and foreign languages. In addition, I began teaching undergraduate and graduate students and faculty about using library resources for their research.

A few years later, because I had some knowledge of French and Italian, I was asked to be the book selector for French and eventually became coordinator of foreign languages generally, meeting with foreign language selectors on a regular basis as needs arose. Finally, I was asked to be coordinator of the humanities, calling and overseeing meetings of all the humanities selectors to discuss humanities purchases, policies, procedures, and concerns. I now truly had a position in an academic library that went beyond any expectation I could have had.

The Unique Opportunities in Libraries

I feel a deep gratitude toward the library profession — largely because of the wonderful flexibility and vision of my supervisors, a ready and warm acceptance on the part of my colleagues, the interesting nature of library work as a whole, and perhaps a measure of old-fashioned good luck. But also my patience and alertness to opportunities were rewarded. If you let your talents be discovered in a natural way, you will no doubt be surprised at what you can accomplish with a little patience and with respect for those with whom you work. My library, like most in the country, employs a wealth of multitalented people whose skills are just waiting to be fully tapped to address a wealth of library needs.

Collaborating on Library Publications

GWEN GREGORY *and* MARY BETH CHAMBERS

You could argue that librarians are collaborators by nature. They frequently work in organized teams, and they often enter into shared resource agreements with other libraries. A quick look at the library literature today reveals more journal articles written by multiple authors than by single authors.

Certainly, anyone publishing the results of a complex or large-scale research project will be inclined to work with others to make the task less daunting. But collaboration may also be just the thing for you if:

- You are in a position that requires you to produce a body of published works (e.g. an academic tenure–track position).
- You are brimming with ideas that you want to write about and see published but lack the confidence or know-how to publish on your own.
- You prefer the team approach in any endeavor, including publishing.

More Than the Sum of the Parts

Collaborating can be empowering. It can boost your professional confidence. Collaborators encourage each other as they work together. They help each other stay focused on the project at hand when a single author might give into fatigue or procrastination. Works of joint authorship have the potential to be information rich because they are products of multiple intellects. When you and your colleagues brainstorm ideas for a written work, you will generate many ideas. When you collaborate, you build professional networks that help you sustain your career in librarianship. With a network of colleagues, you have a knowledge base and a support group to draw upon to further your professional development.

Create Synergy

For many people, talking with someone else is a great way to further develop ideas. If you like to think out loud, you can do this with a partner to develop an article or other publication. You can meet periodically to discuss progress or refine your research. You can also pool your strengths by working with a colleague from a different specialty—a reference librarian with a cataloger, for example. You will each bring unique skills to your project. Whether you work in the same library or in different institutions, interacting with your colleagues and writing together can open up all sorts of possibilities.

Lend a Hand

Are you an old hand at publishing? If so, you have experienced the joy of communicating your ideas to others and the gratification of seeing your name in print. Moreover, you have learned many important skills. You have taken your work through the research, writing, and editing phases. You have worked with journal editors, book editors, and/or peer reviewers. You experienced their constructive feedback—for better or for worse! Consider sharing your knowledge and expertise with less-experienced colleagues. The collaborator-mentor relationship is mutually rewarding. The junior collaborator gets a chance to work with a pro who can provide valuable guidance and encouragement. The senior partner experiences the pleasure of helping a junior partner launch his or her publishing career.

Find Ideas for Research and Publication

Be vigilant; ideas are everywhere. In fact, a good source of ideas is your own work environment. Brainstorm with your colleagues. Is there a problem or an issue at your institution worthy of a formal investigation? If so, you may want to embark upon a systematic review of the literature to see how other libraries are dealing with the same or similar issues. This literature review could become the basis of a publication that would be beneficial to librarians in other places. On the other hand, if your literature review does not reveal the answers you seek, you may want to consider undertaking a research project to learn more about the issue. Publishing the results of your work would fill a gap in the existing literature. Have you worked on a project in your library that was innovative or unusual? If so, why not write about it? Articles in professional journals can also provide ideas for topics. No doubt you have read an article that intrigued you because it related to your own work or professional interests. If a related article would fill a void in the literature, why not produce a unique publication of your own. Many authors of published articles make specific recommendations for further research in a given area. If an idea resonates with you, pick up where others left off.

Where to Publish?

Consider journals that cover your research topic or your area of librarianship. Journal publishers always provide instructions for authors. They are usually available on the publishers' Web sites. Be sure to read them carefully and abide by them. Some editors will accept proposals for articles before they are written; some will review completed manuscripts only. Also, look out for calls for journal articles or books. Often editors post calls on professional e-mail lists. If you see one for a topic that interests you, you can submit a proposal, but you may have to act quickly. The book or journal issue could fill up fast.

Communicate

Collaboration requires some extra effort. Although collaborating with colleagues is potentially rewarding, it can also have a dark side. If partners cannot agree on how to proceed with a task or how to divide subtasks among themselves, collaboration will not happen, and even worse, conflict among collaborators may result. From start to finish, communication is a key component of the collaborative process. E-mail has made this much easier, but in-person meetings can also be helpful. It is important to agree at the outset of a project on what must be done, how it will be done, and who will do what. For instance, will you work together with your partner(s) on all aspects of the project, or will you establish discrete tasks and then divvy up the work? Who will conduct the literature review? In the case of a survey, who will design the research instrument, whom will you survey (sample population), and who will compile and interpret? Who will be responsible for writing the article for publication that summarizes your work? Where will you publish your work? It is critical to develop a timeline for completing the various phases of the project to keep everybody on task and on time. If you are doing a survey, decide when the survey instrument will be created, when the pilot test will be done if one is needed, when the results will be compiled and analyzed, and when the first draft of the article will be due.

While it is essential to decide these matters at the beginning of the research and publication process, you also need to be flexible because your ideas or tasks could change as your work proceeds. Collaborators are required to be good citizens. When working with others, it is your responsibility as well as your partners' to complete your respective assignments and to keep each other informed of the progress you are making.

Who's on First?

Often authors' names appear on published works in the order of their contribution to the project, with the name of the primary contributor appearing first. When collaborators share equally in the production of a work, they will probably list themselves alphabetically. Authors who work together on multiple publications may choose to take turns being first. Determine the order of authorship on the published work at the outset of the project. At the same time, remain flexible on this matter since primary responsibilities may shift and change in unforeseeable ways as the project proceeds.

Final Tactics

Keep in touch with your team members during all phases of the project. One hand needs to know what the other is doing. Remember that you are contributing to the profession and helping others learn by publishing. Enjoy the synergy you create with your colleagues.

Customers in the Driver's Seat

Ruth A. Barefoot

San José Public Library (SJPL) is finding ways to deliver library services that are new, innovative and very popular with today's customers. In fact, it is because of an innovative service model that we are attracting and keeping new professionals who are looking for a platform to develop and deliver what they already know customers want! And we all know what customers want: to be in the driver's seat. It is a matter of being comfortable with that knowledge because it upsets the framework librarians have successfully worked in for, well forever! We were very good gatekeepers, keepers of knowledge, and protectors of information. Now we see ourselves as partners and collaborators with our customers and their changing needs. I would like to share with you a couple of the components of the service model at the SJPL that helped us move from a transaction-based to a relationship-based service model. A word of caution — this has taken years to develop, so don't try this overnight!

In 2003 our service model innovations were formally evaluated through a Library Services and Technology Act (LSTA) grant. The evaluation consisted of surveys and focus groups with 671 customers, 617 residents, and 53 library employees. The results of what users thought of our customer assistance (and what some of our organizational leaders suspected) showed that customers expect:

- an intuitive service approach. They want staff to know when they need assistance.
- staff to be readily available so they do not have to approach staff seated behind desks
- a welcoming acknowledgement when entering the building
- staff to teach them how to use library resources so they can do so independently in the future

This might be obvious to some, but in San José, as well as in many other parts of the country, this is startling news. We as professionals are highly trained to know what our patrons want and need. In fact, during the formal staff evaluation, employees reported that they disagreed with the statement "customers now expect library employees to approach them," in spite of being in direct contrast to the customer survey. The evaluation also found that staff:

- felt that they were not providing good customer service if the user can meet their library needs independently
- saw assisting customers with technology troubleshooting as addressing problems instead of an opportunity to empower customers

- did not feel prepared for their new roles and were interested in training that would help them to be more successful

SJPL leaders asked a staff focus group to come up with working principles that would define where our new ideological alignments are. There are four San José Way Principles:

1. Customers First
2. Teach Customers
3. Reinvent Environments
4. Enable Staff

Asking staff to put customers first was very easy for some, most of the time. For others it was amazingly difficult as a matter of daily routine. Remember the days when we would arrive at work, review the daily schedule and be relieved when we saw that we were scheduled for two desk hours? Why would we prefer working "in the back" over the face-to-face customer service we, as an organization, are known for? What we now face in our organization is balancing the need to be:

- "out on the floor" in front of customers versus developing new and innovative programming or services using technology
- In the building and among our coworkers versus out of the building where yet more customers are
- getting the word out on what we do versus collaborating with new partners to develop a synergistic level of service to the community

We want our customers to thrive not just survive in the 21st Century, so we must look at these relationships and determine what our staff needs to embrace them.

When first developing the new business model for SJPL customer service, we took small steps and performed little pilot programs to get data regarding customer and staff behavior. Various work teams took one area and refined what they did to fit with our four principles, all the while remembering that customers want to be in the driver's seat. A few of the areas refined were:

- backroom work processes
- centralized hiring
- centralized materials processing
- cross training for all staff
- customer assistance guidelines
- librarian duties

Librarians have always done a great job developing services in the past, knowing what to do when. Why should it be different now? It is different now because the rate of changing resources is so fast that librarians are juggling the transition from the old library model to the new one and their priorities are clashing.

Customers versus Organizational Loyalty

Recently, library organizations took careful assessment of where they were and where they wanted to be as a resource. Some were faster at adopting or changing or transferring to new models than others. Nevertheless, we all know we have to adopt the 21st-century library model that celebrates many key attributes including:

- librarians who help foster environments where customers can and do "learn how to fish"
- librarians who work in collaboration with customers to deliver what the customer wants
- librarians who help preserve the customer's right to get what they want over what they need
- librarians who help foster an exciting learning environment and promote staff ownership to customer service where everyone has an equal role
- increased customer service training to improve consistency and quality
- developing an appropriate referral system for customer questions
- developing levels of expertise and scheduling them when needed
- embracing a continuously changing environment of resources
- increased programming to target diversity and age groups
- increased collaboration with internal and external partners

The San José Way service model takes into account the library's new and changing resources and its very dynamic customer groups. Over the last several years the SJPL staff has been very resilient in managing a vast array of ideas and pilot trials in order for us to identify the perfect service model. We knew it needed to approach library service delivery in a new way that included the new technology and changing customer needs. The San José Way helps the customer plug into resources on their own and get staff help in a much more intuitive fashion.

We've come a long way from the old comfortable quiet library where we sat at our desks ready to deliver perfect customer service haven't we? We've gotten out from behind the desk and out of the back rooms to engage customers on their turf and on their terms.

Statistically the customer has really come a long way as well by:

- raising our gate counts by 42 percent over the last five years
- increasing participation in programs 75 percent over ten years
- increasing paying fines online 35 percent in two years
- increasing circulation by 200 percent over ten years

What is the big transformation though? Our full time equivalent has only risen 17 percent over ten years! Customers have really moved into the driver's seat, doing more for themselves. Seventy-two percent in a resident survey rate our service at good to excellent!

Librarian as Author

Yet Another Thing They Didn't Teach Us in Library School!

Kathy Barco

A bookstore clerk led me upstairs to where the owner had just finished showing a customer the mystery book corner. The clerk said "Susan, there's an author here to see you." I looked over my shoulder to see who the clerk was referring to. There was nobody there. He was talking about *me*!

This incident in the Moby Dickens Bookshop in Taos, New Mexico, is just one of the memorable experiences I've had since becoming the coauthor (with Valerie Nye) of *Breakfast Santa Fe Style: A Guide to Fancy, Funky and Family Friendly Restaurants*, published in 2006 by Sunstone Press.

Paging Dr. Spock!

There are a lot of similarities between writing a book and having a baby. The biggest one is that after a long gestation period, your creation appears and you get to take it home. But it doesn't come with a manual that tells you what to do next. Like parenting, "authoring" is a lifelong learning experience. Welcome to the wonderful world of marketing!

Ya Gotta Have a Gimmick — The Cover Story

I had become oblivious to the display on how to "customize your favorite photo" at my local photocopying shop. But I was jolted by a blanket featuring the photo of a little league baseball team. Suddenly I had a vision of a jumbo version of our book cover. A quick Internet search paid off with details on where to order a "photo throw blanket." Six weeks later the mail brought what we like to call the "large print" version of our book: a 50 by 60 inch woven piece of art. Displayed on an easily assembled portable stand, the tapestry provides an attractive backdrop for appearances at bookstores and libraries. And it's a great conversation piece.

We held our first nonlibrary book signing in the same place the photo for our cover was shot: the historic La Fonda Hotel in Santa Fe. Of course we brought our own backdrop. A snapshot taken that day appears on the Photo Album page of our Web site.

We also made book bags decorated with an ironed-on color image of our cover (look for fabric sheets that go in your inkjet printer). We each carried one for months before the book was published (and still do!), and we give them away as door prizes during book signings.

Full-color postcards of our cover, with our URL and contact info printed on the back, have proved to be our most versatile marketing tool. We provided addressed mailing labels to a bookstore that promoted our signing by bulk mailing out over 200 of our postcards. At Christmas we punched a small hole in one end of each card and sent it out, describing it as a "combo thank you/holiday decoration (note hole just right for an ornament hook)." It was a real thrill to see our postcard hanging on the tree of more than one bookstore!

Charlotte's Not Alone on the Web

The designer of our book also developed our Web site. We provide the content, and he handles the updates. We include our URL (www.breakfastsantafestyle.com) on everything: handouts, bookmarks, e-mail signature blocks, etc.

All the bookstores that carry our book appear under "Where to Buy." "Meet & Greet" lists upcoming author appearances. The "Photo Gallery" speaks for itself.

Since both Valerie and I are librarians, we couldn't resist including a recommended reading list with each restaurant reviewed in *Breakfast Santa Fe Style*. We sent free copies to several of the authors whose books we mention. In return, we asked them to write a blurb that we could use right away on our Web site and which will eventually appear on the back cover of our second edition. Their gracious responses can be found under "Breakfast Buzz" on our Web site. Since the restaurant business is volatile, we note name or location changes, even closings, on the Tasty Tidbits page.

Promotion — Gentle Pressure, Relentlessly Applied

We keep track of all the contacts we make: authors, reviewers, bookstore owners/events coordinators/buyers, writers' group members, etc. We let them know about recent reviews and/or upcoming appearances by e-mail or snail mail.

We follow up on everything. Although this is very labor-intensive and needs constant diligence, it pays off big time!

Book Signings

For book signings Valerie and I often dress alike and always wear our squash blossom necklaces—a touch of Santa Fe Style and another conversation starter! As we sign books for people, we say things like "I'm putting in some high-tech, state-of-the-art, repositionable bookmarks, also known as stickies, to mark the introduction and the book list. Feel free to move them around to your favorite restaurants or ones you want to try next." We also slip low-tech bookmarks that say "Signed Copy" or "Autographed" and feature our URL and e-mail address into each book. These are things that folks can repeat or show when they're describing their book-signing experience to friends.

Miscellaneous Tips

- Participating in "group" therapy. We started going to meetings of the New Mexico Book Coop shortly after we came up with the idea for our book. Contacts in this group, plus a wide variety of speakers at monthly gatherings (publishers, bookstore managers/buyers, Web marketing experts) have proved invaluable. Writing groups, book discussion groups, even groups of librarians are other potential sources of support/constructive criticism/encouragement.
- Learning about marketing. We combed our libraries' collections for how-to books on marketing, such as *Jump Start Your Book Sales: A Money-Making Guide for Authors, Independent Publishers and Small Presses* by Marilyn and Tom Ross. We attended authors' talks on the subject; especially one titled "What Writers Need to Know about the Brutal Truth of Book Promotion" by award-winning New Mexico mystery writer Michael McGarrity.
- Donating. We've donated copies of our book to several silent auctions. This is an inexpensive way to be sure that a lot of people will have a chance to see the book.
- Cross-pollinating. Val and I are busy bees. In addition to our librarian jobs, we do lots of other career-enhancing activities, such as presentations at regional conferences. So far our repertoire includes "Banned Books Exposed" and "An ISBN of One's Own: Eating Grilled Chocolate Sandwiches for Breakfast, and Other Incredible Things We Had To Do To Get Published!" We use these occasions to promote our book. Conversely, when we're doing library or bookstore signings, we promote our presentations.
- Writing. Magazine and newspaper editors who received review copies of our book have contacted us to see if we'd be interested in writing articles for their publications. We've each gotten interesting assignments this way, and the byline or author bio often includes the phrase "author of *Breakfast Santa Fe Style.*"

In case you're wondering, the owner of the Moby Dickens Bookshop in Taos bought six copies of my book, and I no longer look over my shoulder when I hear the word *author*.

When Is a Librarian
Not a Librarian?

When She Is a Student,
Professor, Fellow, Mentor...

Cathy Carpenter

There is a great deal of anxiety about how academic libraries can stay relevant in the "Internet as library" Google world. It's not just the library itself that has an image problem, but librarians as well. We bemoan the negative librarian stereotype with our colleagues but do we do anything about it? Instead of focusing on traditional marketing methods to promote our library resources and services to our constituents, perhaps we should try another approach.

If we spend time outside the library and assume more roles in our campus community that have nothing to do with being a librarian, we can increase our visibility, respect, and relevance. I have assumed several roles within the Georgia Institute of Technology community that has changed students and faculty perceptions of librarians and what we have to offer. During the last four years, I have been a student, professor, fellow, mentor, volunteer, and voter registrar.

Student

When I first started in my position as the subject specialist for the Georgia Tech School of Public Policy I wondered how I could get a better understanding of the types of research conducted by the school's faculty since their areas of expertise are multidisciplinary. I also wanted to get to know the faculty. I decided to audit Foundations in Public Policy, the introductory graduate school course. Each week one of the professors came to class and discussed his or her background and research interests with the students. Some of the faculty already knew me but for most this was the first time we met. The faculty were impressed that a librarian would be interested enough in their research to take time away from work to audit this class. It helped the faculty see me in a different light and not just as the library person they complained to when they couldn't get access to an electronic journal. Taking the class was also a good opportunity to network with the students. I had wondered if I could stick out in a class of younger students but since many of the graduate students were older working adults, I fit right in. I was able to connect on a more personal basis with students who would later see me as the person to consult with when conducting research for their thesis. Later, during spring semester, I was overwhelmed with scheduling research consultations with students.

Professor

After having been a student, I then had the chance to be a teacher. Each semester, I teach several one-time library research classes for both undergrad and grad students as a guest lecturer. But for the past four years, I have taught a one-semester, one-credit elective class called GT1000: The Freshman Seminar. The course covers topics such as time management, study skills, library research skills, career research, resume writing and group presentations. The class usually averages 30 students.

I was surprised by how much time preparing lesson plans, grading assignments and calculating grades took. Just trying to remember student's names was difficult, so I brought a camera to class and took photos of the students and posted their photos on WebCt online courseware. The students loved it but never knew I did it so I could remember their names. I don't know who learned more that first semester, the students or me.

It had been a long time since I was a college student, and I didn't fully understand the pressures of freshman students, who were used to being in the top 10 percent of their high school class and now were struggling just to get a C. The 18-year-old students also had the extra challenge of living on their own for the first time. I remember the first time a student called me Professor Carpenter, and I thought, "wow, is he talking to me?" I often see my previous students around campus or in the library, and we will chat for a while. I enjoy seeing them change and mature over the years and feel satisfied that I have changed their impression of librarians to a hopefully more positive one.

Faculty Fellow

Since I was a regular teacher of the Freshman Experience course, I was able to participate in a Teaching Fellows program on campus for new faculty who had been teaching for less than five years. It is an annual program that our Center for Teaching & Learning sponsors with about 15 faculty participating. We met once a week and learned about ways to enhance our teaching. I was able to meet with faculty from all departments and schools on campus, which provided a rich opportunity to connect with faculty whom I would have never met. We discussed not only our professional lives but also our families. For our last meeting together, I did a presentation called "What's New at Georgia Tech Library," where I featured several new library services and resource that the faculty did not know about.

Mentor

I was asked by a former student of mine to serve as a freshmen partner one year. A freshman partner is a member of the faculty or staff who officially serves as an adult mentor to a group of freshman students who live together. I had 15 girls under my wing who turned out to be savvier than I ever was at that age. I would meet with them in their dorm dining halls for lunch and we also went to some local restaurants and movies. I am not sure what perceptions I changed. Since I have a teenage daughter myself, I think the girls saw me as a nonjudgmental mother substitute who just happened to be a librarian.

Volunteer

For the past few years I have volunteered to serve on the Georgia Tech Women's Leadership Conference, which is sponsored by students with the assistance of faculty and alumni. The conference is for all female college students in the Atlanta area. We have a keynote speaker and offer a number of workshops on topics ranging from "How to Get Promoted on Your Job" to "Yoga for Relaxation." I have enjoyed getting to know not only the students but also the alumni of our institution, who, one day in the future, might donate to the library!

Voter Registrar

Probably my most personally gratifying role was as a voter registrar. I organized a voter registration drive on campus during the 2004 presidential election. I knew of the dismal voting rate among 18- to 24-year-olds and saw that the only people registering students on campus were the student political parities. I felt there was a great need to register students who wanted to vote but who were not affiliated with any party. After meeting with the Georgia secretary of states office who administers voter registration, I learned that average citizens can register students. I met with the student officers of the Student Government Association, and we were able to staff a table outside the library to register students as they walked by. Many students said they were glad we were there and that they wanted to register but didn't know how or where to go. Within two weeks we registered over 500 students.

These aren't the only ways to assume alternative roles on your campus; many academic librarians serve on campus faculty committees. A librarian with an English literature background could serve as an editor for the student yearbook or other publication. It is common practice at many universities for librarians to partner with other units to bring exhibits, academic or cultural programs to the library. We are only limited by our imaginations. Think outside of the librarian box and market yourself!

Think Outside the Cases

Strategies for Developing Online Exhibits

MERINDA KAYE HENSLEY

Now that the digital world is coming to people in their own homes, librarians can rethink the traditional library exhibit. Does your library have special collections that could be shared with the world? Online library exhibits can showcase special collections, highlight unique collections or examine a captivating theme or controversial topic. When patrons cannot travel to your library, take the library to them.

How Is an Online Exhibit Different?

- Longevity. Libraries rotate their exhibits on a regular basis. Online exhibits are often released in tandem with in-house exhibits. How many times have you said to yourself, "I wish I could have seen that exhibit?" An online exhibit can be viewed for as long as the library chooses, allowing patrons to visit the exhibit many times over and at their own leisure.
- Broader Audience. Consider that a child in Asia could be viewing your antique children's books. A scholar in Europe could peruse your local musical scores from the late 1800s. The possibilities are endless. Use your imagination.
- Audio and Video. Museums and libraries can add new dimensions by including pertinent sounds bites and video to their exhibits. For example, you can create a podcast interview with a local community member who donated genealogical papers to your library.

Homegrown exhibits don't have to be as fancy as those produced by the Library of Congress. Exhibits can be as creative as you want them to be or as simple as a few images with accompanying text. As you build your skill set, your online exhibits will be more robust and reach more people.

Questions to Ask

- Who is your target audience? Children, the local community, scholars abroad? Your design should meet the needs of the intended audience. For example, if you are showcasing children's books, make sure there are lots of clear and easy-to-read images.

- What do people want to see? You could scan book covers and write short descriptions of the book, or you could showcase certain excerpts from the book that are particularly unique. Are there images that complement the written material? Your exhibit should have a distinct theme that will intrigue your visitors.
- Do you have the time? Although you should not be intimidated about creating an online exhibit, you should be prepared to invest your time and energy.
- How long will the exhibit be available? The exhibit could supplement an in-house exhibit with audio and/or video, with both to be taken down at the same time. Or, the online exhibit could be maintained into the indefinite future, an archive for future visitors to find in their serendipitous travels on the Internet.

The Technology of It All

If you find technology intimidating, find someone to help you. Read. Ask questions. You don't have to be a technology whiz to create an online exhibit, but you will need to know, for example, in which format to save your images. Photos are best saved as a .jpg file. This helps to preserve the color and integrity of the photo for online viewing purposes. You didn't know that? There is a learning curve if you've never done this before. There are lots of great books that deal with the technology of digital projects. Be patient with yourself and don't be afraid to ask for help.

Technology Tips to Get You Started

- Say it with me, "Metadata!" This will help Web crawlers find your new exhibit. Label all the available details about each item including dates, author, place, publication information, size, format etc.
- Anticipate the questions. Visitors will inevitably have many questions, and it is your job to foresee as many of them as possible. This could be in the form of an FAQ or short essay. Take this opportunity to put your library's historical artifacts in context for the viewer.
- Be prepared to update your exhibit. One of the most positive features of the Internet is that it can be updated instantly. If you receive new or additional information, consider adding it to the exhibition.
- Present the materials in their original condition. You may be tempted to Photoshop an image, but that would be changing the integrity of the memory. There is charm in that small tear at the bottom of the photo and visitors will enjoy getting a real feel for the integrity of the item.
- Strive for the highest quality possible. It will pay off enormously in ease of use and the clarity of images. There are many high-quality scanners available for a reasonable price.
- Provide resources for further reading. Perhaps you sparked the curiosity of your visitor; now is the time for a reader's advisory.
- Be consistent in the overall presentation of the exhibit. Each page should have the same look and feel to it. It can be disconcerting to a visitor if they feel like they have left the exhibit. To remedy this, always open outside links in a new window so that visitors will know they have entered the open Web.
- Be sure to provide contact information. Viewers need to know where to go if they have questions about the exhibition.

• Just in case, back up your work. Save all images, text files, audio files etc., in a several places, including on a secure server and on disk. Even though you may still have the items in your library, preserve the time you invested in digitizing.

• Don't forget to market your exhibit. Just like programming initiatives, your online exhibit needs exposure. Advertise, call the local paper, tell your friends.

• Always seek permission and be cognizant of copyright! Do your homework.

Words of Encouragement

Be creative. Your online exhibit can be anything you want it to be. For example, Communal Cuisine: Community Cookbooks 1877–1960, highlights recipes in rhyme. These poems were digitized and blown up for bulletin boards as well as added to the online exhibit. Unlike the limited space in your gallery cases, an online exhibit has an unlimited amount of room.

Second, step away from the notion that this has to be a perfect, high-end exhibit. Recognize that your library has treasures to share with others across the country and across the world. Once you publish one exhibit, you will gain experience for creating a better one next time.

Oh, and give yourself credit. You did a fabulous job!

Examples of Online Exhibits

The Chicago Fire (www.chicagohistory.org/history/fire.html)

Communal Cuisine: Community Cookbooks 1877–1960 (www.library.uiuc.edu/learn/Exhibit)

Frontier Photographer: Edward S. Curtis (www.sil.si.edu/Exhibitions/Curtis)

Library of Congress Exhibitions (www.loc.gov/exhibits)

Victorian Entertainments: "We Are Amused": An Exhibit Illustrating Victorian Entertainment (www.library.uiuc.edu/rbx/exhibitions/Victorian%20Entertainments/home/home.html)

For Further Reading

Kalfatovic, M. (2002). *Creating a winning online exhibition: a guide for libraries, archives, and museums.* American Library Association: Chicago.

The Traveling Museum Exhibition

A Resource for Learning

MARGARET LINCOLN

The cover story of the November 2005 issue of *American Libraries* proclaimed the "power of exhibits" in partnering to illuminate, educate and persuade. The Louisville Free Public Library in Kentucky was commended for hosting "A Broken Landscape," an exhibit on HIV/AIDS, in 2004. The article further praised the traveling exhibitions of the American Library Association's public programs office, which regularly draw large audiences and stimulate civic participation.

Traveling exhibitions programs have also been developed by prominent museums and other cultural institutions. The U.S. Holocaust Memorial Museum (USHMM) lets institutions nationwide bring the history and the lessons of the Holocaust into their community through traveling exhibitions. The USHMM program allowed me as a practicing library media specialist with the Lakeview School District in Battle Creek, Michigan, to be involved in a worthwhile outreach project beyond the scope of my daily job responsibilities.

Battle Creek, Michigan, is home to some 53,000 residents, many of whom have not had the opportunity to travel to Washington, D.C., to visit America's national institution for the documentation, study, and interpretation of Holocaust history. The city, therefore, has been fortunate to host two USHMM traveling exhibitions. I am pleased to share with you some background about this successful partnership between the museum and our city.

Life in Shadows

In 2002 I participated in the USHMM's Museum Teacher Fellowship Program and wrote a grant to the W.K. Kellogg Foundation, bringing the USHMM traveling exhibition on Oskar Schindler to Battle Creek's local Temple Beth El. Following our successful hosting of the Schindler exhibition, the city's Art Center was selected as a site for another traveling exhibition. "Life in Shadows: Hidden Children and the Holocaust" was on display in the fall of 2005. This exhibition explored the remarkable history of children who went underground to escape Nazi persecution and destruction, often aided by the courageous actions of righteous gentiles and other rescuers. "Life in Shadows" traveled to only two other venues in the United States: The Spertus Museum in Chicago and the Museum of Jewish Heritage in New York. Funding for the Battle Creek exhibition was secured from the W.K. Kellogg Foundation, the Battle Creek Community Foundation, the Marshall Community Foundation, the Battle Creek Rotary Club and other donors. An Ad Hoc Art Center Committee (which I chaired) was in place for 18 months and oversaw all aspects of fundraising, organization of supporting events and publicity for "Life in Shadows," including the design of a page on the Art Center of Battle Creek Web site (www.artcenterofbattlecreek. org/shadows/index.html).

A full array of cultural events complemented the exhibition. Pierre Sauvage, a Holocaust child survivor and documentary filmmaker affiliated with the Foundation of Le Chambon (the French village that rescued thousands of Jewish adults and children during World War II) opened the exhibition. He showed his Emmy Award–winning film *Weapons of the Spirit* and addressed a gathering of adults, students, and educators on September 8, 2005.

The incomparable Theodore Bikel (star of stage, screen, and television and a renowned musician) appeared in a concert with the Battle Creek Symphony on October 8, 2005. Miriam Brysk, a Holocaust survivor, hidden child and artist based out of Ann Arbor, Michigan, displayed her powerful mixed-media work in a supplemental exhibit at the W.K. Kellogg Foundation. Author Miriam Winter, who chronicled her moving story as a hidden child in Poland during World War II in her memoir *Trains*, spoke at Willard Public Library in Battle Creek. Rene Lichtman, a Holocaust child survivor who heads up the Michigan chapter of the World Federation of Jewish Child Survivors of the Holocaust led a panel discussion comprised of other Michigan residents who also survived the Holocaust as hidden children.

Educational Outreach

In addition to supporting cultural events, the "Life in Shadows" project included a strong educational outreach component. In May 2005, a Holocaust Educators' workshop was offered to 50 Michigan teachers who had signed up to bring classes to the exhibition so that they might better prepare their students for viewing "Life in Shadows." Stephen Feinberg, head of national outreach in the museum's Education Department conducted the workshop. Attendees participated with no costs to their school district and received professional development (PD) credit along with stipends for purchases of instructional materials recommended by the USHMM. Lesson plans focusing on the topic of hidden children were shared with participants along with Holocaust instructional materials found on the Mandel Fellowship Teaching Resources Web site at http://mandelproject.us. This site features lesson plans and book reviews submitted by past museum teacher fellows and was developed from an advanced funding project which I conducted for the museum in 2003.

When "Life in Shadows" officially opened at the Art Center of Battle Creek on September 6, 2005, a full schedule of 72 separate classroom visits had been organized. Forty-six retired school teachers served as volunteer docents. Students responded in writing to reflection questions, expressing a variety of emotions:

> I will always remember the words of the children who went through the Holocaust. And I will never forget the look on their faces, confusion and disbelief.

We are truly lucky to be free and in America. And it's only been sixty years since this crazy madness happened.

The actual artifacts made it more interesting and made the knowledge connect to us. To think that 1.6 million children died. The exhibit truly impacted my life.

As school groups participated in organized visits to the exhibit, Holocaust instruction was also impacted in the classroom. At Lakeview High School, English classes incorporated the reading of Elie Wiesel's autobiographical memoir, *Night*, into the curriculum. I set up an Internet blog at http://nightwiesel.blogspot.com so that Lakeview students could share their reflections upon reading *Night* with students some 720 miles away at Cold Spring Harbor High School in Long Island, New York.

A research component was associated with Battle Creek's hosting of a traveling museum exhibition. The USHMM had made available an online version of "Life in Shadows" on the Museum Website at www.ushmm.org/museum/exhibit/online/hiddenchildren. Through the cooperation of teachers who brought classes to view "Life in Shadows" at the Art Center of Battle Creek, I studied the educational value of the exhibition in its online and on-site versions by considering three scenarios of classroom visits: students who viewed only the online version of "Life in Shadows"; students who viewed only the on-site version of "Life in Shadows"; and students who viewed both the online and on-site versions of the exhibition. This research was carried out through my participation in an interdisciplinary information science doctorate program of the University of North Texas in Denton. An online survey instrument to obtain student response to both versions of the exhibition was developed through one of my research methods courses.

Conclusion

We in Battle Creek, Michigan, were honored to bring this extraordinary traveling exhibition from the U.S. Holocaust Memorial Museum to our community. The exhibition saw over 8,160 visitors, with 3,800 junior and senior high school students in attendance from all over the state of Michigan. Our attempt to share the lessons of the Holocaust did more than impart knowledge. It raised an awareness of our responsibility to protect and care for all those who are targeted by hatred, discrimination and violence. We believe that students and adults gained a heightened awareness of a most tragic period in the history of humankind.

Reference

Morton, Norman. "Beyond public exhibits to partnerships: Louisville library gets more bang for its public relations programming buck through collaboration." *American Libraries*. Nov. 2005: 42–45.

When the Olympics Came to Town

The Rewards and Challenges of Creating a Large-Scale Exhibition

Connie Lamb *and* Russ Taylor

When it was announced that Salt Lake City would be the 2002 Winter Olympic Games site, we, a social sciences librarian and the reference librarian in special collections at Brigham Young University's (BYU) Harold B. Lee Library, suggested an Olympics exhibit. Initially the idea was to honor Leona Holbrook, a BYU physical education professor, who was the first woman to serve on the U.S. Olympic Committee. As we learned of other BYU faculty and students who had an Olympic connection, it became obvious to us that we could tell a much broader story. There could be, we thought, two or three dozen BYU people who were Olympians. The more we searched, however, the more we found and the project grew to include nearly 100 BYU-affiliated students and faculty who represented their countries at the Olympic and Para-Olympic Games.

Our work, as curators of the exhibition, involved hours of research and writing, the stress of constant deadlines, and the frustration of trying to locate materials for display. But the result was an impressive exhibit set up around the library's central stairwell — a place visible to everyone coming into our three-million-volume library. The exhibition, titled "BYU and the Olympic Games: An International Connection," ran from October 2001 to April 2002. It included a list of Olympians, their country of origin, a sampling of artifacts (including gold, silver, and bronze Olympic medals) set in cases, flags of many of the countries represented, and large panel (four by eight feet) action pictures of some of the athletes.

We were able to create such an extensive exhibit by using six *P*s: planning, preparation, presentation, publicity, postexhibition activities, and purpose.

Planning

Planning starts with an idea that must be developed into a detailed proposal to the appropriate entity (administrator(s), committee, etc.). At BYU this entity is an exhibits committee, and we worked with them throughout the process to:

- decide the breadth and depth of the exhibit
- explain the purpose (education, entertainment, etc.)
- complete planning documents
- obtain funding (we received support from the library and the Physical Education Department)
- build a collaborative effort between curators, administrators, graphic designers, etc.

Preparation

Preparation includes many decisions such as what to include and how to organize the exhibition. The things that must be done in advance include:

- designing a layout for the entire exhibition
- creating contracts for the loan of materials and a procedure for tracking loaned items (to ensure that items are returned to the proper donors)
- gathering materials from donors
- preparing display props, cradles, etc.
- using mock-ups of cases to finalize layout
- writing the scripts for captions and panels

Presentation

Presentation is the "meat" of the exhibition. Aspects to consider are visual appeal, aesthetics, how to best present the desired message, flow of the exhibit and the viewers, and security. Other important considerations are:

- laying out materials for the most effective display
- moving cases, panels or other props into position
- putting items and captions together
- securing all elements of the exhibition

Publicity

As the saying goes, "if you build it, they will come," but only if they are aware of it. So publicity and public relations are important elements to a successful exhibition. The following are some options for advertising an exhibition:

- flyers and mailings
- newspaper articles
- radio or TV spots

- banners
- lecture series (one or more lectures related to the exhibition is a way to draw people to view and understand the exhibition)

Postexhibition Activities

For a temporary exhibit, the take down and cleanup are inevitable, although difficult after all the effort that went into setting it up. Decisions must be made about what to do with items created for the exhibition and how to preserve a record of it. Consider these steps:

- Take pictures or videos of the exhibit before taking it down to create a print and/or digital archive of it.
- Take items out of cases and off panels/walls.
- Return items to their proper homes.
- Find storage space if that is needed.
- Clean the area where it stood (wall patching or painting may be needed).

Purpose(s)

Focusing on the statement of purpose is important throughout all the planning activities. What message do you want to convey to the viewers? How does it benefit the organization, persons involved with it, and the visitors? Our overall goals with our Olympic exhibit at BYU were to educate and entertain. Since the Olympic Games generates international interest, we wanted to show the international connections of BYU Olympians, educate our students and faculty about the Olympic Games, and stimulate interest through bringing the Olympic Spirit home to the BYU community. Specifically, our purposes for mounting this exhibit were to:

- recognize BYU Olympians for their dedication, sacrifices, and accomplishments
- bring people into the library
- establish strong working relationships with other university departments (physical education and public affairs, for example)
- build a strong archive of material on student and faculty Olympics participation
- strengthen intralibrary collegial relations
- emphasize the role of the library as the center of learning on campus and in the community
- create positive public relations and goodwill for the library

Conclusion

While we put in countless hours researching, writing, gathering materials, preparing materials for exhibit, and laying out the exhibit cases, we found our experience tremendously satisfying. It was gratifying to find our exhibit so popular with students, faculty, community members, and visitors to the Olympic Games. On numerous occasions television crews used the exhibit as a backdrop for reporters covering events. This was particularly true for international media, who would position themselves in front of posters of athletes from their countries.

Several of the highlighted athletes had recently died, and our exhibit served as a memorial to their lives. Families came to see how their husbands/fathers/brothers had been honored and paused in almost reverential stillness at the eight-foot-high posters and the cases of uniforms, medals, and magazine and newspaper articles documenting the lives of their loved ones. For us, the exhibit area became a place of celebration and contemplation — holy ground, as it were.

We documented our exhibit with numerous photographs and videos. But perhaps the most satisfying record was a comment book we placed at the end of the exhibit. Reviewing the comments, we feel a sense of pride and satisfaction in the work we did. Here's a sampling:

> Thanks for the wonderful exhibit... Seeing the disabled do so much and succeed is an example to me that I can do anything I set my mind to. This exhibition touched my heart and brightened my day. Thanks.
>
> The whole idea of the Olympiad seems much more personal. Thanks for making it so much more real!
>
> Fantastic!

Large exhibits may initially seem daunting, impossibly difficult, or too time-consuming. Our experience, however, has proven — to us, at least — that with a talented team (including exhibit professionals) they *can* be done and that they are well worth the time and effort. Our advice to others is not to be put off by difficulties or the demands of the project. The end will be satisfying and the outcome highly appreciated by others.

Good luck and have fun!

Libraries and Literary Clubs

The Perfect Match

LISA A. FORREST

Many libraries struggle with the question of how to best market their resources. We all know that simply acquiring interesting materials for your collection is no guarantee that your library will actually be used. As librarians, how can we ensure that our resources are being optimally utilized? The E. H. Butler Library of Buffalo State College in New York has found a unique way to bring students into the library, market literary resources, and promote creativity. Through poetry readings, workshops, and campus-wide poetry projects, E.H. Butler's Rooftop Poetry Club helps to provide real meaning to a seemingly endless sea of information. Literary clubs are an easy and inexpensive way to market your library and make real connections with your patrons. Are you interested in starting a club of your own? There are a few things you can do to get off to a good start.

First, decide what kind of literary club you want to establish. For me, it was only natural to use poetry as my marketing tool. Consider what you are most passionate about — short fiction, biographies, graphic novels — and use your energy and leadership to excite others about your library. Keep in mind your current collection and resources that you have available (now just might be the time to dig out the record player and old vinyl poetry recordings). At the same time, be open to expanding your library's current holdings. Your future club members will be more than willing to suggest titles to add to the collection!

Words Are Cheap

Besides the cost of refreshments, literary clubs costs next to nothing to run. Our club relies heavily on local talent, including student-led workshops and faculty readings. Local guest poets are usually eager to freely share their work, especially if there is an opportunity to promote their work and sell books to a crowd. We've held student-led workshops on journal making, Middle Eastern love poetry, vocal delivery of the poem, and personal essay writing. You can never go wrong with hosting an open-mic event. We like to have themes for our open mics, like poems of thanks at Thanksgiving or winter poems in December. For Valentine's Day, we held a sonnet contest. The possibilities are endless!

Meeting of the Minds

Once you've decided on what kind of club to establish, find one or two interested people to join you as founding members. Call a meeting and brainstorm possible names for your club. Don't underestimate the importance of coming up with a catchy title, preferably something short. Our club (named after our main meeting place, the library's rooftop garden) is most often referred to as "Rooftop." You should also figure out the basics: who will be allowed to join your club, when and where you will meet, activities that you might do as a club, and a mission statement. We began our membership drive with an open-mic reading. Keep a list of ideas generated at your first meeting — even if they seem far-fetched. With a little collaboration, you never know what will be attainable later.

Marketing

We started out by simply posting a flyer announcing the club's conception and the upcoming open-mic reading. Since then, we've expanded our marketing to include a useful Web site, announcements in campus and community newspapers, and trendy looking advertisements. Student members volunteer to post flyers around campus. I promote the club in my library instruction sessions. As a librarian, you are in a natural position of leadership. It's important that you collaborate with like-minded folks on campus and in the community. We work closely with the English Department, student clubs, and our local literary organization.

Incorporate Library Resources

Let's say you've brought folks into the library for a workshop on journal making. Now is the time to bring out all of those interesting books on papermaking and book binding. Valentine's Day open mic? Bring out the sonnets! For each event we hold, we create a list of Related Books at Butler on our Web site. We also have links to all of our literary databases and a pathfinder of online journals listed on our club's Web site. To further our collection development efforts, we ask each member for their favorite book of poetry. If we have the book, we link to the catalog record from our Web site. If we don't have it, we order it. This way, we are ensuring that our patrons have a real say in the development of our poetry collection. Think creatively! We've used discarded book jackets to decorate handmade journal covers, old catalog cards and topographical maps to write poems on, and obsolete 35 millimeter slides to create a multimedia poetry project.

Use Technology to Your Advantage

Librarians have always been known for their openness to using new technologies. At Buffalo State, the poetry club was a forerunner in using pod casting to promote our events. The club also has their own blog, which is linked directly to the library's home page (www. buffalostate.edu/library/rooftop). Each member of our poetry club has their own Web page, complete with bio, digital photo, and a sample of their work. Everyone is a published poet!

When we first started to host reading events, we borrowed our audio equipment (a mic and a small amp) from the instructional resources office on campus. There are a variety of freely available software applications for sound recording and editing. We used Audacity (http://audacity.sourceforge.net) and a laptop computer to record our pod casts. Once the club was flying, we were able to support our request for our own audio equipment, which also included a portable flash drive recorder.

Archive

Although we weren't sure in which direction the club was going initially, we took photos. These photos came in handy when we started our Web site, giving the club real legitimacy. Since then, we have photographed every major club event. We also began recording and pod casting our reading events, which has been a wonderful addition to our Web site. You will probably want to keep track of meeting attendance as well. It might come in handy if you ever need to ask the higher-powers for future funding.

Don't Give Up

It has taken our club time to become fully established on campus. Don't take it too personally if attendance is less than what you hope for at first. Only four people showed up at our initial meeting. Since then, we've had events that brought in as many as 50 people. Developing a personal connection with members is imperative to your club's success. I've found that students in the club often come to me for writing and publishing advice, and general research help. If I see a member in the library, I make it a point to personally invite them to the next event. It's these personal connections that help to make our library a unique place and keeps students coming back!

The Life Stories Project

Collecting Oral and Written Histories

Diana Brawley Sussman

Almost every time we speak we tell a story. In 2006 a network of libraries in Illinois simply listened. We conducted our Life Stories Project in celebration of 75 years of National Library Service for the Blind and Physically Handicapped (NLS; www.loc.gov/nls), a free Library of Congress program which loans audio and Braille books and magazines to anyone who finds it difficult or impossible to read regular print due to any visual or physical limitation or organic learning disability. We, the Network of Illinois Talking Book and Braille Libraries, are part of that national system. This project seemed a good fit for looking back on our history and forward into our future.

There are, however, many reasons to collect oral or written histories:

- to commemorate, explore, or even mourn an event or era in the community's history
- to explore a theme or shed light on a community issue. One theme that naturally arose for us was disability, particularly vision loss. Another library may tap into the shared experience of an immigrant community, an annual festival, the effect of a major industry closing or the urbanization of a formerly rural community. Narrow the focus by targeting a theme or reaching out to a particular group or present an open-ended memory project to the entire community, allowing themes to arise naturally, creating a diverse patchwork of voices.
- to promote the library. Collecting patrons' stories provides a great everyday outreach opportunity or preparation for a referendum.

There were two main aspects to our project, an anthology and a series of life stories workshops. Producing an anthology requires the following steps:

1. Develop submission guidelines to outline what type of stories are sought (length, theme), and from whom. Also address:
   - format such as electronic, typed, handwritten, Braille, recorded, or video. Consider participants' access to computers, disabilities, etc.
   - submission deadline
   - permission form requiring signature and contact information (to edit, publish and distribute participants' written or recorded words for the purpose of sharing them in a newsletter, presentation, press release or anthology in any format)

- when/how/whether participants will be notified of receipt, publication, rejection
- whether submissions will be returned. If so, require a self-addressed, stamped envelope and strongly suggest the author keep a copy of the submission.

Literary journals provide further examples of submission guidelines. The Web site Lit-Line (www.litline.org) offers links to several journals.

2. Notify target participants through newsletters, media, etc.
3. Develop a reviewing system for selecting stories. This could involve a formal rating system, a conversation among volunteer or staff reviewers, or a single editor. Decide to what degree, and to what end, you will or will not edit submissions for length, grammar or content.
4. Determine distribution options, such as:
   - reference and circulating library copies
   - copies to contributors
   - copies to volunteers, board members, city/state officials, community partners, press
   - copies for sale
5. Transfer materials to desired format(s), such as print or audio. Here are some tips:
   - Shop around for printing and binding prices. Some state, system, or larger libraries offer printing services.
   - Inquire at local or university presses as an alternative to self-publishing.
   - For transcribing audio files to text, our local public radio station recommended trying the captioning software used by television stations to insert closed-captioning into video. The National Center for Accessible Media offers an apparently free and user-friendly software called MAGpie. Commercially available products include MacCaption and CaptionMaker. Other options include pay services and asking staff or volunteers to listen to audio, transcribing it to text manually.
   - Consider audio format options, such as CD, cassette, MP3, online podcast or .wav files.
   - Decide whether to edit together original audio, have volunteers or actors read stories, or do a combination of the two.
   - Investigate partnerships with local public or commercial radio stations, state or local talking book libraries (some have recording studios; see www.loc.gov/nls/find.html), and with Radio Information Service (available in some states; talking book libraries can refer).

In conducting life stories workshops, we focused on collecting memories rather than teaching people how to construct or edit written stories. Because our patrons are print-impaired, we provided plastic writing guides to lay over notebook paper, and black sharpie markers to help visually impaired participants to write. We suggested they bring their own adaptive writing aids, such as magnifiers or portable Braillers. However, while we invited participants to write down ideas, most simply spoke and listened.

It's easy to get people talking. I'd explain the project, distribute permission forms, read allowed a sample story, then ask them to sit back for three minutes and make a mental list of memories, of whatever floods to the surface, however magnificent or mundane. That's all it took. When asked to share what came to mind, they did. I asked them to state their name each time they spoke so I could attribute each story to the correct person, although some stories lapsed into group conversation. Workshops lasted about 90 minutes, no matter the group size, which ranged from about 12 to 30 participants. If the memories dried up, I'd ask a question or two. I asked for memories involving certain senses, smells, tastes, sounds. Food provoked strong memories! I asked about childhood or people they admired. Each group set its own tone. For more memory provoking questions or activities there are several books available on memoir writing. Some authors include David and Carl Marshall, Bob Greene, Elizabeth Stone, and Denis Ledoux.

We digitally recorded the in-person workshops using a laptop with free Audacity software (http://audacity.sourceforge.net). We used an inexpensive free-standing computer microphone. Jeff Williams of our local public radio station, WSIU, suggested Adobe Audition (formerly Cool Edit Pro) or Sound Forge. They are popular recording/editing software in the audio industry. He said most audio editing software should work with anything that produces a .wav file.

Because not all patrons could attend in person, we offered phone workshops. Conference calls can be expensive, so we used FreeConference (www.freeconference.com). Rather than a toll-free call, participants paid their regular long distance rates for the call. We simply put the call on speakerphone and recorded it through a microphone.

We also offered an online workshop using OPAL, Online Programming for All Libraries (www.opal-online.org). OPAL uses Web conferencing software from Talking Communities, which allows a group to speak, text-chat, and share Web pages. Conversations can be recorded and archived. Participants need almost no computer expertise, and the software is accessible to blind users.

Our patrons are geographically dispersed throughout the state and our books are delivered by mail. Transportation is an issue in rural areas, particularly for seniors and people with disabilities. Rather than ask people to come to our library, we offered most of our workshops to existing groups. We worked with Centers for Independent Living and Illinois' Bureau of Blind Services to locate low-vision support groups. Those agencies often provide transportation to their support groups, and members are accustomed to attending those events. This ensured a guaranteed audience. We worked with public libraries and the Illinois School for the Visually Impaired to gather participants as well.

WSIU aired a 20-minute segment about the project, and short segments featuring patrons' stories aired periodically over the next few weeks. The station provided us with CDs of the radio programming, agreed to share the files through their statewide public radio listserv, and shared them with our Radio Information Service stations, which air programming specifically for print-impaired listeners. They even suggested we invite a small group of patrons to record stories in the station.

To review similar projects, please visit the following:

- National Public Radio: StoryCorp (http://storycorps.net)
- Library of Congress: American Folklife Center (www.loc.gov/folklife)
- Philadelphia: The Autobiography Project (www.autobiographyproject.com)
- Library of Congress: American Life Histories: Manuscripts from the Federal Writers' Project, 1936–1940 (http://memory.loc.gov/ammem/wpahome.html)
- The Story Circle Network (www.storycircle.org)

Local Hero

STEPHEN FESENMAIER

In February 2006 I was honored as one of 38 "History Heroes" by nine different statewide history organizations in West Virginia. There was a ceremony at the State Cultural Center on History Day at the legislature during which history groups from around the state came to tell the state's legislators about their efforts in preserving the state's history. Two groups on whose boards I serve were also exhibiting — the West Virginia Labor History Association and the South Charleston Museum, which nominated me for the award.

During the last 18 months, I have been showing films about West Virginia history on a twice-monthly basis at the South Charleston Museum. Thousands of people have attended the films, sometimes up to 300 a night, a full house for the restored LaBelle Theater.

Every librarian should become a history hero, promoting their local area using films, videos, books, people, and anything else they can find to encourage people to learn more about their history.

You can meet all of West Virginia's history heroes on the West Virginia Division of Culture and History Web site at www.wvculture.org/history/histhero.html.

University Film Society

I began my film career as a work study student at the University Film Society in Minneapolis at the University of Minnesota in 1972. I eventually became a director and spent my evenings and weekends showing films from around the world. I also promoted any and all local films, ranging from animation by Susan Pitt to independent features like David Burton Morris's *Loose Ends*. During my six years at the University Film Society, we presented a wide variety of films, including erotic films that paid the bills for the rest. *WR: Mysteries of the Organism* is my favorite film. My favorite book is Amos Vogel's *Film as a Subversive Art*, which was recently reprinted. "WR" is on the cover of the book.

Cinema Antitherapy

I wrote my first master's thesis in library science on cinema antitherapy. An excerpt of it was published by *Film/Psychology Review*. As a result, I was interviewed by *Behavior* magazine and live on ABC Radio in Detroit. Unfortunately, my thesis was rejected, and I had to write another one. The second thesis was on film selection policies in public libraries.

West Virginia Library Commission Film Services

I attended the University of Michigan Library School in 1977 and specialized in film librarianship. I had planned on creating the first master's thesis on video about Minnesota's many small publishers, but I was hired in June 1978 at the West Virginia Library Commission to head the last 16-millimeter film library created anywhere.

Fred Glazer, chosen by *American Libraries* magazine as one of the 100 greatest librarians of the 20th century, called me after Don Roberts, a well-known AV librarian and activist, told him about me. I began work on September 14, 1978.

I immediately began a media blitz, both with libraries and the public. Eventually I began writing for various statewide magazines beginning with the *Appalachian Intelligencer*, a local zine. I moved on to writing for the *WV Arts News*, and a weekly column for *Graffiti* magazine called "Film Nuts." In 1987 the U.S. Department of Education chose our film program as a model for statewide 16-millimeter film programs, publishing a book on model programs called *Check It Out*.

For our film program I bought interesting foreign feature films, independent films, and other items that did not make it to the rural communities in the state. I would also buy popular films, like *Star Trek*. Our most popular film of all is *Greatest Heroes of the Bible*. We published a 20-page quarterly *WVLC Film Services Newsletter* that was sent to every public library in the state. It included discussions about various West Virginia film programs, reprinted film articles from local and national publications, and original articles written by myself and the staff.

We also offered an annual workshop for new librarians at our Marshall Workshop, spending two hours showing clips of films. We also printed numerous flyers and posters. The early motto for the department was "When the Lights go out in WV public libraries, the fun begins," and we presented each of our more than 170 libraries as "library cinemas." National Public Radio did a ten-minute story on our program in November 1987.

Working with Local Filmmakers

The key to promoting local filmmakers is to show their films anywhere possible, and to help them make their films in any way possible. I have written many letters to filmmakers, promising to purchase a copy of their film and to show it in West Virginia public libraries. I cofounded the WV Filmmakers Guild in 1979. In 2001 I cofounded the West Virginia Filmmakers Film Festival in Sutton. We have showcased West Virginia films and filmmakers, including Morgan Spurlock, a native of the state and known for his film *Super Size Me!* At the festival a "WV Filmmaker of the Year" is chosen, helping to raise local and national awareness of West Virginia filmmakers. The 2005 WV Filmmaker of the Year, B.J. Gudmundsson, worked with the Pocahontas County Free Libraries on two feature documentaries, helping them win an IMLS National Library Service Award in 2003.

Bhopal and Buffalo Creek

Parts of two important films were shot in my office. One was the key scene for a film on the Bhopal disaster that can now be seen in *Litigating Disaster* from First Run/Icarus and the other was an interview with Ken Hechler about the long-term effects of the Buffalo Creek disaster. We helped make films, not just show them!

The Website

I post film descriptions about West Virginia and Appalachian films at a Web site maintained by AppLit at w.ferrum.edu/applit/bibs/WVFilmIndex.htm. This Web site may be the most important thing I have done to promote WV films. People from around the world, including major filmmakers such as Lars von Trier, famous for *Breaking the Waves* and *Dancer in the Dark*, found me through the Web site, sending a researcher to WV to prepare for making his recent film, *Dear Wendy*. Hundreds of people who grew up in the state, college professors, filmmakers, and others have found these films by finding them on the Web site.

Highest Pinnacle

Presently I am working with WV's leading civil servant, retired congressman Ken Hechler, on his film biography. Russ Barbour, a leading WVPBS filmmaker, was commissioned by Hechler to make the two-hour biography, with funding provided through Marshall University Libraries. I also help Hechler with Web research since he is not a computer user. I have known Hechler ever since I came to the state and bought a 16-millimeter print of the film of his best-selling book, *The Bridge at Remagen*. Last spring I screened *Remagen* at the South Charleston Museum as part of a local Armed Forces Day celebration, marking the 60th anniversary of the end of World War II. I helped Hechler produce two videos available at the Remagen Museum in Germany.

Teaching and Outreach Using Archives and Special Collections

SHARON CARLSON

Once viewed as the domain of "serious" researchers, archives and special collections are being used by an increasingly broader audience. This coincides with the professional literature encouraging more outreach as well. Typically, library instruction is linked to the reference functions within a library system, and one rarely thinks of the role of archives and special collections in this context. The use of archival materials in teaching students of all ages remains a vastly untapped area.

There are some drawbacks to teaching from the archives or special collections. The materials can include items that are unique and rare. Sometimes these materials have significant monetary value and may be vulnerable to theft. They may also be fragile and have special handling requirements. While it may be enlightening to introduce a class to the Civil War through diaries, should you really pass around unique 145-year-old diaries to a group of students?

Despite these drawbacks, the use of archival or special collections materials can enhance the education of students at all levels and provide benefits for both students and educators. Archives and special collections can often provide local perspectives on national and international issues. Well-developed assignments that require students to analyze content and bias can contribute to critical thinking skills that will benefit students. The use of archival and special collections in assignments can be a tool in combating plagiarism. Using archival and special collections as the basis of assignments makes it more difficult for students to plagiarize and virtually impossible for students to purchase commercial products to complete class assignments.

For some excellent guidelines for document analysis see the National Archives and Records Administration's Web site at www.archives.gov/education/lessons/worksheets.

Finding Your Audience

The most successful instruction and outreach programs depend on knowing potential users and their needs. Collaboration with a teacher or professor is almost always necessary because students rarely become enamored with special collections on their own. Some things you can do include:

- Become acquainted with professors teaching in areas where your collection can support.
- Offer to provide an introductory session for the teacher or professor.
- Offer to create or collaborate on a student assignment.
- Become acquainted with high school history teachers and learn about their primary source needs.
- Learn about regional competitions for National History Day. Students enrolled in grades six through 12 are required to use primary sources for successful entries. Contact supervising teachers and offer assistance with primary sources.

Success Stories

Since the mid–1990s, the instructional activities at the Western Michigan University archives and regional history collections have increased from about three groups of students a year to an average of one class each week from October through March. The activities range from informal and fun exercises to introduce students to the types of materials found in the archives and special collections to multiclass meetings in which students delve deeply into the collections and analyze and compare a variety of documents. A couple of the more successful assignments are outlined below.

University Newspaper Assignment

History majors at Western Michigan University are required to complete the three-credit-hour course, Historians in the Modern World, which introduces them to the profession and to related research, analytical, and presentation skills. It is a large class composed primarily of freshmen and sophomores who have never before encountered archival or special collections. A PowerPoint presentation highlights some of the types of materials found in the Western Michigan University archives and regional history collections. Some materials, such as duplicate copies of yearbooks and postcards, are actually passed around for students to examine. Students are also introduced to their assignment, which is to select the issue of the *Herald*, the university's newspaper which dates back to 1916, that was published closest to their own birth date and to answer the following questions:

- What is the date of the newspaper?
- What are the major headlines and news stories?
- Does the issue contain any editorial or editor's columns? If so, what are the topics and do you detect any bias?
- What products are being marketed to students? How much do the advertised products cost?
- What are your general impressions?

This assignment, created by the director of undergraduate studies in the History Department and the director of the archives and regional history collections, has three objectives: (1) require students to physically use the archives and regional history collections, (2) introduce students to the use of microfilm, and (3) have students critically examine a historical document. The assignment is very popular with the students.

Artifacts of the Elders

In 2005, librarians at Western Michigan University developed and implemented an orientation session for high school students vying for the prestigious four-year, full-tuition Medallion scholarship. The objectives of this event focused on basic library skills, including searching the catalog and library Web site, finding books, learning about search engines, and becoming familiar with what constitutes plagiarism. An additional objective was to familiarize these potential students with the vast array of library holdings. Librarians developed events for student teams of four to six members to complete in 20 minutes. The Artifacts of the Elders event introduced students to archival and special collections.

Students were given an assortment of materials from the university archives to examine. All were in original formats but were duplicate copies. The items included a 1913 schedule of classes, a female student's rule book from the 1950s, a 1944 yearbook, and a literary magazine from the 1960s. After examining these materials, students were asked to answer a series of questions. Some of the questions concerned the cost of tuition in 1913, the impact of World War II on Western's campus, and rules for female students in the 1940s. Students completed a worksheet that had a cryptogram. The solution to the cryptogram led the students to the next set of clues and the portrait of Western's first president in the library rotunda. This activity proved to be one of the most popular events of the evening. Since the orientation session, this exercise has been modified for groups visiting the archives and regional history collections. It remains a popular exercise for student groups. While it is fun, it also introduces students to the scope of materials that may be held in an archive or special collection within a larger library system.

Conclusion

Using archival and special collections in teaching and outreach provides numerous benefits to students, educators, and parent institutions. Today's students have grown up believing that anything worth finding is available electronically. Using archival materials is an eye-opening experience and introduces them to the wider array of information that exists. Educators may use unique primary sources to better illustrate concepts and in some instances combat plagiarism. Incorporating these materials in outreach and teaching also provides a public relations tool for libraries to distinguish themselves in this era of approval plans and subscription-based databases which are making institutions increasingly homogeneous.

How to Start Your Own Blog

NICOLE C. ENGARD

Blogs are everywhere you look nowadays. You hear about them on the nightly news; you read about them in the local paper. Most importantly, librarians all over the world are starting their own blogs and encouraging others to do the same. You want to jump on the bandwagon, but where do you start and how much will it cost? What does having a blog mean to you and your library?

Don't worry. I was once where you are, and I didn't have this handy little guide to tell me what to do. As it turns out, starting your own blog is not as complicated as you may think; in fact, you can start your own blog for zero dollars down and zero dollars a day (if that's what you're looking for), and it will only take a few hours of your time to set up.

First you need to answer a few questions:

- How much are you willing to invest (time and money)?
- Do you have any programming or Web design skills? If not, do you know someone who does that can help you out?
- Do you or your library pay for a domain name and host? Do you want your blog to be on your own host?
- Do you want your blog to be private or public?

Choosing the Right Blogging Option

Number one option to consider: cost. Most of the popular blogging packages are free or are available for a small monthly fee. Since my blog was for my own personal use, I decided to start with a free option. This allowed me a chance to learn the ropes and gather an audience. If your blog is for your own personal use, it's best to start with a free option, then you can always upgrade once you get the hang of things. Free, hosted blogs include Blogger (www.blogger.com), WordPress (www.wordpress.com) and LiveJournal (www.livejournal.com).

How do you choose? If you want to be able to password protect your blog so that only people with the password can access it, LiveJournal is the only package that offers you the option of a public or private blog. Other than that, all three offer relatively similar options; it's a matter of which you're most comfortable with, and since they're all free, sign up for as many as you want and give them a test drive. What did I choose? I started with Blogger and stuck with it for about a month. Then I gave WordPress a test run and decided I liked it, but wanted to run it on my own server.

Another great thing about the free options: You don't need any programming knowledge. All three provide their users with a library of premade templates and easy-to-use text editors that allow you to bold, italicize and link your text without knowing any HTML. If you do have programming skills, you'll have the ability to customize some features of your blog on your own, but there are limitations. How do you get around the limitations? You install the software onto your own server.

To Host or Not to Host

Free and low-cost options that can be installed on your own server include WordPress (www.wordpress.org), Moveable Type (www.sixapart.com/movabletype), b2evolution (www.b2evolution.net) and LifeType (www.lifetype.net). These options require that you or someone on your staff has some programming knowledge (including PHP and/or Perl) and HTML (including Cascading Style Sheets) skills. By going this route you allow yourself more control over the look and feel of your blog, as well as preventing ads or unwanted logos from appearing on your site. Also, by hosting the blog on your own site, you have the option of installing it to a private or password-protected directory — allowing you to control who reads the content on your blog, no matter which package you choose.

If this is your personal blog, you'll need to buy a domain name and find a hosting package. Domain names are cheap. Yahoo! Small Business (smallbusiness.yahoo.com) offers amazing sales at least once every couple of months; I got my domain for only $2.99 a year. If Yahoo! isn't offering a good deal when you're ready to purchase, GoDaddy (www.godaddy.com) offers some of the lowest everyday prices around.

Finding an affordable and reliable host can be more difficult. There are thousands of hosts to choose from, all of them offering different features. I like to check with host comparison sites like CompareWebHosts.com (www.comparewebhosts.com) and Web Hosting Talk Forums (www.webhostingtalk.com) to see who has good reviews and offers the features I need. If you're a savvy shopper you can find hosting for as little as $2 a month.

Getting Noticed

So now you have your blog all set up. How do you get other professionals to notice it? You'd be surprised how quickly the members of the biblioblogosphere (librarian bloggers) will notice your site. Somehow, without any advertising on my part, my blog was noticed and posted about within one week of its birth. What if you don't want to wait to get noticed? Well, there are several sites where you can list your blog for free, such as:

- Internet Public Library: Blogs (www.ipl.org/div/blogs)
- Library Weblogs by Libdex (www.libdex.com/weblogs.html)
- Open Directory (dmoz.org/Reference/Libraries/Library_and_Information_Science/Web logs)
- Technorati (www.technorati.com)

Each site offers instructions on how to add your blog to their lists.

Most important to getting noticed (other than posting on a regular basis) is to offer easy access to your RSS feed. RSS stands for Real Simple Syndication, and it is the easiest way for people to keep up with multiple blogs—including yours. Every time you post something new on your blog, your RSS feed will automatically be updated.

All of the packages mentioned above offer RSS feeds, and their help files will tell you how to access them. With Blogger your feed's address will be yoursite.blogspot.com/atom.xml, whereas with WordPress it will be yoursite.wordpress.com/feed. You can submit your blog's RSS feed to blog search engines by using a service like Pingoat (www.pingoat.com) or Ping-O-Matic (www.pingomatic.com). These sites notify popular search engines that your blog has new content. Some blogging packages will automatically notify these services for you; Blogger, for example, is owned by Google and so your blog will be indexed by Google's Blog Search (blogsearch.google.com) on a regular basis.

Keep on Learning

You probably think you're done now that your blog is up and running and you have an audience, but you're not. Part of being a member of the biblioblogosphere is continuing education. I recommend subscribing to a few librarian blogs to keep up with new technology and library news. There are also blogs like RSS4Lib (blogs.fletcher.tufts.edu/rss4lib), which will keep you up-to-date on RSS-related news and tools specifically for libraries, and Performancing.com (www.performancing.com) whose tagline is "Helping Bloggers Succeed."

The best way to find blogs like this is to use blog search engines like Technorati, and by taking a peek at what other librarians are subscribing to. I started my list of subscriptions by importing other librarians' lists of feeds into Bloglines (www.bloglines.com) and then paring the list down based on my interests. Then I made sure to include my list of subscriptions on my blog, What I Learned Today (www.web2learning.net), so as to help new bloggers like you.

In a way, a blog is a natural extension of a library; it is a way to share information with others, which is at the very foundation of what we do. Your blog can be used as a form of advertising, as a newsletter and even as a method of communication between librarians and patrons. In the end, your library blog will be what you make of it.

Me Publish? I Don't Have a Clue

How to Get Published Online

MELISSA AHO, ERIKA BENNETT, *and* SUSAN WAKEFIELD

Have you read with envy a wonderful book review? Perused an article online and muttered to yourself that you could do better? Sure, but where do you start? Whether you are still in school or have been working for years, your unique perspectives or experiences could be topics of articles. In essence, anyone can publish online, you just need a good idea and a little motivation.

The first step is to consider why you'd like to publish. Do you enjoy reading books and would love to share your opinion? Would you like to advance your career? Are you looking for resume or CV enhancement? Do you need to publish for tenure? Or do you just want to see your name in print?

There are a number of online publication venue options. Find a topic that you can specialize in or explore the professional literature to see what topics are cutting edge and where you might be able to find a niche. Don't be discouraged if you don't find any articles on your topic. You might just have a new area to explore. Online publishing will help hone your writing skills and will enrich your life. Below we discuss online articles, book reviews, blogs, and submitting your online publication.

Online Articles: Journal and Web Magazines

There are a wide variety of online publications. After writing your article, decide if you want your work published in a peer-reviewed journal, magazine, or other online publication. Luckily, in today's wired world there are always new publications to choose from. Depending on your area of librarianship; you have a lot of options available.

One of the most difficult aspects of writing an article can be avoiding procrastination. Enlisting a coauthor can help keep your writing on pace, in spite of work and family responsibilities. Your coauthor(s) can be great motivators and will bring a fresh perspective to the topic.

Assign one person the job of shepherding the project. It isn't a pretty job, but your article will actually get completed if one person encourages everyone to keep working, to submit their information at regular intervals, and to provide revised editions to everyone.

Keep in mind that sometimes it is best not to argue over the smallest details but to get the piece submitted. Once your article is selected, the journal editor may ask for corrections or make her own editorial changes. Let go of your pride and let the work develop. Here are two Web sites that can help you get started:

- LIScareer.com (www.liscareer.com/write.htm)
- *Ariadne Magazine* (www.ariadne.ac.uk)

Online Book Reviews

Book reviewing provides one of the best ways to become published. Many publications have online book reviews to supplement their print reviews. Journals will periodically request book reviewer submissions. They often ask for a writing sample. (This is where having coauthored an article or written a book review for a class can come in handy.) If you haven't written a book review, try to get one under your belt. It can be distributed through your local school district, neighborhood newspaper, an organization you belong to that publishes a newsletter, etc. Remember, read book reviews in the journal you are writing for, so that you are familiar with the style.

You can send a request to write book reviews to the book review editor of an online journal. However, the most effective way to start publishing reviews is to apply when a journal calls for reviewers on their Web site or in their print journal. Keep your eyes open on listserves and blogs, because editors will often put out a call for reviewers or even send out a list of titles they would like reviewed.

With book reviews start small, with a 175 to 200 word review. Then work your way up to 500 or 1,000 words. Each journal will specify their requirements for submission, including writing style and format. Never go over the required word count. Editors hate cutting down a review. So, be professional and submit the number of requested words.

Keep in mind that book reviews usually have a deadline. DO NOT volunteer to write a book review if you don't have the time to fully and carefully read the book and write up your review.

Finally, a fringe benefit to reviewing books, in addition to being published, is that you get to keep the book after you are done. Here are two Web sites that can help you get started:

- Library Journal (www.libraryjournal.com)
- Beyond the Job (http://librarycareers.blogspot.com)

Blogs

Blogs or Web logs are the hottest personal publishing option today. If you decided to create a blog, you will want to maintain a fine balance of professional usefulness and entertainment. Remember, most blogs have a life of about three months. So consider how long you want your blog to last. Most good blogs post at least once a week. Are willing to make that type of commitment to your blog? Contributing to someone else's blog or starting a blog with a couple of like-minded people may be a good way to begin.

Start marketing your blog after you have a significant amount of content by linking to sites that will interest your readers. Then list your blog on the many blog directories. Some are specific to the library world.

If you are planning to blog, remember future employers will be able to read your posting. This can happen long after you've moved on from your blog or current thoughts. This may be a positive or a not-so-positive development. So be careful of what you post. Web sites that can help you get started include:

Where to start:

- Blogger (www.blogger.com)
- WordPress (http://wordpress.com)
- LibDex (www.libdex.com/weblogs.html)

Your Online Submission

When you e-mail your online article or book review to the journal editor, set the sending option to alert whether the e-mail arrived and if it was opened (if you have this feature). Always blind copy yourself on the e-mail. Consider printing out a copy for your file, too. You never know when your computer will crash.

Editors are swamped with submissions. If you don't have the capability in your e-mail program to know when and if your writing was received, send a friendly e-mail to the editor mentioning the date sent and that you are interested in knowing the turnaround time. Being harsh or aggressive will not win you any friends. The publishing world is small and your reputation will get around to other editors.

With the above suggestions, you'll have a good pool of places for potential online publications. Make sure you expand your journal search by including other areas that may apply to your potential topic, such as education, business, careers, regional, and social issues.

Conclusion

Publishing online is like everything in life, start with small steps. Build your way up from a 100-word book review to a 1,000-word article. Coauthor the first article or two to see if you like writing articles. The more you write the more comfortable you will become as an author.

Keep in mind that getting published online may lead to getting published in print. You can use your publications from online venues to help launch future opportunities. Publishing online can lead to a rewarding experience both personally and professionally. Good luck! Now go out and write!

Outreach and Information

Blogs in the Academic Library

Diane L. Schrecker

Blogs, or Web logs, have replaced not only personal Web pages, but also some organizational Web sites in this age of Web 2.0 technology (O'Reilly, 2005). How prevalent are blogs? According to Technorati's "State of the Blogosphere" there are approximately 120,000 new blogs created daily, averaging 1.4 blogs per second (Sifry, 2007). Librarians are finding inventive ways to connect with patrons and have found blogs an invaluable resource for outreach, collection development, and information. This essay presents information to consider before creating a blog, suggests online tools for enhancement, and highlights two blogs currently used by Ashland University Library's Instructional Resource Center (IRC).

Blogging: Quick and Simple

Creating a blog is quick, easy, and often free, as blog hosting services provide necessary software applications. A recent Pew Internet report on blogging lists LiveJournal, MySpace, and Blogger the top three tools preferred by surveyed users (Fox, Lenhart, 2006). Before making a software choice, consider:

- Will the blog reside on your organization's server or will it be hosted on the blog server? Pros and cons exist for both choices; a host server may have maintenance or usage outages but also offer the ability to blog from any Internet connection without firewall concerns.
- Are you familiar with blogging? Explore blog Web sites and evaluate what each has to offer users; ease of use, blog layout, and additional indexing options are desirable. Investigate technical support and help pages provided by the blog site.
- What type of blogosphere presence does your organization want or need? When using the blog server, the name and URL will reflect the server and not your library.

If you are new to blogging, start with your blog on the host server, as the choice to move your blog to your own server can be made at a later date. Generally speaking, it will take longer to make the decision on what blog site to use than it will to set up the blog. Overall steps include creating an account with the service, choosing a name for the blog, and selecting a design template. Of the three tools mentioned, four Ashland University Library and IRC blogs have been created with Blogger and reside on the Blogger server with a blogspot.com address.

Enhancing Your Blog: The Sidebar

Blogs layouts are commonly divided into at two sections: a main body, displaying blog posts in chronological order, and a sidebar of permanent information. Adding information significant to your library in the form of widgets, snippets of code inserted into sidebars, will personalize your blog.

Listed below are just a few of the resources available for enhancing the visual appeal and usability of blogs, as well as providing statistical information to help determine blog usage. Mix and match them with other textual information, such as library hours and contact information to personalize your blog and create interest.

- LibraryThing (www.librarything.com): Free to 200 entries, this online social catalog permits users to create collections of books. The LibraryThing widget maker can turn your list into a visual treat for your patrons by displaying book covers. New to LibraryThing is LibraryThing for Libraries.
- WidgetBox: Widgetizing the Web (www.widgetbox.com): Set up a free account and browse the catalog for tools. Investigate the "blidget." It will make your blog a small widget capable of being added to any existing Web page or other blog.
- Feedburner (www.feedburner.com): Burn your feed, create user-friendly subscription "chicklets" for your blog, and view user statistics. Basic (free) and upgraded (for a fee) accounts are available.
- StatCounter (www.statscounter.com): View real-time statistics on your blog using invisible coding. Basic service is free, and expanded service is available.
- Technorati (www.technorati.com): Claim your blog, create tags for posts that will link to other blogs, search other blogs, and create sidebar widgets.
- WorldCat Beta (www.worldcat.org): From OCLC, a search box widget.

Information and Book Reviews: Two IRC Blogs at Ashland University

Presenting current information regarding the IRC and its various collections is a vital aspect routinely charged to the "What's New" and "Handouts" sections of the IRC Web site. However, as the collection continued to grow, handouts, lists, and e-mail notifications became cumbersome additions to both the IRC Web site and the faculty e-mail in-boxes. It became apparent an IRC blog, offering a chronological record of purchases, quick access to the information, and a searchable index would be useful. The following goals were determined:

- Include news and information with a focus on collection purchases for the IRC, such as juvenile books, activity books, education titles, manipulative kits, software, audio books, and IRC reference items.
- Replace publication of yearly book lists. Post all collection purchases as they become shelf ready with each entry's heading specific to the book genre represented.

The first entry to the IRC blog (http://auircbookblog.blogspot.com) was posted June 10, 2005. Two years and 502 posts later, the blog continues to be a viable platform for providing information to IRC and library patrons. Blog appearance has changed significantly over time with new sidebar widgets, RSS feeds, and the university color scheme; the basic purpose continues to be providing news and information. As is often the case with technology endeavors, subsequent brainstorming resulted in a number of blog ideas being discussed and dismissed even as others were successfully instituted yet failed. Last spring a second IRC blog debuted focusing on children's literature and book reviews.

The IRC Book Review blog (http://ircbookreviews.blogspot.com) was created to complement the library juvenile collection. With content beyond news and information, specific attention was given to purpose and goals, resulting in the following structured sidebar categories for the review blog:

- Instructional Resource Center: Basic facts and contact information.
- About This Blog: How to find reviewed books, recommended books for review, introduction to blog comments, and an explanation of Technorati tags.
- AU Library Juvenile Collection: Description of the juvenile collection, review resources used to select books, and library collection development policy.
- More Information/Reviewing Books: Bibliography resources for reviewing books.
- Catalog and Library Links: Links to library databases, a library catalog search widget, and a WorldCat search widget.
- Internet Resources: Children's literature blogs, online review sources, and book awards.
- Blog Information: Blog comment policy, library disclaimers, list of reviewers, use of book covers, and copyright statements.

Initial goals for this blog were the inclusion of reviews written by librarians and College of Education faculty, weekly postings, and the possibility of student reviews written in conjunction with various children's literature courses. Falling well short of projected numbers, there are currently 47 reviews posted on the blog, with a significant amount crafted by one librarian. However, feedback on this project is positive both on and off campus with blog statistics supporting its continuation as a review source and feasible marketing tool.

Not every library blog is destined to be a success; some have limited scope and appeal, while others lose interest or readership. Ashland University Library and the Instructional Resource Center have had a total of four blogs. Two are successful, one had limited use and was abandoned after a year, and the fourth is being evaluated for deletion. All of the blogs have been learning experiences in the field of blogging and Web 2.0 technology. After all, the next IRC blog might be created tomorrow.

For Further Reading

Castro, E. (2005). *Publishing a Blog with Blogger*. CA: Peachpit Press.
Richardson, W. (2006). *Blogs, wikis, podcasts, and other powerful web tools for classrooms*. Thousand Oaks, CA: Corwin Press.
Stone, B. (2004). *Who let the blogs out?: A hyperconnected peek at the world of Weblogs*. New York: St. Martin's Griffin.

Bibliography

Fox, L. & Lenhart, A. (2006, July 19). Bloggers: A portrait of the Internet's new storytellers. *Pew Internet & American Life Project*. Retrieved from www.pewinternet.org/PPF/r/186/report_display.asp.

O'Reilly Network. (2005, September 30). What is Web 2.0? Retrieved from http://oreillynet.com/lpt/a/6228/.

Sifry's Alerts. (2007, April 5). The state of the live Web, April 2007. Retrieved from www.sifry.com/alerts/archives/000493.html.

Setting Up a Quickie Wiki

NICOLE C. ENGARD

What is the first word you think of when I say wiki? *Wikipedia*, right? There is so much more to wikis than just the Wikipedia. Wikis are a great way for a group of people to collaborate on a single project — if two heads are better than one, imagine how great 10 or 20 or 40 would be. They are also an easy way for people without programming skills to create an interactive Web site in almost no time at all.

So, where do you start? I started with the infamous Wikipedia. I decided I wanted to learn more about how wikis worked, so I found an article in the Wikipedia that interested me and I clicked "edit." The beauty of wikis is that anyone can edit the content without having to register or sign in (if the site owner chooses). Once on the editing screen I was able to see the syntax (special coding) others had used to format the page. I'll admit there was a lot to learn and all wikis have different rules. Some wiki packages, like JotSpot (www.jot.com), come with WYSIWYG (What You See Is What You Get) editors that enable you to see exactly what your page will look like as you edit it. With services like these, the learning curve is significantly reduced. Unlike JotSpot, Wikipedia is powered by MediaWiki (www.mediawiki.org/wiki/MediaWiki) and uses its own brand of syntax.

If you would like to learn in a slightly easier (and still free) environment, Peanut Butter Wiki (pbwiki) (www.pbwiki.com) is the place to go. Pbwiki offers free, password-protected wikis hosted on their own servers; for this reason I am going to walk you through the basics of setting up a wiki using this service.

Visit pbwiki and click "Get a free wiki." Simply choose your wiki name and enter your e-mail address, and you are on your way to your first wiki page.

Defining Your Settings

Once you have created your wiki, you need to change a few of the settings. When you visit your wiki (yourname.pbwiki.com), you will see a button on the top that reads "Settings." The settings include your site's title, description, passwords, look and feel, and much more.

You will notice that a password is required for your wiki. If you would like your wiki to be edited by anyone you can just provide the password on the front page for all to see. This is how I have seen it done on some of the conference wikis I have visited. If you would like your wiki to be private, you can change the Public/Private settings and then go to the Sharing options to get the URL to send to the group you would like to be able to see the page.

With your test wiki, I would recommend seeing what each option does for you. Try out the different free skins and decide which color scheme you like best for your site.

Learning the Syntax

Once your wiki is set up you will have a default start page that will point you to more help, including a quick syntax/style guide, a tour, and tips on how to start a new page. To create a new page using pbwiki you can either click the button that reads "New Page" or you can simply create a link to the page from your home page by typing your page title in square brackets.

Each of these options takes you to a different page. If you click the "New Page" button, you will be taken to a form that asks you for the title and gives you the choice of some premade templates. Templates make it easier for beginning wiki users to learn syntax and to format pages. If you start your page this way, you must remember to create a link to your page from one of your existing pages because, unlike most Web sites, which use folder structure to define navigation, wikis use links.

Once you are a bit more experienced you may decide to create a page just by adding a link. For example, to create a page titled "My First Page" you type "My First Page." Once you submit that change, click the link to "My First Page" and you will be taken to an empty form where you can edit the page.

At first it all seems a little confusing and a bit cumbersome (if you ask me), but you will get the hang of it. The key to learning is experimenting. Play with the different templates and syntax until you get used to creating lists, using tables, and changing fonts, etc.

Other Wiki Options

Once you have gotten the hang of creating and formatting pages, you may decide you want to upgrade to something like MediaWiki. In order to install MediaWiki, you need access to your Web server. Some PHP and MySQL knowledge would not hurt either. Why upgrade? A package like this gives you more control and more features, while still costing nothing.

To help you choose the right package for you and your library, Wikipedia has a comprehensive comparison chart (http://en.wikipedia.org/wiki/Comparison_of_wiki_software) that lets you compare features, functionality and price side by side.

Uses in Your Library

Now that you know how to set up and use a wiki, how is this knowledge going to help in your everyday life? The uses for wikis are only limited by your imagination. At my library, our entire staff intranet is a wiki.[1] This allows the staff to edit every page regardless of their

HTML knowledge. Since our intranet stores information for all of our staff, it only makes sense that all of our staff be able to edit the pages.

Another great use of a wiki is to keep meeting minutes.[2] After a meeting, someone can put their notes on a wiki page and then the other meeting participants can come in and add their comments, notes and ideas. This way there is an interactive document for keeping track of all of the information for that project or meeting — no more searching through e-mails with vague subject lines to find out what others thought about the ideas presented at the meeting.

A wiki also crosses office boundaries. Want to share your ideas with people in other branches, other libraries, or people in other countries? Wikis can do that. Putting a wiki on your library Web site would allow your patrons and the world (if you so choose) to include their own resources to share with others.

Your Very Own Wiki

You are now ready to start your very own wiki. The key things to remember are:

- Be Creative. Find areas in your work and life where it would be great to have help and create a wiki for that task
- Be Fearless. When working with free packages, you have nothing to lose but time. Try new things, play around with features.

To get you started here are a few wikis for and from libraries that have been pretty successful so far:

- Wikis for Libraries

  ➤ Blogging Libraries [www.blogwithoutalibrary.net/links/]
  ➤ Library Instruction Wiki [http://instructionwiki.org]
  ➤ Library Success: A Best Practices Wiki [www.libsuccess.org]
  ➤ LISWiki [www.liswiki.com]

- Wikis from Libraries

  ➤ The Biz Wiki (www.library.ohiou.edu/subjects/bizwiki)
  ➤ SJCPL's Subject Guides (www.libraryforlife.org/subjectguides/index.php/Main_Page)

Notes

1. Engard, Nicole and RayAna Park. "Intranet 2.0: Fostering Collaboration," *ONLINE Magazine*, vol. 30, no. 3, May-June 2006, p. 16.
2. See the Virtual Reference SIG Wiki (http://vrsig.pbwiki.com).

Webmaster 101

Building a Personal Web Site

JENNIFER JOHNSTON

I'm a webmaster. Not for my library, or any other organization or company, but for my professional self. After I graduated from library school, I felt that having a Web site showcasing my vitae, projects, and other accomplishments would demonstrate my comfort with computers to future employers. Not only was I right, but I've also found that it's also a great way to connect with other librarians and advertise the library where I work.

Getting Started

Before you install Web authoring software, brainstorm your Web site content. Decide what information you want to include and why. If strictly professional content is your goal, stick to it; only include information that you want employers, students, editors or publishers to see.

After sketching a rough draft of your content, you should have an idea of how elaborate your Web site will be. I envisioned about eight different pages for my site and wanted to keep things fairly simple; these factors—along with my familiarity with Microsoft products and slight experience with Web authoring software—convinced me to use FrontPage to build my first Web site offline. It was a good decision for me, but keep in mind that Dreamweaver is an excellent program as well. Also know that you have the option of creating your Web site online, using services such as those from Geocities or Tripod.

After deciding how you want to design your Web site, you'll need to select (and purchase) a domain name and hosting service. Services vary depending on price, reliability, and services offered, so do your research. Linda Roeder's articles for About.com regarding personal Web pages (http://personalweb.about.com) extensively cover these issues in easy-to-understand language.

More About Content

Every Web site needs a homepage; in webmaster lingo this is called the index page. Because this is usually the first page people visit, it's imperative to make a good impression. I embellish mine with a library or book-related quote, and try to change the passage every couple of months. Other ideas include a particularly powerful image or a short introduction to your Web site.

A brief biographical statement could also be incorporated into a home page, though I chose to keep mine separate. This was mainly because I wanted to include a picture of myself on the Web site, but didn't want to have that picture be the first thing people saw; a biography page seemed to be the perfect solution to this. When creating your biography, try to keep it succinct; author bios at the end of reviews or articles are good examples. Mention where you work, outstanding accomplishments, and any associations and committees to which you belong. Maintain a professional tone, but keep in mind: This doesn't mean you can't have fun. For instance, the pictures I include on my biography page are all taken in book-related places, such as Hay-on-Wye, Harvard University's Lamont Library, and my personal library at home.

Another important element of a professional Web site should be your resume or curriculum vitae. Though I'm now working in public libraries, I worked in academic libraries longer and wanted to include my teaching experience and publications in my resume; I find vitas better suited to this.

Depending on what your resume includes, you can then link from within the resume page or construct a separate page or pages for certain sections. For example, you can embed links to reviews that are listed under publications on the resume page, or simply create another Web page titled "Publications" that lists your writings and create hyperlinks there.

Consider also having a projects page that details programs and activities you're currently cultivating. I believe this is a good way to demonstrate and document one's experience in libraries. My projects page includes everything from book exhibits to art databases to author readings, and I also post pictures whenever possible for added significance.

Another page you might want to include in your Web site is one describing interests and hobbies, but this can be tricky. Again, if a professional tone is what you're after, make sure your interests somehow correlate with your library knowledge.

The last element you'll want to include in your Web site is contact information. Decide how you want someone to reach you: work address, phone number, and an e-mail address are all possibilities; I chose to list my e-mail address only. When listing an e-mail address, know that if you type the information out, such as "librarian123@library.com," computers can harvest your e-mail address for spam. One way of eliminating this is to create a Mail To form.

What Not to Include

There are two items you should consider *not* posting on a Web site: family pictures and unrelated hobbies. Including pictures of family members shares a glimpse into your private life, one you might not want just anyone to see. I believe that publishing family pictures or interests or hobbies that aren't related to your profession digresses from a professional appearance.

I admit: A previous version of my Web site advertised my affection for bargain book collecting and building model biplanes, from which I linked a bibliography I created in library school. I've since removed both hobbies after feeling they were too personal and now simply keep a list of books that I've finished and enjoyed, titled "Recent Reads." I believe this book list is especially well suited to my current job in the public library setting.

Making It Pretty

The best advice here is: Less is more. Start out using only two different types and sizes of fonts for text and keep the colors within your Web site to a minimum.

Interesting graphics enhance well-written, organized text; however, don't post too many pictures on your Web site, since doing so will make it more difficult for users to navigate your site, and for Web pages to load. Many Web sites offer free graphics; my favorites are those for educators, since they often have pictures related to library and information science. A simple Google search for "free clip art for educators" brings up several of the sites that I've found useful. You might also explore other ways to embellish your Web site using video or sound clips. (Because I've had such success with my first Web site, I've since enlisted the help of a professional graphic artist; my goal is to take the graphics to the next level, while keeping the concept and structure of the site as I'd originally designed it.)

Maintenance

Once you've fashioned your Web site, don't stop there. After uploading it, troubleshoot the site to make sure all links work, text is readable, and formatting lines up correctly. Trained webmasters have various secrets to ensure Web sites will appear the same on all computers, but if you're an amateur like me, simply open your site on different computers, in different browsers, such as AOL, Internet Explorer, and Netscape to ensure everything looks good.

Finally, keep your site up to date and do this regularly so you don't have to make a lot of changes at once. I've created a simple Word document where I can log in information I need to add and to which sections. This tracks all my changes so I don't forget — or repeat — any modifications to my Web site.

Being your own Web site manager doesn't mean you have to be a computer whiz. I'd never used a computer until my second year of college and hadn't created a PowerPoint presentation until my final year in library school. But with the right planning and a little bit of patience, you too can become your own Web site manager.

PART 5. VISION IMPAIRED

Seeing Through Others' Eyes Grant Project

BOB BLANCHARD

Increasing public awareness of the assistive technology available at Des Plaines Public Library was the focus of a successful grant project in spring 2004. Titled "Seeing Through Others' Eyes," the project also funded programs for the public about visual impairments, training for library staff, glossy brochures of the assistive technology (AT) the library offers and the library's start-up collection of descriptive videos.

The Need and Intent

A large and growing pool of potential users of the library's AT devices and services provided the inspiration for the grant project.

According to the 2000 census, the City of Des Plaines, a northwest suburb of Chicago, has nearly 57,000 residents, of which 17.7 percent (or 10,105 people) are age 65 or older. In 1990, the percentage of seniors was 15.4 percent, or 8,195 residents. According to Prevent Blindness America, in 2002 about 23 percent of all Illinois residents aged 40 or older had blindness, vision impairment, cataracts or glaucoma, and it was determined that about 6,600 Des Plaines residents in that age range would have one of those conditions. This statistic does not count the many people in Des Plaines who may have sight-robbing macular degeneration or diabetic retinopathy. Of course, sight impairment also affects the younger population. All of these people could benefit from what the library has to offer.

The intended audience for the project was persons with visual impairments, as well as their family members, friends and caregivers. The expected benefit, which was fulfilled, was increased public awareness and usage of the library's AT.

The Programs

The library's grant proposal was approved by the Illinois secretary of state and state librarian's office. After receiving the $4,895 Library Services and Technology Act grant, four programs were planned, all scheduled within three weeks in March 2004, which was Save Your Vision Month.

First, Dawn Maxey, the Illinois representative of Guide Dogs for the Blind Inc., spoke about guide dogs and the independence the trained animals can provide for their masters. Maxey, who is blind, and her guide dog, Lea, fascinated the audience by demonstrating basic commands and describing situations in which Lea is especially helpful.

Three days later, on a Saturday morning, the library hosted its first vision fair. AT vendors and nonprofit agencies that serve visually impaired individuals had booths for the public to visit. About 50 people attended and learned about the AT the library offers and local merchants sell. Representatives of Prevent Blindness America, the Guild for the Blind, the Chicago Lighthouse for Persons Who Are Blind or Visually Impaired, the regional Talking Books center, and the local organization for persons with disabilities also participated. Pharmacy students from the University of Illinois at Chicago fulfilled a public service requirement by explaining causes and symptoms of eye disorders.

The following week, two representatives of the Des Plaines Lions Club presented a program titled "Etiquette for Interacting with Visually Impaired Persons." Topics included how to address a visually impaired person, how to offer help and how to interact in common situations. The Lions members certainly knew their stuff — one was totally blind by age seven but has not allowed his disability to be a burden, and another had taught persons with visual impairments for more than 30 years. Outside of the vision fair, this program attracted the greatest number of attendees.

The final program was presented the next week by Chicago writer Beth Finke, author of the memoir *Long Time No See*. Finke started losing her sight in her early twenties, during her honeymoon. The book describes her frustrations and her victories while coping with her blindness. The audience learned that persons may allow life-altering events to change their lives in positive ways, and the attendees asked several questions about her writing process.

In all, the programs attracted about 100 people to the library. Many attendees became more knowledgeable about visual disorders and the ways people successfully live with those disabilities.

Other Benefits

With remaining funds, the library purchased a start-up collection of more than 70 descriptive videos, in which a hushed voice describes the scene, the actors' nonverbal cues, certain actions and other aspects of what is happening in the movie.

Also, an AT vendor trained two library staff members on the use of the popular AT software programs JAWS and MAGic with Speech. JAWS reads aloud words and Internet links that are on a computer screen, while MAGic magnifies the images on the monitor and also has an audio component. The training gave staff insight into the software the library provides for individuals with special needs.

An attractive four-color brochure explaining the library's assistive devices and services was designed by the Public Information Services staff. The 3,000 copies of the "Access-Ability" brochure — set in large type — were printed locally, to promote Des Plaines business and to keep some of the grant funds in the city. In addition to describing AT devices and software, it outlines services, including delivery of library materials to homebound patrons and deposit collections for senior residences.

Members of the target audience were reached by the four programs, and people today still benefit from the grant project. One patron reported that the guide dogs program had a profound effect on her life. The woman, who had recently become visually impaired, obtained more information about guide dogs and subsequently applied for training. In an e-mail to presenter Dawn Maxey, she wrote, "You actually made it possible for an individual to acquire the independence needed to maintain a normal lifestyle."

The library community also benefited from the grant project. At the 2004 Illinois Library Association's annual conference in Chicago, I presented a poster session, at which librarians learned about the grant and its effect on the population of Des Plaines. The visits were followed up with mailed packets that included the AccessAbility brochure and a list of vision fair participants. In 2006, I responded to an Ohio librarian's query, posted on the prtalk listserv, regarding services to adults with special needs. I sent her those same informational brochures.

Continuity

An update was created and inserted into the AccessAbility brochure because the library added portable magnifying machines. The brochures will be distributed to local health-care professionals, social service agencies and organizations, senior residences and nursing homes, and others who provide services to older adults. The goal of this mass distribution is to make potential users and the people who serve them aware of the AT devices and services at our library.

A more extensive brochure listing several local AT vendors and service agencies was produced and made available in 2007.

Subsequent vision fairs were held at Des Plaines Public Library in 2005 and 2006. In 2007, a group of library outreach staff from five public libraries in the area collaborated to present a vision fair at a location central to the suburbs served by those libraries.

The Vision Fulfilled

The grant project successfully fulfilled its purpose — to educate the public about the assistive technology the library offers for in-library and home use and to increase the uses of our AT devices. A growing number of patrons check out AT machines, mostly magnifiers, and can borrow them for eight weeks. The library intends to increase and improve its AT collection in the future. Library staff members also will be kept informed about the library's AT collection. But, most of all, the public is more aware of some of the specialized services at our library.

Technology for Visually Impaired Patrons

BOB BLANCHARD

"This is a godsend!" one Des Plaines Public Library patron said while viewing an image of her great grandson — a boy she had never seen before. She was looking at the color photograph in her condominium with the aid of a closed-circuit television lent by our library.

Providing assistive technology to patrons with visual impairments, both at the library and inside their homes, is one of the great joys of my job. Assistive technology (AT) is defined as a device, machine or computer program that people with disabilities use to improve or maintain their quality of life. In the case of libraries, most AT typically is for persons with visual disabilities, although libraries also offer AT for persons with hearing, physical and mental disabilities. This essay focuses on AT for people with visual impairments.

Des Plaines Public Library serves the City of Des Plaines, a suburb northwest of Chicago. According to the 2000 census, the city has a population of more than 57,000, and nearly 18 percent is age 65 or older — the prime age range for the onset of visual disabilities including glaucoma, macular degeneration and diabetic retinopathy.

Some of our patrons with visual issues were avid readers, and the loss of their vision is heartbreaking because they now have difficulty enjoying the written word. This population may benefit from our closed-circuit televisions (CCTVs) and portable magnifiers. A CCTV is a significant improvement over the standard magnifying glass. It includes a camera and a monitor (either black and white or color) and greatly enlarges print materials. Newspapers, magazines and mail are easier to read. The space between the CCTV's moveable platform and the monitor allows patrons to view labels on prescription bottles and to write checks. Some people even use the machine to view their needlework!

The library has three CCTVs that circulate. I deliver the machines to the homes of people holding Des Plaines library cards.

All of the library's AT has an eight-week loan period and can be renewed once. When a CCTV is not in a patron's home, it is ready to use in a carrel on the library's popular materials floor. Our circulating CCTV with color monitor was purchased by our Friends of the Library. Another CCTV, which was donated by the family of a lifelong library patron, has a very large color monitor and a permanent place on the Reference Services floor.

With all their wondrous capabilities, CCTVs are not designed to be portable. However, the library has a set of portable viewing machines for loan — a Tiemann Group Traveller, purchased by the Friends of the Library, and an even smaller QuickLook machine. Both can be used in different modes, just like most CCTVs: color, black on white background, and white on black. These machines are convenient for doing classroom work, reading letters and reviewing menu choices in restaurants. One teenager used the QuickLook for reading his homework assignments.

In early 2007 the library installed the latest versions of computer software that magnifies and "reads" images or words that are on a computer screen. JAWS is perhaps the best known and most widely used screen-reading software on the market. MAGic with Speech is a screen magnifier with an audio component. Our library has JAWS on one computer, which also has the Internet and Microsoft applications. MAGic with Speech, because of its dual capabilities, is installed on ten computers throughout the library. At least one computer on each of the library's four floors is equipped with MAGic.

Our staff is trained on MAGic with Speech and JAWS and will continue to be made aware of new developments in the library's AT via training, e-mail and the staff intranet.

Awareness of the machines and their availability has expanded through a consistent public relations campaign of news releases, Internet postings and newsletter articles, but word of mouth and in-library demonstrations are the best ways we increase the usage of AT. Library staff, especially those at the circulation, reference and readers' services desks, need to be familiar with the library's AT, so they can refer people with disabilities to me. Staff members also are encouraged to be attuned to the needs of patrons who have visual disabilities, so that staff may suggest using a magnifying machine or enrolling in the Talking Books program.

Targeted programs, such as a guide dog demonstration, a presentation about etiquette for interacting with visually impaired persons, and a talk by a blind author, and vision fairs have helped increase awareness of the library's offerings to persons with disabilities.

At the vision fair, people may meet with AT vendors and inspect the latest products available. The public may also visit representatives of organizations that provide services for persons with visual impairments. The Des Plaines Public Library held its first vision fair in 2004 as part of its Seeing Through Others' Eyes grant project. The fair featured nine exhibitors, including one vendor, the library itself and representatives from organizations as varied as Prevent Blindness America to the area's Talking Books program to pharmacy students from a local university. The 2005 fair expanded to include five AT vendors from the Chicago area, four service organizations and the library. The following year's fair included vendors of assistive technology for various disabilities, not just visual impairments. For 2007, programmers for older adults from five libraries collaborated to plan the fair.

How can your library start and promote an AT collection? Here are a few basic steps:

1. Determine the need in your community. How many persons have visual disabilities? How many potential AT users might there be in the near future?
2. Talk with staff at other libraries that offer their patrons AT. What do they have? Do some devices circulate? If so, what is the circulation policy for AT? What devices must stay in the building? How often do patrons use AT?
3. Find reputable AT vendors. Staff members from other libraries may be able to tell you their experiences with vendors in your area.
4. Find potential sources of revenue for AT. The library's operating budget may include

funds for AT devices. Your Friends of the Library group may be interested in providing a public service by purchasing AT. Community organizations, such as your local Lions Club, may also be potential partners.

5. Plan a public relations campaign to let the public know in advance that your library will carry AT.

6. Once the AT is purchased and installed, host an open house to introduce the public to the wondrous machines and/or software.

7. Produce a brochure about your AT devices and include information about vendors and social service agencies that can assist persons with disabilities.

8. Post AT information on your Web site and keep the site updated.

9. Keep your staff members abreast of the latest changes in the library's AT collection. It is particularly critical for circulation staff members to know about the library's AT, since they often receive the most inquiries. They particularly need to know what the library offers and with whom the patron needs to consult.

AT manufacturers are coming out with more innovative adaptive equipment and software each year. Millions of baby boomers are entering their 60s, and the demand for AT likely will become greater and the devices more sophisticated, especially since many boomers are computer savvy. It will be exciting to see what equipment and software AT manufacturers offer in the future to meet the needs of the boomer generation and the generations that follow.

The Art of the Picture Book Conference

Partnership Beyond Library Walls

DIANE L. SCHRECKER

Eighteen months ago this conference was a simple collaborative idea; put together a few sessions, find an extraordinary keynote speaker, and bring together professionals interested in picture book art. Surely, we reasoned, this would appeal to a wide range of people in the fields of art, education, librarianship, and even publishing.
— *The Art of the Picture Book Conference program*

Partnerships and collaborations are an integral part of successful academic library programs. Plans for an innovative venture at Ashland University began during the fall of 2005 and culminated with a successful May 2006 conference featuring a unique celebration of art and the picture book. This endeavor provided an opportunity for Ashland University librarians, College of Education faculty, and Ashland City School District teachers to join forces, forming a conference planning team. Teachers, librarians, artists, publishers, and anyone interested in picture books, attended The Art of the Picture Book Conference and enjoyed a two-day celebration of the genre. This essay provides a short synopsis with highlights of the conference and suggests a few tips for readers interested in pursuing a conference project.

Conference Planning: Behind the Scenes

The Art of the Picture Book Conference was initiated by two faculty members, professors of children's literature and art, who came into the library's Instructional Resource Center and proposed a concept; prepare a conference offering that will bring together art, instruction, and the library to celebrate picture books. Could it work? Was there interest? Discussion ensued, ideas flowed, and basic concepts, such as theme and logo, became reality. When permission from the university was obtained, it was time to convene a planning committee. Listed below are suggestions for organizing a committee:

- Remember Goldilocks: Committee size should not be too small or too large; it needs to be just right. A small committee may find it difficult to handle the stress of conference planning, and it may be hard to schedule and manage a large, broad-based committee.
- Committee chair and/or cochair: Final decisions will need to be made and signatures are required on speaker contracts and other documents. A committee chair is a necessity for things to run smoothly.
- Choosing the committee: Ask for and solicit volunteers who have diverse talents. Not everyone is interested in budgets or has the creative flair for design or marketing. Create an idea expansive committee.
- Conference experience: Find people with previous conference planning experience to be a member of the committee, or to consult. It will make things go smoothly.
- Regular meeting times: Meet at regular intervals to keep conference proceedings current.
- Committee communication: E-mail, especially when committee members work at the same institution, is almost an instant form of communication. Create a group or listserv to make one message work for everyone.

Of these five suggestions, choosing the committee members is key to planning success. During the eighteen months prior to the Art of the Picture Book Conference, our planning committee went through several personnel changes. It was a challenge, and often an obstacle, to meet and overcome. If not for a strong core of planning committee members, a successful conference would not have been possible.

Conference Programming: Decisions, Decisions

Keynote speakers, in this instance authors and illustrators who are able to create attention and draw attendees to the program, are a fundamental part of any conference program. The Art of the Picture Book Conference featured the exceptional talents of Denise Fleming, Ted and Betsy Lewin, Dominic Catalano, and Benjamin Sapp of the Mazza Museum. Program committee members determined the conference theme components of "Celebrate, Educate and Appreciate" should be interpreted to include illustration, as well as the artful layout of a book. This expanded definition integrated "using picture books successfully in classrooms, libraries, and other settings to teach and analyze, to listen and enjoy" (Art of the Picture Book, 2006). As a result, proposals received in answer to the conference call were from a divergent group of authors, artists, K–12 teachers, college instructors, preservice teachers (students), school librarians, public librarians, and academic librarians. Thirty-six breakout sessions covering a wide range of topics were subsequently offered during the two-day conference.

These elements are the most visible results of decisions made by the planning committee, however, they provide only a surface glimpse of conference particulars discussed, dismissed, and designated throughout the programming process. Consider the following topics:

- Timeline: Detail various deadlines, expectations, and assigned tasks.
- Proposals: A call for proposals is only part of the process; determine how many programs to accept, how to review, and the format or structure to use for submissions.
- Budget: Will the conference be self-supporting or is there a need for outside vendors, grants, or donations from within the university?

- Freebies: A giveaway for conference attendees that is a tangible reminder of their day.
- Scheduling: Management during the day is crucial; determination of keynote speaker times, limits for sessions, break and food scheduling, and providing free time is vital.
- Programs: Offer attendees a professionally printed program. It will assist in the execution of daily events and provide presenters with tangible evidence of their participation.
- Subcommittees: It may be necessary for more than one person to handle aspects such as food, publicity, proposal reviews, and technology.
- Technology: Detail technology that will be made available to presenters and assign someone to troubleshoot during the conference.

Conference Marketing: Using the Internet

Relying on flyers, handouts, and posters for conference marketing and advertising is an expensive proposition. It was determined that while these items were fundamental to publicity, budget constraints made this type of marketing a fiscal challenge and early committee determinations to utilize the Web as a major promotional tool was fundamental to our success. The conference Web site, available on the Ashland University server at www.ashland.edu/~artpicbk, debuted a full year prior to the conference, generating widespread interest. Web site concept, design, and implementation were handled by the conference webmaster, but Ashland's Information Technology Department proved to be an invaluable asset for Web consultation. Its staff set up space on the server, created a network e-mail account for the conference, and facilitated online forms. Every aspect of the conference, from speakers to online proposal submissions, was included on the Web site. A brief overview is presented below and may serve as a starting point for other conferences:

- Main page before the conference: An index of the entire conference.
- Main page after the conference: An archive tool detailing conference proceedings, photographs, and session handouts.
- Speakers: Photographs with biographical information supplied by the authors and illustrators for the conference.
- Program: Links to the conference program with sessions and maps.
- Presenter page: Information, FAQs, news and updates for session presenters.
- Registration: Registration pricing, deadlines, and payment options.
- Location: Conference location, parking options, nearby restaurants, hotels and directions.
- Sessions: Abstract and presenter information for all sessions.

Following the conclusion of the conference, comments from attendees, both in person and via evaluation forms, provided invaluable feedback to the planning committee. Pleased with the outcome, the conference planning committee has considered repeating the collaborative endeavor in the future.

For Further Reading

Dempsey, B. (2005, February 15). Literary festivals, library style. *Library Journal.* Retrieved from www.libraryjournal.com/article/CA502013.html.

Williams, W. (2003, February 15). Booking authors: Advice from the pros. *Library Journal*. Retrieved from www.libraryjournal.com/article/CA273960.html.
Tips for booking an author: From the publisher's viewpoint. (2005, March 1). Random House. Retrieved from www.randomhouse.biz/libraries/authortips.

Bibliography

The Art of the Picture Book (2006, June 7). Retrieved from www.ashland.edu/~artpicbk.
Welcome to the art of the picture book (2006). Conference Program: *The Art of the Picture Book Conference*. Ashland, OH: Ashland University.

Breathing Life into Your Library

Hosting the Perfect Author Event

JENNIFER JOHNSTON

After five years of working in college and university libraries, I made the leap into public libraries and accepted a full-time position in reference services. As luck would have it, I was also given the opportunity to manage adult cultural programming, mainly in the form of author readings. The library currently offered other types of adult programming — computer classes, tax assistance, a book discussion group — but the last visit from a prominent writer was about three years prior to my arrival.

As any zealous book-loving librarian knows, this new responsibility was a dream come true, but I quickly found it much more challenging than I ever could have imagined. I hadn't taken any classes about public libraries in library school, and certainly didn't learn how to plan and arrange author visits on the job in academic libraries.

However, I eventually navigated through the confusion, and this is what I discovered along the way as an author event coordinator.

Know Your Library

Before approaching an author about a library visit, you need to brainstorm about library resources: who, where, and how much. Determine if you'll be the sole person arranging presentations, or if a committee will be in charge of different aspects; this will definitely help you decide how elaborate of a reading you can host. In my situation, I handle everything except the graphic design and room preparation, and this helps me feel less overwhelmed.

Next, decide where the reading will be held. The size of the room will impact a number of things, including what kind of author you invite and amount of publicity you do. If your library doesn't have the capacity for a large audience, consider teaming up with a school, college, or organization to use their facility.

After you mull over these details, find out if programming is allotted a certain amount of your library budget; if it's not, don't panic. Simply investigate other options: your library's Literacy Department, the Friends of the Library organization, local business sponsorship, charging admission, and applying for state, federal, or community grants, such as those from Poets & Writers, are all possible alternatives. It might be helpful at this time to draw up a programming budget detailing what costs you're looking to cover, such as honorariums, travel expenses, publicity, room rental, and refreshments.

Know Your Community

Before you begin inviting authors, it's imperative to know what your community likes and wants. This ensures your event will be well attended and widely effective. Two resources can aid in this: demographics of your community and library user statistics. For example, my library serves a large population of 189,000, where the majority of the people are low-income, Spanish-speaking residents; in addition to this, patrons check out mysteries more than any other genre. I try to use this knowledge when deciding which authors I think our community would most enjoy.

Another way to find out what your community wants is by asking them. Develop a survey that can be mailed or distributed at the circulation desk, or pass out an evaluation sheet after other programs for patron suggestions.

Finding Authors

There are many, many ways to locate authors. If your library doesn't have a large budget for author visits, hosting a local author can often be cost-effective, since you won't have to pay for travel or lodging expenses. Start your search at local colleges and universities in your area for possibilities, or see if your state has an online directory of writers.

Other ways of finding authors include:

- Book festivals. They're a great way to meet authors and entice them to visit your library. The Library of Congress's Center for the Book (www.loc.gov/loc/cfbook/bkevents.html) lists literary festivals by date.
- Web sites and online directories. These are just a few places that have helped me find authors for my library: Poets & Writers (www.pw.org/directry), Bowker's Bookwire (www.bookwire.com/bookwire), Romance Writers of America (www.rwanational.org), and ALA's Authors @ Your Library (www.authorsatyourlibrary.org).
- Publishers' Web sites. Bookmark them and periodically check which authors are touring in your area; several, such as HarperCollins, Picador, and Algonquin have an e-mail newsletter or author alert that will let you know which authors are currently on tour in or near your area.

Inviting Authors

Once you've selected an author, choose the best way to contact her or him. Most authors now have Web sites listing their e-mail and/or phone information. I usually prefer e-mail, simply because of time constraints. It allows time for me to prepare the letter, and the writer to mull over the written details. Some of the bigger names—Terry McMillan, Alice Sebold, Neil Gaiman—prefer arrangements to be made through their publisher or literary agent. Instructions about who to contact is usually on the author's or publisher's Web sites.

As far as the content of the initial contact goes: Try to be as general as possible. Explain who you and your library are and why you'd love for her or him to come visit your library, but try to steer clear of specific dates and times; I think this shows respect for the author's schedule and demonstrates your flexibility.

Publicizing Authors

In this day and age, it's all about marketing, which is why this next step is crucial to a successful author visit. First of all, if you have someone who handles the artistic design of publicity materials, skip to the next paragraph. If you'll be the one taking on this job, I suggest coming up with a basic design that can be easily turned into invitations, flyers, or posters, and serve as a template for later events.

Mail and post your invitations and flyers to the typical places: libraries, coffee shops, colleges, universities, and community bulletin boards—but also try to think of other locations. For example, if you're bringing in an author who would also appeal to teenagers, let high schools know about the event.

Bookstores are another wonderful place to post flyers, which brings up another point: Should you have books available for purchase? I think so. Many bookstores, independent or chain, are willing to participate, and some will even offer to give you a percentage of the profit. Having the author's books available is also a good incentive if your library has a small or nonexistent honorarium to offer the author.

Other marketing ideas, depending on your time and resources, include: posting the event information to a listserv; e-mailing invitations to members of local book and writing clubs, and other interested people; and informing your local paper about the event so they can run a feature story the week before.

A Final Note

Becoming an author event coordinator has been a highlight of my library career; if I had one last piece of advice to offer, it would be only this: Enjoy yourself! Though planning and arranging author visits can be stressful and overwhelming at times, it's absolutely worth it. Not only are you attracting people to the library, but you're also making the written word come alive for them —and you get to meet famous authors!

For Further Reading

Adult Programming for Libraries: A Manual for Libraries. 1997. Chicago: American Library Association.

Lear, Brett W. 2002. *Adult Programs in the Library.* Chicago: American Library Association.

Ludlam, Jane. 2000. "Presenting Readings and Workshops," *Poets & Writers.* www.pw.org/rw/pres-guides.htm (3 March 2006).

Michigan Center for the Book. *Author Visits at Your Library.* www.michigan.gov/authorvisits (22 February 2006).

Weekly Coffeehouse

Lee Johnson

Every Friday the hallway just outside the high school library at San Antonio Christian Schools is transformed into an aromatic and inviting coffeehouse, complete with an assortment of hot and cold beverages and delicious breakfast and snack items. Christian music provides a welcoming background, and a seating area offers a place to relax and chat or read. Many students prefer to study in groups at the large round tables. A magazine rack is rolled into the hallway to give everyone better access to the wonderful magazines to which the library subscribes. The coffeehouse is a wonderful place to get to know the faculty and students in a relaxed atmosphere and to introduce them to a unique and exciting opportunity involving the library.

The start-up costs for the coffeehouse were minimal, because most of the equipment, such as coffee pots, toaster, tables, chairs, CD player, rolling library cart, and trash can, belongs to the school. The round tables, chairs, and magazine rack are borrowed from the school library. The success of the coffeehouse eventually prompted us to purchase our own coffee pot and a large galvanized bucket for ice to chill the cold drinks.

Three to four students staff the coffeehouse and take care of setup, cleanup, restocking, shopping, and cashier duties. The librarian and the two sophomore advisors coordinate the effort and share all duties with the students. All students from the sophomore class are required to participate in this weekly fundraiser because it benefits their annual trip. The class adviser posts a list each week to remind students of their assignments to bring goodies and fulfill other duties.

In planning to launch the coffeehouse, several important decisions were made, such as:

- Where. The hallway adjacent to the library was chosen because it is spacious yet accessible, and it can be easily monitored and restocked from the library. Spills are also much easier to clean up on linoleum than carpet.
- When. We decided to have the coffeehouse one day each week. It was important not to conflict with other similar weekly fundraisers. We open 40 to 50 minutes before school starts each Friday morning. We are open daily during finals week.
- How. The librarian, faculty advisers and students trade off acting as cashier before school and between classes. We use a cash box with $30 to $40 in change.
- Why. The coffeehouse is a fundraiser for the sophomore class. Profits, which have netted anywhere from $50 to $215 weekly, are shared with the library. The library uses the

income to supplement its budget for purchasing materials as well as promoting reading and the library itself through contests and promotions. Future plans for these funds also include sponsoring author visits, a poetry workshop/rave, and a storytelling festival. The sophomore class uses their portion of the funds for various mission-related projects and trips.

For the first year we made announcements each week informing students, faculty and staff about the coffeehouse. Now that our schedule is well-known, we only make an occasional announcement to advertise new offerings or any change in hours of operation.

At the coffeehouse, pricing signs are taped up on the wall above the food and beverage tables. We also tape small signs on the beverage tables to distinguish between the coffee and the hot water. We leave a cup and small sign on the food table asking patrons to please leave payment for items purchased when there is no cashier. We also post bright red "Coffee House Today!" signs on doors around the school to catch patrons entering in the morning and between classes.

The food, materials, and equipment that we use includes:

- three round tables with two to four chairs at each table
- two rectangular tables (to display baked goods and beverages)
- rolling magazine rack, newspapers
- CD player and CDs
- library rolling cart to hold extra supplies and CD player
- large trash can
- two coffee pots
- galvanized bucket for ice to chill juice/water
- creamers, half and half, sugar, Splenda, Sweet'N Low
- ground coffee, hot chocolate, hot cider, tea, juice, bottled water
- baked goods, donuts, bagels and cream cheese, granola bars, fresh fruit
- twelve-ounce cups and lids, stirrers, napkins
- platters for goodies
- toaster for bagels (optional)
- table decorations

The three round tables are set up against one wall in the hallway with four chairs each. Decorative placemats or cloth napkins are centered on each table and topped with table decorations which vary from week to week. These decorations include silk flowers in pots and in soda bottles. We use holiday decorations as well, such as live poinsettias in December. On the wall opposite the seating area, one oblong table offers baked goods which are frequently individually wrapped and displayed on large platters and in decorative baskets. Another table offers large pots of coffee and hot water, a wide array of teas, hot chocolate, and hot cider, all individually packaged for convenience. A large galvanized bucket filled with ice chills bottles of water and juice. At one end of the hall, a magazine rack offers a variety of magazines while Christian music plays on a nearby CD player. Local newspapers are provided free of charge to our school and we set them out on the tables. A library cart featuring a selection of new books is also be set out in the hallway to create interest and draw readers. These books vary weekly or monthly and usually represent a theme such as a holiday, genre, author, or subject.

Helpful Hints

- I occasionally give out coupons for a free beverage and a goodie to teachers who help me with book fairs and to students as prizes in library contests. Teachers may also purchase coupons as rewards to give to their students.
- We held a contest to name the coffeehouse when we first opened and offered a gift certificate to a local gourmet coffee shop as a prize.
- At lunchtime, leftover baked goods can be sold in the cafeteria for half price.
- Some teachers bring their students down for 10 to 15 minutes at the end of class to get a snack. This practice has led to discussions of current events as well as other academic topics.
- Everyone that helps with setup and cleanup gets a free treat.
- Small candy canes are offered as stirrers at Christmas time.
- Suggestion cards can be offered to invite input regarding how the coffeehouse can better serve patrons.
- High school students are allowed to bring their covered drinks into the library.

Future Plans

- Have the art students paint a mural on the wall in the coffeehouse hallway.
- Have aprons made with our exclusive logo on them for coffeehouse helpers to wear.
- Just before Christmas break, the poinsettia table decorations can be given away as prizes in a drawing for coffeehouse patrons.

World Building

A Comic Collaboration for Academics and Sixth Graders

DIANE COLSON *and* TRAVIS FRISTOE

What do comics mean to you? For some teens, manga from Japan fires their imagination. For others, Charlie Brown's frustrations are part of their morning newspaper reading. And for some local university students, the graphic novel format represents a unique form of storytelling, where they focus their scholarly talents on what comics mean in the midst of culture, industry and literature. The common factor is a love for the highly original combinations of art and text that we know as comics.

Here in Gainesville, Florida, we were lucky enough to host the Conference of Comics in 2007. The conference is a collaborative effort joining the University of Florida with the Alachua County Library District in our shared interest of sustaining a comics literature for the community at large.

That's the lofty-sounding theory behind it. In concrete terms, what we've done for the past few years is bring in interesting comics artists and have them give talks at the university and then workshops in local schools and library branches. This means the artists could be on a panel discussing Deleuze's theory of representation as it applies between panels with professors and grad students one day, and at a rural library showing kindergarteners how to draw their own stories the next day.

It's a winning situation on all fronts. The emergent comics-studies program gets a high-profile forum for their studies; the library gets to highlight its popular and growing graphic novel collection; and local artists of all ages and abilities get the chance to attend hands-on workshops with professionals working in the field. On the library side, both youth services and adult services work together on the scheduling, hosting and logistics.

Planning for the multiday annual conference is a collaborative endeavor and includes making sure that all the programs are free, well advertised and open to the public. The theme of the conference was *World Building*. The artists who were invited to participate were chosen not just for their proficiency and willingness to work with diverse groups, but also for the richness of the worlds they'd created in their work.

The three comics artists who participated in the conference were Dylan Horrocks, Tom Hart and Leela Corman.

Dylan Horrocks lives in New Zealand and is the creator of the acclaimed graphic novel *Hicksville*. *Hicksville* tells the story of an imaginary town that quietly hosts the world's greatest comics library. In 2002, Horrocks won an Eisner Award for Talent Deserving of Wider Recognition. Horrocks has also written *Tim Hunter: The Books of Magic* for Vertigo and *Batgirl* for DC Comics. Despite the extra expense of flying an artist across the globe, all parties agreed that Horrocks's talent would be a real boost to the conference.

Tom Hart started publishing his own minicomics in the early 1990s, eventually winning a Xeric Award to further establish his dedication to a comic's career. His most famous creation is Hutch Owen, a vagrant who lives by his wits in a hostile world. Hutch Owen has been in three of his own books so far and is now the star of a weekly serial. Between Hutch books, Hart explored single, complete stories in his books *Banks Eubanks* and *New Hat Stories*. Hart teaches storytelling at the School of Visual Arts in New York City.

Leela Corman is an acclaimed comics artist and freelance illustrator. She has published two graphic novels, *Subway Series* and *Queen's Day*, and is currently working on a third, *Unterzakhn*, set in the tenements of the Lower East Side. She's appeared in the all-female comics compilation *Scheherazade* and has illustrated for numerous publications.

Full sponsors of the conference were the University of Florida Department of English, the College of Liberal Arts and Sciences, the Alachua County Library District, the Friends of the Library, the Digital Worlds Institute, Alternative Comics, ImageTexT, the Center for Children's Literature and Culture, Gameology.org, CLASSC, and Xerographic Copy Center.

To publicize the conference, the headquarters library created a display highlighting graphic novels and books on drawing. Library staff needed to continually refill the display because circulation of the items was so high. Handbills with the event schedule were part of the display, so that patrons could take home a reminder and actual comics.

The library arranged for the comics artists to visit area schools during their stay. The first visit was to an after-school program at an elementary school. There were about 50 children, from kindergarten to grade five, in an old-fashioned auditorium. The comics artists focused on creating characters from elemental shapes, such as circles and rectangles, which the comics demonstrated. The children enthusiastically participated, helping to recreate characters like Spongebob Squarepants by describing the shapes of each body part. They then tried creating an original character. "Noodle-shape" turned out to be the basis for the creation, with a variety of wavering figures as a result.

The second school visit was a middle school art class. The visit was arranged by the school's media specialist, so the art teacher was unsure of what to expect. She was delighted when three professional artists made their appearance, full of stories about bad grades in art class and childhood dreams of drawing comics. The comics artists demonstrated their individual favored tools for drawing. One of them used a Sharpie-like marker, another worked with an ink pen, and the third preferred to use a brush. Everyone was fascinated by the techniques and by the realization that each artist finds their own best medium. It was a very powerful presentation for the students, who were captivated by the willingness of the talented professional artists to share stories of failure and success.

After the presentation, the teacher sat with the comics artists and discussed her strategies for encouraging the children to develop as artists. The artists had many suggestions about artists that the students could emulate. The teacher was thrilled, commenting many times how this unexpected bounty of inspiration was the highlight of her year.

The workshop held at our headquarters branch library was a similar success. Attendees ranged from kids to adults, curious patrons and hopeful future artists. As with the previous workshops, the presenters handled the diverse crowd well, giving individual attention to each person as they worked on drawing and writing. A few days later, one of the attendees stopped by the reference desk to say how much more confident he felt about drawing since he'd gone to the workshop.

We also had the chance in 2007 to put on a Sunday evening art show at the Downhome Gallery in downtown Gainesville. The show combined pieces from the visiting artists and local people and is walking distance from the library, where we held the keynote speeches. The art show went well, and we're now planning on making it part of our annual events, a pleasant and sociable endnote to a full conference.

In conclusion, the five days we spent with the visiting artists was a success on many levels. We bridged the traditional gap between the university and the community, as well as the divide between high and low art that comics entails, and the usual schism in adult versus children's programming. Both the librarians and the artists were exhausted by the end, but the subsequent feedback and thanks from kids and adults alike made our efforts worthwhile.

CONNECTing for Collaboration

How Six College Libraries Worked Together to Identify Common Information Literacy Outcomes

PAMELA HAYES-BOHANAN *and* MARCIA B. DINNEEN

Since librarians have commitments ranging from teaching to desk time, book ordering and community outreach, being asked to be on yet another committee can often seem overwhelming. We have all been to meetings that were long, accomplished little, and left us wondering what our own role was. However, the librarians who formed the CONNECT group to create the rubric "Common Learning Outcomes for First Year Information Literacy" found that effective collaboration is possible and even rewarding. Our focus is on how meetings can be made effective and engaging in order to create a usable document. We also hope that by sharing our rubric, we can give other librarians a place to start in creating their own outcomes.

History of CONNECT

In January 2003, the leaders of five postsecondary institutions, Bridgewater State College, Bristol Community College, Cape Cod Community College, Massasoit Community College and the University of Massachusetts Dartmouth, each located in Southeastern Massachusetts, formed the CONNECT partnership. This unique collaboration of community colleges, a state college, and a state university was founded with two basic goals: to improve the quality, accessibility and affordability of higher education for students and to promote the economic, educational, and cultural life for all residents of the region. In April 2007 the Massachusetts Maritime Academy, another state college, joined the organization. Additionally, CONNECT was formed to maximize dwindling state funding to higher education and to promote collaboration among the member institutions.

One of the first major accomplishments of CONNECT was the development of a rubric for the teaching of Writing I and II, streamlining course transferability among the CONNECT partners. An annual conference for teachers of Writing I and II continues to reinforce commonalities in the teaching of writing. The CONNECT partnership is also working toward common outcomes for math and other subject areas.

Creating the Rubric

Library directors have also been involved in CONNECT, and at a meeting in the spring of 2006 they called upon reference librarians from each institution to meet and develop common outcomes for information literacy. Librarians from Bridgewater State; Bristol, Cape Cod, and Massasoit community colleges; the University of Massachusetts Dartmouth and Massachusetts Maritime Academy (although the academy was not yet a member of CONNECT) eagerly took up the challenge. At this initial meeting the librarians and directors did some brainstorming to define information literacy. The librarians were then charged with the task of developing common information literacy outcomes for students across campuses.

As librarians, we did our homework and found some examples of rubrics developed by various colleges and universities for information literacy. With these and the ACRL standards at hand, we developed the rubric in just two more meetings, following the initial session with directors.

At the first meeting of the CONNECT librarians, the group realized the necessity of concentrating on a specific aspect of information literacy, rather than trying to develop information literacy outcomes across the curriculum. Consequently, we concentrated on first-year writing classes because these courses are taught and required across all the campuses involved, and because two members of the committee taught first-year composition courses, in addition to being librarians, in their institutions. Both librarian/teachers knew what outcomes would best fit students' abilities and needs. We also had the benefit of having the rubric for first-year writing students created by the English faculty at the CONNECT institutions. To make implementation more logical, the same categories to identify students as novices, practitioners, or experts used in the writing rubric were adopted. We discussed which ideas from our brainstorming session with the directors should be included in the rubric, and which needed to be used later, as students developed more skills. At our second and final meeting, we identified the categories to use in the rubric and decided where each outcome fit.

Our recommendations for effective collaboration are as follows:

- Do your homework. When everyone comes to the meeting having studied the same documents, the meeting will be more productive and, therefore, shorter!
- Know your audience. We knew we would need to communicate our outcomes with people outside the field of librarianship.
- Have a focus. This will prevent you from trying to be all things to everybody.
- There is no reason to reinvent the wheel. The ACRL standards and the rubric created by the CONNECT writing group were invaluable to us.
- Representation from each constituency is essential. Every institution had a representative, including one academy that was not yet part of the CONNECT consortium and subsequently joined.
- Give all ideas the same consideration. Not all the ideas put forth were used in the final rubric, but we understood that all had merit. An atmosphere of active listening and consensus allowed all librarians to know that their ideas were considered fairly.

• Do not have a separate meeting for things that can be communicated via e-mail. Minor changes to language and announcements were taken care of electronically.

The Work Continues

The "Common Learning Outcomes" rubric was presented by the authors to the chief academic officers of the CONNECT institutions in the summer of 2006. With slight modifications, it was accepted and posted on the CONNECT Web site (www.connectsemass.org/ common%20learning%20outcomes%20for%20info%20literacy%20spring%202006.doc).

Work is continuing on campuses to implement the outcomes. At Bridgewater, for example, classes taught by the reference librarians, introducing students to the resources in the Maxwell Library, focus on the common learning outcomes. These classes, requested by individual instructors, involve using the online catalog, searching various databases, differentiating between scholarly and nonscholarly sources, and pointing out the differences between Google, Wikipedia, and Web sites and sources appropriate for academic work.

In her Writing I and Writing II classes, Marcia B. Dinneen has crafted certain assignments toward accomplishing the outcomes. Students in the Writing II classes have had two library sessions. One focused on finding credible film reviews as support for an essay on a particular issue in a provided list of films. For this assignment Dinneen stressed the importance of using national newspapers and magazines to locate the reviews and demonstrated how to use the appropriate databases. Another assignment, defining an abstract word or term, required the students to use a subject-specific dictionary and the *Oxford English Dictionary*. The second trip to the library instruction classroom was to demonstrate searching techniques in the online catalog and to review selecting and using the appropriate database.

Pamela Hayes-Bohanan used the outcomes defined in the rubric in a team-taught, semester-long, first-year seminar called the Psychology of Academic Success. Along with a psychology professor, she introduced students to using and evaluating online and print resources, taught students the difference between peer-reviewed and popular journals, and explained the importance of citing sources.

At Bristol Community College, the rubric has been accepted by the information literacy task force as a basis for making recommendations for implementing information literacy into the general education curriculum. Massasoit Community College has used the rubric to start examining information literacy competencies for a core curriculum that would integrate information literacy skills.

As far as the original group of librarians who developed the rubric, we have maintained contact with each other and are looking forward to developing additional subject specific outcomes.

The authors gratefully acknowledge the work of our partners in this project: Mary Adams, University of Massachusetts Dartmouth; Gabriela Adler, Bristol Community College; Susan Berteaux, Massachusetts Maritime Academy; Jean-Marie Frazer, Cape Cod Community College; and Jennifer Rudolph, Massasoit Community College.

Librarians and Educators in Partnerships

Instigating the Teachable Moment for Information Literacy in Core Education Courses

ANITA RAO MYSORE *and* ELIZABETH CHADBOURN MCKEE

The core concepts of information literacy run parallel in the library and education professions. Librarians assert that "information literate people are those who have learned how to learn. They know how to learn because they know how knowledge is organized, how to find information, and how to use information in such a way that others can learn from them. They are people prepared for lifelong learning, because they can always find the information needed for any task or decision at hand" (The American Library Association Presidential Committee on Information Literacy, 1989). The initial core course, Introduction to Education, in the Curriculum and Instruction Department at the University of Arkansas, is based on the tenets of the scholar-practitioner, defined as one who accesses, uses, and/or generates knowledge; plans, implements, and models best practice; understands, respects, and values diversity; is a developing professional and a lifelong learner; is knowledgeable about teachers and teaching, learners and learning, schools and schooling; communicates, cooperates, and collaborates with others; and makes decisions based upon professional standards and ethical criteria (McGee et al., 2001).

The Challenge

What can librarians and teachers do together to ensure that future educators are capable of finding, evaluating, and conveying knowledge? To begin with, how can we take entering education majors on the path to information literacy?

A Sample Scenario

Nancy is a freshman who wants to major in elementary education. She is taking Introduction to Education and received the course guidelines on the first day of class. Nancy is overwhelmed knowing that she will be required to review four journal articles. How is she supposed to find journals and articles for reviewing? She rushes in a panic to her instructor's office. Nancy's instructor calms her by pointing to the date on the course calendar when the class will visit the university library to learn about library research from the education librarian. Nancy feels relieved. Her classmate Sara, on the other hand, is cool from the beginning. No problem, she thought. I'll just Google that and be done with it in a wink. She was less than excited when she heard from Nancy that they were going to the library. That's a drag she thought ... but she wanted to pass the course.

The authors have faced challenges as described in the scenario, as have many other educator/librarian partnerships. They have good assignments, but find they face in the same classroom students who are underprepared, overconfident, inexperienced, or technology-savvy but have limited knowledge of the variety of information sources and little experience evaluating them. The authors developed a multicomponent, introductory "information-need" energizer to help entering education majors experience the pleasure of becoming "information literate."

The Initial Spark

As the first step, the authors propose motivating the students by engaging their personal need for information. McKee asked students to bring with them to the library presentation a topic of personal curiosity, a concern about which they had a genuine desire for information, or an issue in which they were interested. Since some concerns might be personal, the instructor might take this opportunity to explain the library profession's ethic regarding confidentiality or try to respect any student's wish for privacy in their research topic. A few examples to encourage the choice of topics might be:

- What movie would I like to go to tonight?
- How do I figure out what would be a good used car to buy?
- I need a children's book that I haven't read before for class. How do I choose?

Steps Toward Information Literacy

The next step was the visit to the library. McKee advised students to think about finding information for their personal quest, while she taught them the skills needed to complete their education assignment. The education assignments were designed to make the students scholar-practitioners (and information literate):

- Find definitions of four key terms used in education: *teaching, education, scholar-practitioner,* and *action research.*
- Review four peer-reviewed journal articles on four different topics: an area of interest in education to the students, a practitioner article, a research article, and an article that improved or enhanced the educational environment.

- Write a personal philosophy paper on teaching, consulting books and articles to base the historical perspectives of their school of philosophy.
- Develop a professional portfolio with different items, relying on library sources for at least two items — to review educational videos and books.

McKee outlined the steps of library research tailored to the education assignments. She used a PowerPoint presentation, sample reference books and journals, live database searches, search engines, and Web sites to demonstrate the steps in searching information. The basic content presented included:

- Overviews of information: reference books, textbooks, literature reviews, collected works
- Materials published once: books, monographs, videos, DVDs, documents explaining the content of the library catalog, whether found on the shelves or online
- Materials published in serial (ongoing) form: journal articles, databases, print and electronic formats for full text (e.g. aggregators, Google Scholar, and subject-specific indexes such as ERIC, PsycInfo and others)
- Experts: faculty, associations, scholars, educated people (e.g. doctors, lawyers, engineers, other people knowledgeable in a field, even experienced friends)
- Web sites: the Internet as a medium, not a distinct source, but when evaluated as reliable may provide content from any of the above tangible sources; thus, ability to evaluate becomes paramount

The subsequent step was the practice time in the library's computer lab so students could immediately rehearse, receive individual attention and guidance from their committed instructor and librarian, and acquire research skills for their education assignment.

The Objective Accomplished

The visit to the library got the students started. They rehearsed the skills as they completed their course assignments spread over a semester. They also visualized and applied the components of information research to their personal quest. By incorporating information-seeking skills into daily interests and using the technological approaches young people are accustomed to, we can integrate information literacy into their professional lives.

We recommend that future librarian-educator partnerships use a wrap-up assignment, wherein students turn in their research — the process and product of their personal-curiosity topic to their instructor, providing citations to the articles, books, and Web sites that helped them in their quest.

Lifelong Learning

Information resources are changing so rapidly that updating techniques and sources for students is an ongoing challenge for librarians and faculty. Entering education majors become preservice teachers in their fifth year. They return to the library to hone their information-literacy skills further for their action research projects. They graduate and become in-service teachers. Throughout their careers, they will need to update the information they teach. They also pass on information-seeking skills to their students. For both, they need to be lifelong learners. To achieve this goal we must start by capturing the natural curiosity attached to personal interests; motivate scholar-practitioners to transfer information acquisition and evaluation skills to professional research; and enable them to become proficient lifelong learners and teachers because of their information literacy.

References

ALA American Library Association (2003). Introduction to Information Literacy. Retrieved April 4, 2006, from www.ala.org/ala/acrl/acrlissues/acrlinfolit/ infolitoverview/introtoinfolit/introinfolit. htm.

McGee, C.D., Wavering, M. J., Imbeau, M.B., Sullivan, E.P., Morrow, L.R., Lefever-Davis, S. et al. (2001). Association of Teacher Educators Distinguished Program in Teacher Education Award 2001: Preparing scholar-practitioners in the 21st century. *Action in Teacher Education 23*(3), 5–15.

Teaching and Librarianship

A Winning Combination

DARBY ORCUTT

My students usually forget that I'm a librarian. They often give me valuable insight into the perceptions and problems that they have in using library services and collections because they don't self-censor or feel the need to be polite, and often assume that I share their reluctance to bother a librarian with questions for fear of feeling dumb. But getting to actually *be* the fly on the wall for a change certainly isn't the only reward of teaching.

I love being a librarian, but have the best of both worlds thanks to my supplementary part-time teaching jobs. During my full-time career as a librarian, I have taught five courses in three departments at two universities and only one of these in library science. Most frequently, I teach an introductory world religions course for North Carolina State University's Department of Philosophy and Religion.

Few librarians anywhere teach full, for-credit courses, especially outside of library science, but I know from the questions I hear that it's not necessarily for lack of interest. So, how might you go about getting involved in teaching? I focus on college-level, nonlibrary science instruction here, but the basic principles apply across any context.

First of all, understand the needs and preferences of those who hire part-time teachers. They need to find a candidate who:

- knows the subject matter. Most institutions mandate a minimum level of degree or graduate-level coursework (and no, your MLS doesn't count, as it is a *professional* degree). The minimum, however, is usually only in the neighborhood of 12 to 15 graduate credit hours in the discipline. Beyond that, demonstrated familiarity with the field is paramount. A master's or PhD might help you make your case, but so might your publication and presentation record, disciplinary memberships, conference attendance, and simple ability to converse intelligently about the field with academic colleagues.

- knows how to teach. You are best off if you have taught already, even if only as a graduate student or a long time ago. I highly recommend that those with no formal full-course teaching experience seek out a "team teaching" opportunity with an established instructor. Many are more than willing to take on a protégé, especially one who is willing to take on a large percentage of the workload! Many academic departments are willing to give a chance to individuals who show promise as instructors, especially those who already appear strong in many of the skills involved (and, as you'll see below, librarians often bring much to the table).

A teaching job is, in the end, a job. The usual advice regarding any job seeking and application applies. Employers want the best person for the position and, especially for teaching, need employees who can work independently, meet deadlines, and fully comply with the host of regulations governing student interaction and grading. Supply and demand plays a primary role in any job search. You should have realistic expectations about the market and your prospects. Programs with large doctoral programs already have most if not all of the instructors they'll need. The market for teaching literature courses is flooded with untenured PhDs. Nontenured faculty will generally not even be considered for teaching nonprofessional, graduate-level courses. The most opportunity lies in departments with large numbers of introductory or general-requirement-type courses.

Librarians make good teachers. Whether you are making your case to a potential employer, or are already hired and preparing to teach, you should know that your experience and perspective as a librarian probably gives you at least three unique advantages. Librarians:

- value learning,
- take an environmental approach, and
- emphasize tools.

Contemporary educational theory privileges learning over teaching. The old model of the scholar at the podium imparting knowledge is long gone, replaced by a concern with fostering student development. As servants of our users, we librarians have always sought to promote such learning, encouraging students to understand processes for finding information.

The very word *librarian* reflects our link to a place. And whether the place is physical or virtual, we invest tremendous resources in ordering that space in ways that will be useful, engaging, and appealing to our users. Librarians craft environments for learning. The best teachers do likewise, designing course content that facilitates student interaction, feedback, understanding, and engagement. The customer-oriented ethic of librarians means that we constantly and efficiently evaluate, adapt, and improve environmental contexts, including recognizing and helping circumvent barriers to learning which individuals may experience.

Most significantly, librarians emphasize tools for learning, from specific resources for the task at hand to more general and transferable techniques for engaging information sources. Perhaps because of my training as a librarian, I find myself using a tools approach in the classroom, seeking to equip students with intellectual, conceptual, and theoretical "tools" that will serve them well even long after the course's end. One of my main pedagogical goals in teaching the introductory Religious Traditions of the World course, for example, is to develop in my students an ability to understand new religious ideas or traditions they may encounter, through knowing how to ask good questions, being able to (at least tentatively) place religious content into larger and cognitively useful frameworks, and appreciating the ways in which historic, cultural, social, political, and other factors influence and interweave with religious thought, practice, and expression.

Introductory or survey courses most neatly match the librarian's propensity for thinking in terms of shaping a learning environment conducive to equipping students with tools necessary for continued learning. These are also, by the way, the very courses which often prove most challenging and/or least interesting to subject-specialized tenure-track faculty.

Yet despite the fact that your full-time profession prepares you well for it, don't underestimate the challenges of teaching, of which time management is but one. Some key and potentially challenging differences between librarianship and teaching revolve around the areas of:

- relationship
- evaluation
- goal setting

The relationship between teacher and student differs tremendously from that between librarian and user. Ours is a service profession, and we rarely if ever stand in a relationship of institutionalized power over our customers. Additionally, especially when it comes to our student customers, we rarely enjoy anything like the extended, accretive teaching opportunities available to classroom instructors. In teaching, one can afford to be more patient while a student grapples with a concept over a period of time.

Grading best represents the (at least perceived) power of the instructor over the student. Librarians, as discussed above, tend to focus on environmental factors, and our very ideals guide us toward not passing judgment on our users' needs, intelligence, etc. But, teaching requires evaluation of the performance of *individuals*. I recommend clear standards (however strict), clearly communicated. Students ultimately value perceived fairness more highly than any particular grade.

Formally and informally, teachers must set goals for every student interaction (in or out of class) in order to take advantage of teachable moments and to make wise use of time. Planning lessons in advance and setting reasonable goals for student learning means not only work, but also careful choosing of one's battles. I learned early on that I could not teach both the content of my course and the basic writing skills lacking in most of my students' papers. Many librarians could benefit from conceiving of their own patron interactions similarly, shunning the desire to educate a user all at once, in favor of driving home one vital concept of information literacy.

Being a librarian *and* a teacher gives me a better sense of the full process of student intellectual and academic development. Being a librarian makes me a better teacher, and teaching makes me a more effective librarian.

What Is a Curriculum Developer Doing in Special Collections?

Anita Rao Mysore

I hold a rather unusual job at an academic library: curriculum developer in the Special Collections Department at the University of Arkansas Libraries. My unique assignment is to develop curriculum materials using the primary and secondary sources in the university libraries' collections, especially in our Arkansas archives.

The University of Arkansas Libraries hold a wealth of materials: more than 1.7 million volumes of books and bound periodicals; over 5.4 million microforms and government documents; over 18,000 print and electronic journals; thousands of maps and manuscripts; and audio and video recordings. Among the treasures held by the Special Collections Department are: writings and personal papers of prominent civic leaders, writers, educators, musicians, journalists, architects, photographers, military veterans, conservationists, and agriculturalists and records of organizations with a community, state, and international focus. Examples of individual collections housed in special collections are the papers of Senators J. William Fulbright, Dale Bumpers, and David Pryor; architects Edward Durell Stone and Fay Jones; composers William Grant Still and Florence Price; writers John Gould Fletcher and Frank Arthur Swinnerton; political cartoonist George Fisher; and folklorist Mary Celestia Parler. Other examples of collections pertain to the international exchange of scholars, agriculture, environmental initiatives and concerns, women's studies, the Civil War, the civil rights movement, Japanese Americans interned in Arkansas, and Arkansas maps.

Objectives for Curriculum Development

The primary objective in developing curriculum materials is to assist teachers of Arkansas history in K–12 schools. In 1997 the Arkansas General Assembly adopted Act 787, a bill which for the first time outlined a series of requirements for teaching the state's his-

90

tory to Arkansas public school students. School districts and teachers throughout the state are working to implement this law, but a lack of focused instructional materials makes this a slow and difficult process. Some teachers have openly expressed the need for support resources for teaching Arkansas history.

Many people are aware of the negative aspects of the state's history such as the 1957 Little Rock Central High School integration crisis or the 1919 Elaine riot; but they are less aware of the outstanding contributions of the state's diverse populace. The curriculum package I am assigned to create, educates students about the state's notable people, exciting events, and positive accomplishments. The ultimate objective is to instill a sense of pride in the students about the state, as a part of the national historical experience.

My specific duties include producing various series of educational posters to highlight leaders in Arkansas history; developing lessons in compact disc format; designing appropriate curriculum materials using the broadside and map collections; and assisting the departmental director in planning and conducting seminars and in-service training for teachers. I also make presentations about Arkansas leaders to public school librarians, teachers, and students.

Sharing Our Heritage Poster Series

One of the ten poster series I am developing is Sharing Our Heritage: Amazing African-American Leaders of Arkansas. African Americans have been part of Arkansas history since arriving with French hunters and trappers in the late 1600s. Since then African Americans in Arkansas have played major roles in building the state. The ten leaders featured in the poster series are from the fields of agriculture, business, civil rights, education, law, literature, medicine, science, and sports.

I will discuss a poster that features Silas Hunt, the first African American student admitted to the University of Arkansas Law School, to illustrate the curriculum components on it. The portrait of Silas Hunt and his biography adorn the front of the poster. On the reverse of the poster is a preface to the poster series, followed by a concise description of the University of Arkansas Libraries and the Department of Special Collections. The diversity statement of the University of Arkansas is also presented; indeed the poster series is testimony to this commitment.

Other curriculum materials on the poster include:

- a glossary of terms
- supplemental information
- a lesson plan
- an assessment
- resources for additional reading
- a timeline

How to Use the Poster in Teaching

The curriculum materials on the poster afford flexibility in teaching. If a teacher wants to use the poster for only one class period of 55 minutes, he or she can teach the biography and review student learning with questions from the assessment segment of the poster, constructed to meet the diverse capabilities of students. The questions in this section are modeled after the Grade 8 Released Reading Items of the Arkansas Comprehensive Testing, Assessment and Accountability Program (ACTAAP) Benchmark Examination, which consists of eight multiple-choice questions and one open-response item with a grading rubric for the latter.

For the teacher who wants to use the poster for more than one class period, longer and more detailed supplemental information about Hunt's role in integrating higher education in Arkansas is provided on the poster, accompanied by a suggested lesson plan. The lesson plans in the poster series have been developed using the constructivist principle, which lets students construct knowledge by questioning, interpreting, and analyzing information. Activities in the lesson plans involve students in developing skits, preparing speeches, and conducting and presenting research findings within cooperative learning group settings. These activities accommodate the broad spectrum of strengths and needs of all students. Relevant Arkansas History Curriculum Standards have been identified in the lesson plans— teachers can easily determine how the lesson plan meets the state's curriculum frameworks. The glossary defines terms used in both the biography and the supplemental information.

Given teachers' busy schedules, the poster is designed to be comprehensive so that teachers do not have to search for additional resources for content, teaching methods, or assessment. For those teachers who wish to have more material, there is a bibliography section. Also, given the different learning styles of students, a timeline is provided for visual learners.

Posters in the Age of Interactive Media?

At the time of this writing, three posters have been produced. I have sought feedback from preservice and in-service teachers, who have found the posters extremely beneficial in teaching Arkansas history. They are eagerly asking when the entire poster series will be available for them and their students. One frequently asked question is "Isn't the use of posters obsolete in the age of interactive media?" In response, I quote James S. Kinder in his book, *Audio-Visual Materials and Techniques* (New York: American Book Company, 1950):

Posters in their multitudinous forms are everywhere about us. Indeed, one cannot go to town, or to the doctor's office, post office, railway station, museum, library, school, ball park, store, filling station, or take a ride on a street car or subway train without seeing and being influenced by posters.... The poster has come to be an expressive form of American art. Its direct appeal is understood by the practical American people.

More than half a century later Kinder's statement still applies. Classroom posters create an atmosphere for learning and motivate students. They also foster curiosity in students. Moreover, practically speaking, they provide a long-lasting visual presence in the classroom — without any need for electronic equipment to display. Posters of historical leaders add a touch of reality and bring a sense of here and now to the classroom. It has been satisfying to know that our posters with instructional aids— available in a single portable medium — are successfully filling a curricular void for teachers of Arkansas history.

Grant Writing

LORIENE ROY *and* SARA ALBERT

Grants are one way that libraries can receive at least temporary funding to extend or introduce new services. True, applying for grants can involve a large amount of time and effort on your part, but it can be very rewarding if you are awarded a grant that will allow you to develop your program idea.

Grant writing starts with a winning, innovative idea that must be packaged according to a required format. Your concept should serve as a model project, highlighting activities and a standard of possibility to which other libraries might strive. In other words, your grant proposal should not be a request for run-of-the-mill expenditures. Remember that grant applications are usually evaluated by reviewers, often other librarians, who will provide input to funding agencies on what they deem is deserving of grant funding. This essay provides some tips on how to convert a concept into a successful, funded grant. We assume that you have identified one or more sources of grant funding and that you have a fundable project in mind.

Getting Ready

Read the Grant Application — More Than Once

Start writing your grant by becoming familiar with the process you will need to follow. The process can be thought of as a board game, with each step of the application process representing a position on the board. The grant writer(s), reviewers, and funding agencies are the game pieces, and the grant requirements are the rules of the game. Play special attention to deadlines. Some grants require the submission of a letter of intent — a notice that you plan to submit a full grant application. Federal grants often list an estimated "burden" or number of hours needed to complete an application. Knowing this burden will help you block out time to complete your proposal.

Assemble Your Team

Nowadays, few successful grant applications are written by a single person. Some funding agencies welcome, prefer, require, or give stronger consideration to proposals that reflect collaborative work. Consider assembling a team to write your proposal. At a minimum, ask one or more careful readers to provide feedback on your drafts. If you submit a grant proposal with another individual or agency, investigate the documentation that you might need to confirm this relationship; some grant proposals may require letters or memoranda of agreement.

Find Samples of Funded Grants

Many funding sources have Web sites that provide substantial information about the grant application process and, often, samples of grants funded in the past. Use these samples for guidance in preparing your application, although you should be cognizant that the process may change over time. If samples are not available on the funder's Web site, then seek published reports of funded projects. Most projects are required to stipulate that they will disseminate findings through presentations and publications.

Constructing Your Proposal

Give Your Project a Name

Give your proposed project a recognizable name and repeat the name frequently in your narrative. Your project name should resonate with readers and serve as a hook. Envision the name of your project on a Web site or a promotional product such as a mouse pad, pencil, mug, or T-shirt.

Prepare Your Narrative

The narrative portion tells the story of your grant. Here you set the stage, identify your constituents' needs, and introduce what you would like to do to meet goals and objectives in alignment with your project mission. Your narrative will also delineate the evaluation process. Evaluation is usually both formative (ongoing evaluation during the program) and summative (conducted at the end of the project). In some cases you may need to provide samples of the data collection instruments that you might use. You may be required to document your experience and training in conducting research with human subjects. Some funding sources require outcome-based evaluation. In that case you will explain how you will observe and measure changes in skills acquired and/or attitudes and behaviors as a result of the presence of your program. Similarly, you may need to describe how you will share your results with the larger community.

Repeat and Emphasize Key Phrases

Funding is often awarded for grant proposals that focus on specific clients or targeted services. Make sure that your proposal meets the grant intentions and reiterate this clearly in your proposal. At the same time, be able to defend that your proposal addresses the target funding areas.

Prepare the Funding Portion

To calculate a benchmark funding level, determine the maximum grant request, divide by the number of years of funding, and subtract your indirect cost rate to determine the amount you might request per year. Your university or city authority will set your indirect cost rate. This is equivalent to your overhead rate and will cover the cost of hosting the funded project through supplying space and utilities such as heating, cooling, and electricity.

Some grant proposals require that you supply a certain percentage of the funds needed to manage the prospective project. This is called contributed or matching funds. You might not be able to leverage other grant funds as contributed costs. The most common contributed cost is the amount of staff time (and associated fringe benefits) you will contribute to the project. Remember that any one staff member cannot be paid for more than 100 percent of their time. Your institution might also set a maximum amount of time that any one employee might contribute.

You may be required to identify the sources you used to calculate certain figures that appear in your budget. Sometimes your budget is accompanied by its own narrative. This may be referred to as your budget justification. Here you explain how each budget line (such as salaries and wages) contributes to the project and how each is calculated. For example, you may need to indicate that travel estimates are based on state-contracted airfares. Materials/supplies requests may be based on vendor-supplied estimates. Report individual budget lines in whole numbers. Meet with your financial analyst early and often.

Stay Within the Maximum Word Length

The grant guidelines will stipulate the maximum total length of the grant proposal, and sometimes the length of separate segments of the proposal. Do not exceed the allowable word count and make sure that you cover all required elements within this limit.

Before You Submit

Consider Ways to Improve Readability

Consider how to incorporate white space, bold text, underlining, and bulleting in your text. You might have room to include one or more graphics. Since reviewers may spend less than an hour on the grant application that took you perhaps 40 hours to prepare, you want to make it easy for them to read and understand it.

Avoid Overreliance on Library Jargon

Make sure that your text is easily understood. Ask a novice reader if he or she can readily comprehend your proposal and your word choice. Do not assume that reviewers will share your professional background. At the same time, you usually will not provide an extensive bibliography of related publications with your proposal; instead, you will refer to other writings and/or research results that directly relate to and support your proposal.

Review Your Narrative

Reread your narrative alongside your budget request. Ensure that figures match and are logical. Read for consistency. Do not pad your budget to provide funding that is not necessary for the project.

Finally, follow the funder's instructions for submitting your grant application. Submit your hard work, record the date when grant winners will be announced, and consider what will happen if you are not funded — and if you are!

Grant Writing and How One Grant Turns into Two

VICTORIA LYNN PACKARD

My foray into grant writing started very innocently. I was looking at the ALA Web site at www.ala.org and read about the traveling exhibit, "Alexander Hamilton: The Man Who Made Modern America." It sounded fascinating and something very appropriate for South Texas. The exhibit was funded by the American Library Association (ALA), the National Endowment for the Humanities (NEH), the New-York Historical Society, the Gilder-Lehrman Institute for American History, and the National Park Service. Applications were accepted through all of these sources, but only 40 libraries were selected to participate in the traveling exhibition. We were one of the lucky ones and the only one in the Texas A&M University system.

Texas A&M University–Kingsville (TAMUK) has a student population of approximately 6,200 students, 62 percent of whom are Hispanic. Kingsville, Texas, is a small rural community of 26,000 people. We are approximately two hours south of San Antonio, north of Brownsville, and east of the Mexican border.

We were very interested in the Alexander Hamilton exhibit because of the exposure it would bring to students and the surrounding community. The exhibit is in seven sections and encompasses various areas of Hamilton's life. They are:

Section I. His World
Section II. Alexander Hamilton: Immigrant
Section III. Alexander Hamilton: Soldier
Section IV. Alexander Hamilton: Lawmaker
Section V. Alexander Hamilton: Economist
Section VI. Alexander Hamilton: Futurist
Section VII. Alexander Hamilton and Aaron Burr: the Duel and Hamilton's Legacy

The student population of TAMUK is relevant to the Alexander Hamilton exhibit because he was the first among the Founding Fathers to advocate for minority rights. He was very opposed to slavery. Our students, their families, and the community would appreciate learning about his fight for equality.

Alexander Hamilton was a self-made man who had to work hard for all he received, much as our students do. Most of our students come from an area that has the country's highest rate of poverty. As stated previously, our student population is 62 percent Hispanic. Many are the first in their family to attend college. Many of our students have rarely traveled to north Texas and even fewer have traveled out of the state. This fact is also true for members of the public who attend the exhibition and programs. This exhibit is a way to expose the students, their families and the public to American history during an exciting time for our country. Alexander Hamilton is an excellent role model. He can show how a person can come to America from another country and through hard work become someone to be proud of, a role model for young people. These are some of the concepts I stressed in the grant.

This was the first time the James C. Jernigan Library at TAMUK had received an exhibit. As a result there was no infostructure in place for the myriad of projects needed to be done for the exhibit.

Before writing the grant, I approached the Robert J. Kleberg Public Library director Robert Rodriguez to see if he would be interested in partnering with the Jernigan Library, and he was very interested. Once we had a partner, I approached the colleges of history, language and literature, communication, political science, business, and the university archives. All were interested in participating, and the exhibit became one of the largest intercollegiate collaborations on campus. Two professors from each college provided many different programs. I left presentation formats open to the professors so there are lectures, panels, student paper presentations, and discussion forums.

There was one mandatory meeting held at the New-York Historical Society. While there I learned about a play called *Alexander Hamilton: In Worlds Unknown*. It is a four-act play for one to six actors portraying Alexander Hamilton throughout his life and mirroring the exhibit. The play uses Hamilton's own words and writings. Our committee was very excited about the play, but we needed money to produce and pay the fees.

Our problem was the original grant did not award money with the exhibit. This is how one grant became two. I researched various grants available and found the Humanities Texas Grant which funds many grants in the humanities. It was a much more detailed grant involving a budget, cost analyses, and other paperwork. After discussion with the Theater Department to secure their participation, I applied for the grant. I heard a few months later that we were awarded the money to promote and produce the play *Alexander Hamilton: In Worlds Unknown*.

Throughout the writing of two grants I learned the following things:

- Each grant is different and requires different responses. In writing the grant, stress how it will benefit your community.
- Find a partner. Grant organizations like to give money to groups. The more participation the better.
- Contact local area schools. You will need committee members and helpers. Here's a great place to find them.
- Find speakers. Friends of the Library (we do not have one, but the public library did), Boy Scouts and Girl Scouts, and local experts can give talks.
- Get committee members and rely upon them. You cannot do this on your own, it will drive you crazy.
- Make sure you have plenty of letters of support. Use a wide variety of sources in the community.
- Look at other grant sources. Search the CFDA (Catalog of Federal Domestic Assistance), Grants.gov, and other print and Internet sources.

- Make sure your grant application fits the grant. Nothing irritates grant organizations more than receiving a proposal that does not meet the grant intentions. If you send them another application someday, they might remember you.
- Contact the grant agency. I did and they were very helpful. They can give you tips on how to improve your grant.
- Watch timelines! I cannot stress this enough. If a letter of intent is due on a specific day, make sure it arrives by that date.
- Get feedback. Have many people read your grant and get ideas from them. You have read the grant so many times it makes sense to you, but maybe not to someone else.

Before I started writing the grant, it seemed easy. Just write a grant and people will give you money, right. I know better now. It's a process. You complete each question completely no matter how many times you already answered it before.

In the beginning, someone told me that grant writing is a leap into the realm of fantasy, a place where you plan for things to happen a year or two in the future. This was the hardest for me to fathom. I kept thinking, how can I write a grant in 2005 and not have the exhibit until 2007? Presenters leave the area, change their minds, or want to do something totally different for their presentation. The last one happened to me. All you can do is take great notes, attempt to plan for all contingencies, stay flexible, and try not to do it all yourself.

On March 1, 2007, when the exhibit opened, I took a deep breath and enjoyed the exhibit, the play, and all the events. Maybe I'll write another grant proposal one day.

Ace the Presentation, Win the Job

ROBERT P. HOLLEY

A presentation as part of the job interview process serves several goals. First, it may be the only chance for members of the library and even the wider community to meet the candidate. The audience will often be asked to submit a comment sheet on the candidate's performance. Second, most library positions require some type of public speaking, including teaching short courses, giving training sessions, making presentations to administrators and the public, or answering questions one-on-one. Judging the candidate's ability to speak in public, both from prepared remarks and extemporaneously, is therefore a valid test of future job performance. Third, the presentation gives candidates a chance to show off their knowledge of the topic and their ability to develop a persuasive argument.

Choice of Topic

Most likely the library will assign the candidate a topic that is broad enough to give some flexibility in developing the presentation. The openness of the topic offers the first test for the candidate. If there is any doubt, candidates should be sure that they understand the topic and ask for clarification if they don't.

The Audience and Time

Candidates should also not assume that the audience will include only librarians. If faculty or the members of the governing board are invited, it may be necessary to explain library jargon. Support staff can also play an important role in this part of the interview; any trace of elitism will not be well received. The candidate should also ask for an estimate of the number of attendees to be sure to bring enough handouts and to have some sense of the size of the room where the presentation will occur since intimate surroundings call for a different delivery than a large lecture hall. It also helps to take into consideration the time of day for the presentation. If possible, the candidates should try to get it scheduled at a peak energy time for them whether they are larks or night owls. As for the audience, presentations before or after lunch and near quitting time pose special problems of hunger, sleepiness, and eagerness to leave that the candidate should take into account.

Length

The candidate should be absolutely sure about the expected length of the presentation and whether this length includes time for questions. Staying within the allotted time is an important test of the ability to understand and follow directions.

Practical Matters

The candidate should let the library know about any technical requirements and make sure that they can be met. While the candidate may presume that the library will have the correct version of PowerPoint, the "right" browser, and a high-speed Internet connection, it is always better to ask. The candidate should prepare for all sorts of disasters by having any presentation materials accessible in at least three ways— CD, portable storage device (floppy, flash drive, portable drive, etc.), and e-mail. Sending the files to at least one e-mail address is especially important in case luggage, purse, or briefcase gets lost or stolen. Finally, the candidate should be prepared to give the presentation without any technical support as a worst case option. A poised candidate in such a situation will gain a large quantity of employment points.

Developing the Presentation

There are multiple ways to develop a successful presentation. The most important factor is to avoid dullness. This is possible with both traditional and more creative strategies. Candidates should consider their personalities and styles and choose a method that they are comfortable with. While traditional presentations can win jobs, creative ones can become part of institutional memory. In one library, stories are still told of the candidate who applied the principles of winning baseball games to libraries.

The candidate should have done enough research to know the general stance of the library in question on the topic. If the director/dean of the library is an expert on outreach to undergraduates, arguing for more attention to faculty and graduate research is a risky strategy unless the research shows that the library wishes to change direction. Another way to show knowledge of the library is to cite the published research by those in the audience or to acknowledge their interest in the topic, though such references carry some risk of being considered as toadying. One method to appear erudite without overloading the presentation with scholarly references is to distribute a critical bibliography in print either before or after the presentation.

Candidates who are unaware of the dangers of "bad" PowerPoint presentations should read at least a few articles on the effective use of this software package. Remember that the candidate should be the focus of the presentation rather than the PowerPoint slides. A slide show with dense text that the candidate then reads is one of the surer ways to put the audience to sleep.

Before the Presentation

Candidates should ask for time to check out the equipment and room before the presentation. It is also reasonable for candidates to ask for a brief break to collect their thoughts immediately before going on stage.

The Presentation

The one recommendation that cannot be stressed too highly is: *Applicants should not read their speeches!* Instead, candidates should practice ahead of time so that they know the content well enough to follow the outline of their talk while still leaving room for the spontaneity that comes from speaking extemporaneously.

Not reading the text also makes it possible for candidates to make eye contact with the audience and to monitor reactions to their presentation. If members of the audience are falling asleep, fidgeting, or showing signs of hostility, candidates should do what they can to adjust their presentations. Perhaps a question to the audience, a poll of responses on an issue, or some other interactive device might rekindle interest in the presentation. If members start looking at their watches, this may be a sign that the candidate has exceeded the allotted time. On the other hand, positive body language such as heads nodding in agreement can be a sign that all is going well.

Questions

The candidate should leave sufficient time for questions, probably 10 to 15 minutes for the average job presentation. Strong candidates should welcome questions as a way to show that they can think on their feet. As in other parts of the interview, candidates should be careful to avoid answers that commit them to specific actions if they should get the job. Candidates should also be on the lookout for questions such as, "You do agree, don't you, that the library should avoid purchasing controversial materials for young adults?" that lead the candidate to respond in one way when the questioner is looking for the candidate to disagree. It is acceptable for candidates to say that they don't have an answer or that they haven't looked into that aspect of the topic.

After the Presentation

The time after the presentation can be a dangerous point in the interview for some candidates. Those who find public speaking a draining experience should ask for a bit of time alone to regroup. Asking to use the restroom is an effective way to get a few peaceful minutes. Those who find public speaking energizing may be even more at risk since they may need to come down from their manic state. They too may benefit from a few moments of alone time.

Concluding Thoughts

This has certainly not covered all that could be said on this topic. Candidates can consult the extensive literature on public speaking and, more importantly, create opportunities to practice their presentation skills. Toastmasters and similar organizations as well as acting classes are good ways to overcome shyness and to develop a winning public presence.

Presentations

Tools and Tips

ANN MARLOW RIEDLING

I have been honored to speak to numerous school library media specialists—and others—all over the world. I have presented at many conferences locally, nationally and internationally, such as the International Association of School Librarians (IASL) in Ramat Gan, Israel; school media specialists in Waterloo, Belgium; and Department of Defense Education personnel in Asia and Europe. Scary, yes, at first. However, with the proper tools and tips presenting can be an extremely rewarding and fulfilling experience. I hope to provide you with a wide variety of tools and tips so that you will become a confident, organized and inspiring speaker, regardless of the audience or number of participants.

Your Plan of Action

It is always helpful for me to begin with a specific plan—on paper (seeing it in black and white makes it clearer). For me, this plan includes the following areas:

- introduction (snappy!)
- point one (with subpoints)
- point two (with subpoints)
- point three (with subpoints)—I think you are getting the picture.
- conclusion and review of major points

Another simple and direct plan is the beginning-middle-end format in which the "main meet" of the presentation is contained in the middle and is preceded by an introduction and followed up by a summary and conclusion. Also, prior to the talk, ask yourself the following:

- What is the purpose of the presentation?
- Who will be attending?
- What does the audience already know about the topic?
- What is the audience's attitude toward you?

I cannot overestimate the importance of careful preparation. With a lot at stake, you must concentrate not only on the information being presented, but also on the style, pace, tone and tactics that should be used. As a general rule, you should spend one hour or more on preparation for every five minutes of talking.

In addition to the plans above, there are other considerations. First, you must formulate precise objectives. These should take the form of simple and concise statements of intent. Bottom line, if you are not sure at the onset what you are trying to say, it is extremely unlikely that your audience will either. Focus is key! The objective of any presentation is not the transmission, but the reception. Your talk must be geared to the audience. Your message must be understood and remembered. The average person has a very short attention span and a million other things to think about. You must hold their attention long enough to make your points perfectly clear.

I have found that if you lose your audience in the first two minutes of your speech, you have lost them for good. Therefore, spend time — a great deal of it — on your introduction. Who is your audience? What do they want to hear from you? Your job is to do something, anything, that captures their attention and makes a lasting impression upon them. Your opening remarks imply that you understand the problem/situation/issue and that you have a solution; your audience will be flattered by your attention and attentive to your every word. The following are areas that I consider when beginning my speech:

- Get their attention. Pay attention to what your audience is doing. Are they taking off their coats or getting coffee? Wait until they are settled and ready to listen.
- Establish a theme. You must get the audience thinking about the subject of your presentation. Provide a statement of your main objective. Your audience will have some experience or opinions on this, and at the beginning you must make them bring that experience into their own minds.
- Present a structure. If you briefly explain at the beginning of your talk how it will proceed, then the audience will know what to expect. Ultimately, it provides a sense of security and the promise that this speech, too, will end!
- Create rapport. You should plan exactly how you wish to appear to your audience and use the beginning to establish that relationship. Whatever role you choose must be established at the very beginning.
- Plan the ending. The final impression you make is the one that the audience will remember. Thus, it is worth planning your last few sentences with extreme care.

Visual Aids

Most people expect visual reinforcement for any message being delivered. However, there are a few rules that should be followed to ensure that visual aids are used effectively. As with all elements of your talk, each visual should have a distinct purpose. Some visuals reinforce your verbal message and assist in recall; others are used to explain or inform, which can be more easily displayed than discussed; some visuals are simply for entertainment and used to pace the presentation. Keep your visuals simple and professional. All items must be large enough to be viewed by the people in the last rows. Finally, do not merely reiterate exactly what is on the visual. Talk to the audience, not the visual aid.

Delivery

Whatever you say and whatever you show, it is you who will remain the focus of the audience's attention. You have the power to both kill the message or to enhance it to a hundred times its worth. The following deserve attention when presenting:

- Eyes: During your presentation use the duration and intensity of eye contact to enhance your rapport with the audience. If possible, attempt to look at all participants; try to hold your gaze for five seconds at a time. Shortly after each change in position, a slight smile will convince each person that they are acknowledged and that you are ready to begin once again.
- Voice: In an ordinary conversation, you can see from the expression, movement of the eyes, and so forth when something has been missed or misunderstood. In front of an audience, you must make sure that this never happens. The simple advice is to slow down and take your time. It is also important to vary the pitch and speed of your presentation.
- Expression: The audience watches your face. If you are smiling, people will wonder why and listen to find out! This message is quite simple, make certain that your facial expressions are natural, confident and happy.
- Appearance: Your choice of dress should be deliberately made. It is critical to dress for the audience, not for yourself. If they think you look out of place, then you are.
- Stance: When presenting, your stance and posture will convey a great deal about you. Do not allow your stance and posture to convey boredom or indifference. Use your entire body as a dynamic tool to reinforce your rapport with the audience.

There is no substitute for rehearsal. You can do it in front of a mirror or an empty room. Accentuate your gestures and vocal projection.

Conclusion

Once the presentation is over, you should try to honestly evaluate your performance. This can be done alone or with people in the audience (who you are comfortable with). If there are problems, write them down, practice them and address them in your next speech. Practice your next speech. Practice is only productive when you make a positive effort to improve. Presentations can be fun. They are your chance to speak your mind, to strut your stuff and to tell people what you know. With each presentation, you will gain more and more confidence and learn to *wow* your audience!

Booktalking

Wicked Cool Advertising for Your Library

Jill S. Carpenter *and* Christen A. Caton

Picture this: A 13-year-old boy slouches into the library. He looks like any other teenager trying to seem cool despite his presence in a *library*, so you assume he'll head straight for the computers. Amazingly, he makes his way toward the reference desk, and rather than asking for homework help, he says, "So, where's that book you told me about this morning at school? You know, the red one. I want to read it." Or imagine 50 teens showing up for a library program. Do you think this is a fantasy that could only happen in an alternate reality? Booktalking will make that fantasy come true! Booktalking is the Pikes Peak Library District's (PPLD) most successful strategy for marketing to teens.

Booktalking is so important to PPLD that every year more than 11 staff members dedicate an average of 50 hours each, preparing for the semester's upcoming "booktalking season." Booktalkers ransack the catalog and the stacks for any book that might help them connect with teenagers. No genre is ignored, and books are pulled willy-nilly from fiction and nonfiction shelves alike. Every booktalker at PPLD needs to have at least ten booktalks available per semester of booktalking. Dozens of books are evaluated, and at least 20 are read and then either set aside in preparation for writing a booktalk, or consigned to the reject pile of books that might be engaging but won't translate into an interesting booktalk.

Once this winnowing is done, the writing, practicing, and rewriting begin. After writing talks for each book, the booktalkers practice presenting them. This can be done in the car, in front of a mirror, or on a walk around the neighborhood. A good booktalk is not necessarily the best written but the best acted, so booktalks have to be practiced out loud to get a feel for rhythm and intonation. Sometimes, even after writing what seems like a great booktalk on paper, practicing it aloud reveals that the booktalk is flat and boring and must be either rewritten or discarded.

Here are some tips for creating exciting booktalks:

- Know your booktalks so you can look at the class, gesture, and wave your arms around when necessary.
- Vary your voice according to the flow of the book. If the voice of the book is frightened and scared, make your voice soft and your breathing quick. If the voice of the book is a 13-year-old cheerleader, adopt that voice for your booktalk.

- If you are using a climactic part of the book as your booktalk, make sure that the tempo of your speech follows that of the book. Speed up your voice. Speak in a whisper. Lean in close as if you are confiding in the teens.
- Become the character of the book you are portraying. Do you envision that cheerleader twirling her hair? Twirl your hair. Do you envision the frightened character looking around him; paranoid that something is going to jump out at him from around the corner? Look from side to side or stop talking suddenly to listen for noises.
- Knowing your booktalk means more than memorization. Memorization allows you to repeat your booktalk but if you forget a line you're stuck! And it's embarrassing to have to stop and look through your notes! Get comfortable enough with your booktalk so you can change it when you need to.
- Get interactive! The teens should participate more than just listen. For example, have them actually do some of the improvisational games from *My Nights at the Improv* by Jan Siebold. Or, ask the teens what they would do in a character's situation or if they've ever been in a certain situation. Or have them guess what will happen next in a series of events.
- Remember that booktalking is a performance, not a reading.

This sounds like a lot of work, doesn't it? It is. So you might be wondering: Why should I bother? What could I possibly accomplish that will make all the effort worth it? There are at least half a dozen reasons to put in the time and the effort to booktalk, such as:

- Booktalks lure reluctant readers. A boy who thinks anything other than skateboarding is a waste of time might be captured by the story of a skate punk trying to make it in a world that doesn't think his skills are any kind of accomplishment.
- There is very little in library work more rewarding than teens rushing to the library after school looking for the books you booktalked that morning at their school. They might not remember the title or the author, but something in the booktalk grabbed them and you might hear requests for "that book about the guy who can't move but who has super powers" or "that scary one, with the rhyme" or "the book where everyone gets to be pretty when they grow up." Booktalking makes that happen. Honestly.
- By going into schools, library staff members build relationships with both students and teachers. Teachers enjoy these booktalks because they watch their students actually get excited about books. These relationships are why PPLD staff has been booktalking for over 20 years.
- Booktalking in schools gives the library staff a chance to verbally advertise library services and programs. Many teens have no idea the library provides more than just printed material these days. If a program is dependent upon advertising solely within the library, there won't be nearly the number of people aware of it as there will be if you can tell several hundred teens in one fell swoop.
- There is one more reason to booktalk: Fun! It really is fun to booktalk once you get past the butterflies that come with trying out new booktalks for the first time each semester. And not only do the students remember the books they hear about, but they will also remember you. You might be approached at the grocery store or in a doctor's office by a teen who remembers that you came to their school, and then proceeds to tell you how much they either loved or hated one of the books you recommended.

If you think you need to have a dozen booktalkers with endless prep time available to make booktalking work in your own library, it's simply not true. Two staff members can get things started. If you are the only person on staff involved with teen programming, look outside teen services. You'll be surprised at the number of staff who would love the chance to get away from the circulation or reference desk! If the prospect of going through the process of finding good books to booktalk seems daunting, there are resources that can help get you started until you have the confidence to start writing booktalks of your own. The Web site, www.booktalkingcolorado.ppld.org, is full of booktalks already teen tested, so all you have to do is read the book and select your booktalk. And then, of course, practice, practice, practice, so that the booktalk is second nature by the time you are in front of the class.

No matter how many teens we currently serve through our programming, there are always more to reach. Booktalking provides an entertaining and effective way to reach out to teens every school year, to create life-long library users, and to share our love of good books. Whether your teen department is brand new, or well established, booktalking will bring teens into your library!

Attracting High School Students

ALEXANDRA TYLE

Have you noticed that your teen events are filled with junior high students and little or no high school students? Are you interested in getting more high school students involved with the library? The Homer Township Public Library in Homer Glen, Illinois, has found a way to successfully bring high school students into the library, for more than just homework research.

I noticed that our Young Adult Committee meetings usually consist of preteens and only a small number of high school students attended. The high school students tended to form one group while the junior high students formed another. It was becoming evident that the two groups should have separate programming.

After hosting our first summer intern program, I noticed that many of our interns were not our usual young adult activity participants. The teen interns consisted mostly of high school students looking for volunteer hours to present on their resume or college applications. Realizing that many of the older high school students were interested in activities that would benefit their future, I decided to create teen programs that focused on this interest.

Planning

Creating a teen program for your library takes a lot of planning. The suggestions listed below will get you started.

- Set goals. Sit down and think of the goals for your program. What will the participants gain from it? How will the program benefit your library? How long will the program last?
- Determine participant grades/ages. While our library decided to limit our program to high school students, we did include a statement on the application form stating that the library may decide to include eighth graders if all spots were not filled. Remember, high school students may be turned off by the fact that eighth-grade or younger students are participating. They may not take the program seriously. Or perhaps you could limit the program to juniors and seniors, students who are feeling the pressure to plan their futures.
- Decide which teens to invite. Do you want to limit the program to your community's patrons or open it to any interested teenager? Look at your local high school(s). Does

110

the high school only serve your community? Or is there more than one town that feeds into your high school? If it serves other communities as well, you may want to open your program to those communities also. Teens like to go to things with friends and many of their friends may live in other communities.

- Establish a budget. Does your library have the funds to create a budget for your program? If so, how much? Will your speakers speak for free or for a fee? Will you provide food? If so, will it be donated or purchased? Also, will money need to be set aside for promotional tools?
- Identify staffing needs. Does your library have a Teen Services Department? If so, is the department large enough to run the program? This will depend on the number of teen participants. A large turnout may require more staff.
- Decide how many programs to offer. Have at least two or three programs a month, on various weeknights. Teens who are unable to attend programs on certain weeknights because of other activities and/or work will hopefully be able to attend on another night. Letting too much time go by between programs may cause teens to lose interest, forget dates or forget about the program altogether.
- Consider using teen volunteers. Determine what activities or services teen volunteers can assist with. Again, remember some teens will have other commitments. Try to be flexible with the volunteer schedule and timeline.
- Name your event. This is very important. Create something catchy, motivational, and long lasting, especially if your program will be a yearly event.

Presenters

Speakers for your program can be found just about anywhere. Consider the following:

- community leaders (police, fire, or local government personnel)
- local sports teams (coaches, players)
- local colleges (career services personnel, recruiters, instructors)
- corporations (While corporations may not be able to give grant money or sponsor your event, they may be willing to send a speaker.)
- local organizations (Small Business Administration, Counselors to America's Small Business, humanities councils, other speaker bureaus)

Sponsors

Need money? Try applying for grants. Remember, grants can be highly competitive and it may take some time to receive funds. Local companies may be willing to sponsor an event. Restaurants may be willing to donate food. Try contacting teen-friendly restaurants. They may be the most receptive.

Advertising/Promotion

Promotional items for your program should be teen-friendly. Nothing too boring and nothing too cute. Create a logo and make sure it is included on all posters and flyers and on the applications. Also, be sure to refer to your program by name on all printed materials and when talking with others. Places to advertise your program include:

- Local schools, both public and private. Send brochures to administrators, counselors, and school librarians.
- Your library's Web site and blogs. Create a blog post two or three days before the program and include a link to the program schedule.
- Local businesses. They may not have funds to sponsor or donate but may be willing to hang up posters and hand out entry applications.

Staff Participation

Encourage all library staff to make suggestions, before, during, and after the program. Staff members may know of possible presenters or sponsors and can pass along any positive or negative remarks they may overhear about the program. Staff may also view the project more positively if given the opportunity to participate and are more likely to take the extra step to speak positively about your program.

Follow Up

At the conclusion of the program ask teens what they thought of it. Which presenters should be asked back? What type of presentations should be added? You may wish to offer paper surveys at the end of the program or provide an online survey through a Web site, like Surveymonkey.com. If presenters have handouts, ask to keep a couple of copies. Teens that are unable to attend may come in asking about the event.

Most importantly, observe your high school population. Note what they do, and do not, gravitate toward. These observations will help you create programming that will meet their needs and interests.

Innovative Programs for Teens

IVY MILLER

You are a young adult librarian and you have been told it is your job to start some innovative teen programming at your library. Perusing the Web sites of various libraries you find dozens of ideas for "teen" programs. Book discussion groups, guest speakers, and writing workshops—all of it sounds great. However, when you look at the pictures that accompany the program descriptions you notice that something isn't quite right. Do these teens have some kind of glandular problem? Aren't they a little, well, young to be called "young adults"?

Most public libraries consider young adults to be anyone between the ages of 11 and 18. But there is a big difference between an 11 year old and a 17 year old. Programming for children in the fifth or sixth grade is relatively easy. Most of them are only slightly older than the kids in your current children's programs. Parents and guardians are used to driving them to the library for a read aloud or the local pet shop program. When you want to draw in high school students, that's where programming gets more interesting and much more challenging.

The first thing you need to do is establish a Library Advisory Board and invite teens to be the board members. Draw from the kids who have been coming to the library for a while. Advertise in local papers and hang up flyers around your library and in the high schools in the community. Call up your friends with teenage children and tell each teen to bring a friend. Lure them with pizza and community service credit. You want at least four teens but no more than 12. (The pizza bill gets really expensive.) Once you have them in for your first meeting, establish some guidelines:

- When is a good time to meet? Monthly? Bimonthly? Make sure it's consistent.
- Are meetings going to be informal get-togethers or more formal and businesslike?
- How many teens should be on the board?
- How long can a teen serve on the board?
- What is the process for accepting new teens to the board?
- What is the age range for teens on the board?
- What kind of food should be at each meeting?

Next, set a precedent for questions you will ask them at every meeting. Feedback is crucial, although it might be hard to get in the beginning. As time goes on you may want to make these questions more conversational. After you have built trust pose these questions to individual board members. They might feel more comfortable away from the larger group. Questions to ask consistently at board meetings include:

- What do they think of the library's collection? Would they like more music, DVDs or graphic novels?
- What kind of programs would they like to see at the library?

Throw some ideas at them and watch for their responses. Asking teens direct questions is the kiss of death, especially if they don't know you very well. When I first asked these questions I could literally hear the crickets chirping outside.

Then comes the tough part — gulp — do what they say. Well, maybe not everything they say. You don't want mayhem and chaos to take over your otherwise sane library. But doing some of what they ask for establishes trust. If they trust you, they'll bring their friends and the more they trust you, the more feedback they'll give. It wasn't until my third advisory board meeting that I learned my most important programming lesson from a very vocal young lady who said, "I don't want to do anything that even remotely reminds me of school."

Getting to know the teens who come to your library is the single most important thing you can do when programming for young adults. You may have a group of mostly young women who are interested in beauty. Why not have a make-up representative come in and do makeovers or have beauty school students to do manicures? You may have a very rural library where kids are interested fly-fishing or agriculture. Listen and be creative. Most importantly, be a presence in your programs but not necessarily in the program. If there is a room you give the teens for a few hours, let them have it. Even though they may like you and think you're the coolest librarian who ever lived (and you are), they will feel more comfortable with each other. I do not recommend leaving any group of teens unsupervised for any length of time, so make it understood that you will be "popping in" periodically to check on what they are doing.

At my library I found that there were some very distinct groups. There was a group who was very interested in Anime and Mange. I had to do some research to even figure out what these words meant. We established an Anime group, who got together monthly and swapped books, magazines, and Web sites; showed each other their artwork; and sometimes dressed up as their favorite characters. The group was so popular that high school graduates came back to visit when they were in college. There was a fantasy group who liked to play fantasy games and discuss books and characters. Another distinct group was the crafty bunch that liked to knit and "dip stuff in chocolate." Some programs worked really well for the general public. The Red Cross offers a babysitting class in which the kids learn first aid and walk away with a certificate. Open mic night for poetry and/or music is successful in many libraries. Many teens are very socially active, so planning programs around events like World Aids Day or Arbor Day can bring in a lot of teens.

A monthly or quarterly newsletter is a great way to keep in touch with your kids and announce new programs. Some items to put in your newsletter in might be lists of new books and/or a monthly profile of an individual board member. The newsletter is also a way to get feedback about programs.

As a librarian, you know how hard it is to find money for programming. Local community groups might help, but there are a lot of freebies too. Anything that allows teens to get together and hang out with like-minded people will be successful. A cosmetics firm came in to do makeovers for my kids and didn't charge anything. A local candy maker came and gave a short demonstration for free as well. After you've had a few programs, evaluate them to see how well they worked:

- Did the kids enjoy the program? Look for signs—did they smile and laugh or where they quiet the whole time?
- Did they say they would come back?
- Did they say they would bring a friend?
- Did they have ideas for the next program?

Some programs work and some don't. I came up with what I thought was a great program, a presentation by a comic book store owner, a comic book artist, and a comic book writer. I advertised the heck out of it, and only four kids showed up. One of those kids was my vocal young lady who told me, "It reminded me too much of school."

Looking Through the Eyes of a Child

PAM NUTT

Every Tuesday, Mrs. Pepper and her third grade class come to the media center for story time. Story time for third graders you ask? Why yes, they love being read to just as much as my kindergarten class does. So read to them! Montavious, who is one of 15 children in the Blackwell family, hates everything. Montavious is a very smart child, but just hates being told what to do. Montavious's goal for the day was to stay out of detention, which he has everyday. Mrs. Pepper's class came into the library all excited and sat in the circle. The circle is an area in the media center just for story time. Everyone sat down in the circle except Montavious. He decided he did not want to listen to story time today, so he sat with his back toward me, and yes, he was out of the circle.

Well, today, I decided that Montavious and I were going to get along, so I asked him if he would like to choose a book for story time. At first, he did not move or say a word, but then he decided to pick out a book for the class. Wouldn't you know it; it was a book that I've not read before. Me, the person who has been in the media center as long as the dinosaurs roamed the earth. Me, the person who is older than school meatloaf had not read that one lone book. Of course all research tells you not to read anything to the class without reading it yourself first. Did I follow the research suggestions?

Montavious handed me the book. It looked so large, so bright, so clean, I knew it must not be a very good book because all the books in my library are pretty old and loved. All of my Junie B. Jones, Amelia Bedelia, Arthur, and Amber Brown books are worn and need to be tossed due to being read so much. Let's not even mention the condition of books by authors like Dr. Seuss, Eric Carle, and Laura Numeroff. I quickly took the book and began flipping through the pages. It was very bright and had wonderful color pictures about a spider, a tin solider, and an old lady that lost her love years ago.

I began reading the story just as it was written, but it was not long after the first page that I realized that these kids thought Montavious's book was really bad. Montavious began to fidget. It was time to take action, or at least a few liberties. So, I decided to have an evil spider king, who would have a fight with the bugs, and then the bees began to sting the girl, and the ladybugs began to attack the spider, and, and, by the time I finished the story, the kids were clapping and the little girls where happy because the old lady turned back

116

into a little girl again. Well, my story had a happy ending or so I thought. Montavious decided that he didn't believe everything I just read, so very slyly, he asked if he could check out the book. I told him of course he can check the book out. This was the first time he had ever checked out a book in his four years at my school. Mrs. Pepper's class all checked out their books and went happily down the hall, and I was proud that Montavious finally check out a book from the media center. I smiled all day long because I believed that I had finally made a difference and broke through to Montavious.

The next morning, I arrived at school around 7:15 A.M., instead of my usual 8:00 A.M. Much to my surprise Montavious was waiting for me at the check-out desk. He slammed the book down on the desk, pointed a finger at me and said very loudly, "Ms. Nutt, you lied to us!"

"Montavious, what are you talking about," I asked in disbelief. "Why are you talking to me like this?" I could not believe what I was hearing.

Montavious said it again "Ms. Nutt, you lied to us about the book yesterday. I took this book home last night and read it to my mama and there was not a spider king or flying ladybugs or anything like that. Then, I read it by myself to see if I just missed something." I began to wonder if I should have just read the book as it was written. "Ms. Nutt," Montavious said using a calmer tone, but still very upset, "I guess I'm going to have to start reading all your story time stories so I can tell if you are reading it right or not. What do you have to say now?"

I was in such shock, for I had just realized that this child read the book, not once, but twice. This nonreader took a book and actually looked for facts, ideas, and anything that resembled the story I had told his class the day before. Forget that I lied to him about the story (well, I just got creative); he actually read the book. I was so excited about what just happened my face began to glow. My eyes were tearing up. I tried not to choke while I said that I was sorry for lying to him, but maybe he needed to come to the library the day before story time day and read me a book so I could get it right when he came with the class. Montavious told me that if I was in his class, I would be in detention for lying!

For the rest of the year, Montavious would come to the library and read me a book for story time. He began to smile and he loved showing me how to act like the characters in the book. One of his favorites was the *Grouchy Ladybug*, by Eric Carle. Montavious had a rubber face that could make the cutest expressions, and he would get a very deep voice and say "Do you want to fight" trying to portray the ladybug as he saw her. I will never forget Montavious, nor will I forget the knowledge I gained that day that one person really can make a difference.

The moral to this story is never be afraid to try something different and new with your class. So what if you fall on your face or look silly. Children need to see that you are a real person who is trying to reach them by getting on their level of learning. So next time you read to a class try using the following:

- voice inflection
- rise and tone of pitch
- facial expressions
- hand gestures
- long pauses
- dress up as a character in the book
- use puppets (allow the children to be the character as you read the story)

- allow the students to hold the book and turn the pages as you "tell" the story
- use a flannel board (does this date me?)
- use cutouts. (Printshop is a great source to make characters. Print them out, laminate them, and then glue them to Popsicle sticks and use as puppets.)

Personally, I love to listen to someone read to me at the ripe old age of 40-something, and I know that my students love listening to me as the Grouchy Ladybug and not as Ms. Nutt.

Multimedia Story Time

ROBIN BARTOLETTI

Those who work with children, including librarians, teachers and others need to deal with the changing role of computers in learning. One aspect of education that has been affected by computers is language arts, books and stories. Although children love hearing stories simply told by the traditional teller, many libraries have the tools to offer them more in the story-time or language-arts setting. One area that has yet to be explored thoroughly is that of the multimedia story time.

Christine Miller, children's librarian at the Dupont Branch of the Allen County Public Library in Indiana, uses multimedia in several ways in her story times but never for more than five minutes in a 30-minute story time. Miller says

> When doing a story time about monkeys or some other animal, I might use a product such as Mammals CD Rom by Dorling Kindersley to show the children pictures or short video clips of the animal and to provide sound effects. Sometimes I use Bailey's Book House CD Rom and we would make up our own story as a group and play it back. This was especially nice to do with visiting daycare groups because we could print it out and they could take it back to their center. For storytimes about seasons, we would go to the pond in Sammy's Science House CD Rom and watch the seasons change and explore the differences" [Voors and Miller, 1997].

Multimedia story time is beneficial because:

- It encourages learning by
  - ➤introducing children to the library, library staff, and computers.
  - ➤helping to equate books, computers, and the library with fun and enjoyment.
  - ➤creating habits and routines that include books, reading, and computers.
  - ➤providing exposure to print materials and multimedia materials.
- It encourages family literacy and involvement by
  - ➤encouraging interaction between child and adult.
  - ➤modeling read-aloud techniques computer use for both child and adult.
  - ➤creating an awareness of quality in children's literature, Internet sites and software for children.

- It enhances cognitive skills through the development of
  - ➤listening skills.
  - ➤language skills.
  - ➤motor skills through finger plays, action songs, and exposure to keyboarding.
- It encourages socialization by
  - ➤participation in a structured group activity.
  - ➤providing interaction with other children and adults.

Key points to consider when incorporating technology into story time:

- Does the multimedia add value to the story time?
- Does the multimedia promote good listening? Traditional story time activities like finger plays, rhythmic activities, and repetitive songs sharpen listening skills. Technology should add to this experience.
- Does the multimedia encourage creativity and allow children to move beyond listening to share responses and interact with sounds, words, and graphics?
- Does the multimedia link reading, responding, and computer use in an effective way?

Most, if not all, educational software and Web sites will work well on computers with the following components:

- Microsoft Windows 3.1/95/98
- Intel Pentium-class 75 MHz CPU
- 32 MB RAM
- 2.1 GB hard drive
- super VGA PCI video card with 1 MB video RAM
- super VGA color monitor
- sound card
- speakers, CD-ROM, keyboard, and mouse
- A graphical Web browser that will accommodate multimedia formats and Javascript, such as Netscape Navigator, Safari or Internet Explorer
- helper applications (plug-ins) like Real Player, Macromedia Flash Player, etc. for listening to audio files and viewing videos and portable documents
- Internet connection

An LCD data/video or multimedia projector is also suggested. These offer such features as a virtual or remote mouse and video compatibility. The purpose of the projector is to hook it up to the computer and project the images from the Internet or CD Rom onto a screen on the wall for viewing by a group.

Make sure you have clearly defined your learning goal for your story-sharing program. Decide on the type of multimedia activity you want to do to reach your learning goal. Make sure your activity is clearly planned with very specific instructions. Plan at least two back-up activities in case there is a problem with a Web site or the equipment you planned to use (for example, choose three Web sites on a topic or plan a craft as a backup to a CD-ROM). Go to the Internet or CD-ROM ahead of time and try out the activity yourself. Make sure you are comfortable with the technology before trying to use it. Check the links you intend to use the day of the program to make sure they are still active. Some Web sites may have links to inappropriate material. Be aware that current-event sites such as news programs change their content frequently. The clip you listened to yesterday may not be on the site today.

If you are planning to suggest Internet-based activities for parents to do at home, make sure your activities do not rely on complicated or advanced technologies that they do not have. Make sure whatever plug-ins are necessary are available in your organization.

Multimedia Story Time Program Checklist

Several months prior to event:

- develop objectives for story times
- decide on themes/topics for story times
- identify available resources, including multimedia
- purchase needed resources and equipment, including educational software or CD-ROMs
- obtain permission, funding, etc. from administration

One month prior to event:

- assemble materials and make final selections
- set up and test equipment
- identify audience, date, and time
- begin publicizing event
- check any Web sites selected and see if the links are still available
- develop contingency plan with alternate activities in case of equipment problems
- download and install any needed plug ins

Two weeks prior to event:

- schedule equipment assistance if needed
- set up equipment and do a dry run of program with multimedia
- bookmark Web sites to be used in story times
- determine seating arrangements and equipment arrangements

Day prior to event:

- assemble materials
- prepare seating
- prepare and retest equipment, test Web site links
- prepare decorations, displays, exhibits, crafts and handouts

Day of event:

- check lighting, temperature, room arrangement, equipment cords
- check Web site links one last time
- greet guests
- have fun doing the program!

After the event:

- do informal evaluation
- do formal evaluation
- begin planning next program

To see a sample multimedia story time for children ages five to nine, please visit http://arapaho.nsuok.edu/%7Ebartolet/mmstorytimes/samplemmstorytime.doc.

References

Voors, Mary R. and Christine Miller, "Integrating Multimedia Computer Use into Storytimes," *Journal of Youth Services in Libraries*, 10 (3), Spring 1997: 244–252.

Read, Write and Rap

Connecting Teens and Tweens to Poetry through Hip-Hop Lyrics

TAMELA N. CHAMBERS

Iambic pentameter and spittin' lyrics. Is the latter the estranged offspring of heralded poets such as Shakespeare and Wordsworth? An old dog doing new tricks? Ask yourself these questions the next time you gaze in confusion at your teens and tweens as they print and trade lyrics to the latest rap songs or come across forgotten lyrics that are — ahem — a bit objectionable. The potential for educational opportunity is in these experiences.

To capitalize on the educational opportunity you need only to follow these three steps: (1) Take everything that you *think* you know about hip-hop and forget about it. (2) Repeat for poetry. (3) Open your mind and open some books. It's time to reeducate.

Poets of the Past

Did you know that Lord Byron's first book of poetry, *Fugitive Pieces*, was destroyed by an English clergyman who found some of the poems objectionable (Literary Encyclopedia 2005 People, p. 1), and he was once considered to be "mad, bad and dangerous to know"? Or that Shakespeare's *Venus and Adonis* straddled the fine lie between erotic and vulgar (Bedside, Bathtub & Armchair Companion to Shakespeare 2001, pp. 236–239, 4p)? That Dylan Thomas, author of the classic *Do Not Go Gentle into That Good Night*, became a victim of his own celebrity (Contemporary Authors Online 2007, http://galenet.galegroup.com/servlet/BioRC)? Hardly the "romantic death" envisioned for poets, Spanish poet Federico García Lorca died in a hail of bullets; a fate similar to the unsolved death of Tupac Shakur (Authors and Artists for Young Adults 2007, http://galenet.galegroup.com/servlet/BioRC). Since these poets relied on their real-life experiences as muses and art imitates life, is it such a stretch to consider hip-hop artists as our 21st-century bards?

Connecting Poetry and Hip-Hop Lyrics

If you are now able to visualize (with comical musing of course!) the image of Kanye West trading verses with William Wordsworth, you are on the right track. Below are some tips for planning and implementing a Read, Write and Rap program in your library:

- Organize and visualize. Set up a display of books highlighting the works of various poets as well as historical and biographical books on various hip-hop artists and culture. Create a bulletin board that highlights the lyrics of popular hip-hop artists (the clean versions—if applicable—of course!)and the poetry of "required-reading" poets.
- Create and disseminate. Design and distribute brochures highlighting your library's collection of poetry and hip-hop related titles. Create flyers and press releases and send them to your local newspapers. Speak with local school principals to see if you can put an ad in the school newspaper or newsletter. Work with churches and other community groups serving teens/tweens to promote your program.
- Host and boast. Plan a series of poetry/hip-hop related programs. Set aside a week to conduct them. Possible programming ideas include:
  - ➤Hip-hop forums. Invite teens/tweens to bring the lyrics of their favorite hip-hop artist for discussion.
  - ➤Discuss the poetry of select poets and ask the teens/tweens to compare and contrast. Show a screening of a hip-hop documentary, such as *And You Don't Stop: 30 Years of Hip Hop History* or *The Art of Rhyme: Featuring Mos Def and Lord Finesse.* Show a screening of a poetry documentary, such as *The United States of Poetry* or *Slam Nation.* Be sure to provide participants with parental permission slips. Discuss the connections between "old-school" poets and modern hip-hop artists.
  - ➤Writing workshops. Provide space and stimulus to help teens/tweens write their own rhymes. One way to jumpstart this process is to get them to compare themselves to an inanimate object. Another way is to do a "rhyme chain" in which one person says a word and each person in the room has to find a word that rhymes with it. Be sure to have rhyming dictionaries on hand. Take a tour of your library and have the teens/tweens write poetry out of titles on your shelves. Have them read and "rock the mic." They can do this by "book rapping" a summary of their favorite poetry books or by putting together rhymes to promote poetry books chosen by you. For an added twist, make a contest of this and use the book rhymes for an annotated reading list, created by teens/tweens for teens/tweens.
  - ➤That's. My. Word. "Publish" the collective works of your teens and tweens in an anthology. Allow the participants to name their collection. Print copies and distribute them inside the branch as well as to the principals of the schools represented in your program.
- Poetry slam. Allow your program participants the opportunity to showcase their rhyming skills. Invite other community organizations to see your patrons perform. Offer praise and accolades accordingly.
- Take it on the road. Work with your teens/tweens on the formation of a spoken word troupe. Ask local elementary schools and junior highs if the spoken word troupes can perform their work at special assemblies or for select classrooms.

Readin' Is Fundamental

The following is a list of recommended titles to use for Read, Write and Rap at your library:

Crane, Ronald. (1978) *A Collection of English Poems*. Great Neck, NY: Granger Books.

Eleved, Mark. (2003) *The Spoken Word Revolution: Slam, Hip-hop, & the Poetry of a New Generation*. Naperville, IL: Sourcebooks Media Fusion.

Forman, Murray. (2004) *That's the Joint!: The Hip Hop Studies Reader*. New York: Rutledge.

Fricke, Jim. (2004) *Yes Yes Y'all: The Experience Music Project Oral History of Hip-hop's First Decade*. Cambridge, MA: De Capo Press.

Moustaki, Nikki. (2001) *The Complete Idiot's Guide to Writing Poetry*. Indianapolis, IN: Alpha Books/

Schmidt, Michael (1999) *Lives of the Poets*. New York: Knopf.

Sitomer, Alan. (2002) *Hip-hop Poetry and the Classics: Connecting Our Classic Curriculum to Hip-Hop Poetry through Standards-based, Language Arts Instruction*. Beverly Hills, CA: Milk Mug Publications.

Upton, Clive. (2004) *The Oxford Rhyming Dictionary*. New York: Oxford University Press.

The titles listed above are intended to serve as a reference point from which you can begin to plan your program. A good mix of history, social perspectives, criticisms and how-tos will not only help you and your teens/tweens learn the hows and whys of hip-hop and poetry, but also jumpstart the creative process. Teens/tweens will understand the importance of studying classic poets and poetry and see the connection between old school and new school.

Ready to Rock the Mic?

You now have a starting point from which to connect hip-hop lyrics and poetry and to communicate that connection to your teens and tweens. Transform yourself from librarian to "hip-hop-brarian" and make your library hip-hop generation friendly. Whether you successfully convert them into poetry lovers or you yourself develop a liking for hip-hop, your teens/tweens will adore you, their parents and teachers will love you. You will have elevated your "cool factor" and everyone wins!

Splish-Splash Story Time

SIAN BRANNON

It gets pretty hot in Texas, especially when you are stuck inside a small room of a barely air-conditioned library with 30 children and their caregivers during a story time. Come August and September, you would do just about anything to cool off. Nothing sounds better than leaving the library and going swimming. However, you can't do that if you want to get paid for doing your job ... can you?

In the fall of 2005, after a very long and hot summer, the weather-beaten youth services librarians at the Denton Public Library decided to try and accomplish this. Year-round, the Denton Public Library staff conducts various outreach story times at day-care centers and schools around the city; basically, we try to take the education and literacy efforts to where the children are. Well, as it turns out, one place children are in the middle of summer is the local community swimming pool.

The library component of the City of Denton does not fall under the Parks and Recreation Department as it does in some other municipalities. It falls under what's known as "general municipal services." Furthermore, the two sections of the city government have not traditionally worked together in any formal capacity, not in the library's Summer Reading Club events, or in any of the Parks Department's regularly scheduled activities. It was time for new ground to be broken! After securing support from her supervisor, one adventurous youth services librarian attempted to contact the head of the local swimming hole. Luckily for us, and the citizens of Denton, a new water park had just been built on the north edge of town.

The librarian's basic idea was this:

- On a set weekday morning each week during the summer, library staff would arrive at the water park in their swimsuits before it opened.
- Water park staff would allow library staff, parents, and children into the park BEFORE normal operating hours without charging them.
- Library staff would conduct a basic story time of a few books, some songs, and some puppetry for about 20 minutes.
- Everyone would frolic in the wading pools until the park opened, at which time everyone would leave (or pay admission to stay in the park).

At first, the parks and recreation staff was not too receptive about letting librarians and citizens come into the water park before normal operating hours. They were also uneasy about not charging for entry to the park. There was also a concern about scheduling water park staff to work while story time participants were in the park. Furthermore, who would be responsible if any problems arose, such as an injury or a health problem? The library or the water park? For these reasons, the director of the water park tried to put off making a decision as long as possible.

But, who can stop a youth services librarian once she sets her mind to something? After the idea was brought up the first time, and seemingly forgotten, another librarian ran into the water park director at a staff training function. They discussed some of the concerns coming from the Parks Department, and finally were able to come up with a compromise that pleased both sides:

- The program would happen on four set days during one month in the summer.
- No water would be turned on until a certain time.
- The library would be responsible for all publicity.
- The program must be completed and all participants out of the park before normal operating hours began.
- The director would be on hand to serve as lifeguard and to handle any issues that arose.
- The program would take place at a certain pagoda near the young children's wading pool, and all "frolicking" would have to happen there.

So it was settled. It seemed like a tall list of demands at first, but really, each item was easy to work into the overall plan. Splish-Splash Story Time was on its way to becoming a reality!

Four different youth services librarians took over one of the scheduled dates for the story times. Each was responsible for planning, creating, and conducting a 20-minute program. There were a lot of differences between these programs and our regular story times:

- The librarian wears a swimsuit (shorts if preferred).
- The librarian uses a microphone (to be heard over the busy road next to the water park).
- When else do you wear sunscreen during a library program?
- There is the dilemma of whether to get your hair wet.
- The librarian must choose the program materials carefully — they could get wet.
- The librarian must decide whether to bring his favorite host puppet and subject it to chlorine.

Perhaps we were reading too much into these special story times, but it truly was a new idea with a few hurdles to jump. Now, it was time for publicity. The water park is on the north end of town, but publicity was to be distributed between three branches.

Announcements were made during regular children's programming leading up to the first Splish-Splash Story Time. Handouts were made and distributed at programs and at circulation desks at each branch. Whenever a child or parent complained about the heat, we announced the new water park story times!

The first story time was wonderfully successful, with much higher participation than expected. The attendance was over 100 total. Approximately 35 percent were parents. The microphone came in handy for projecting over the large crowd, and it was hard talking over the wind. The second program came the next week, and word had apparently gotten out about the fun. Over 230 participants were there. This was a bit much for the one librarian to handle, but again, the microphone helped a great deal. By the third week, apparently some parents didn't want to be part of such a huge crowd, and attendance was back down around 110. Attendance for the final program during the fourth week was also around 110.

The Parks and Recreation Department aided in the fun during the programs by providing water park admission coupons to attendees. They even asked us if we would extend the program for a few more weeks. Unfortunately, due to other programming commitments, the library was unable to do so. Just a few weeks after the programs ended, the Parks and Recreation department asked the library if it could submit the Splish-Splash Story Time as an entrant for the Texas Recreation and Parks Society's Lone Star Programming Award. This is awarded for innovative recreational programming for a program offered for the first time. We won!

Each librarian who participated in these programs is eager for next summer to come around; they all want to do it again. Maybe each of us can go to a CPR class just to be on the safe side. There will be some changes, however. A longer season is planned; the program's popularity indicated that we need to offer more than four story times. We will also send more staff to future programs; it is hard for one person to control that many people. We also have plans to use collection development money to purchase some "waterproof" books especially for this program. The children thought splashing the librarian was funny!

"El Día de los Niños/El Día de los Libros" Goes to College

Mardi Mahaffy, Susan Metcalf *and* Irene Shown

"El Día de los Niños," or Children's Day, has held long standing in Latin America as the day to recognize and value children. Declared by Mexico in 1925, El Día is celebrated on April 30. In 1996 Pat Mora, a children's author, developed the idea to extend the tradition to the United States and include a celebration of literacy and joy in reading. Several individuals and organizations joined her in the effort, including Reforma (the national association to promote library services to Latinos and the Spanish speaking), MANA del Norte, and the W.K. Kellogg Foundation. Today, April 30 is celebrated in libraries across the country as El Día de los Niños/El Día de los Libros (Children's Day/Book Day) — a day to honor childhood, diversity, and reading.

Made for Each Other

Since El Día de los Niños/El Día de los Libros (often just Día) was started by a children's author, it has so far been promoted primarily by public libraries. This is to be expected, since children services are a prominent part of the mission of public libraries.

But celebrating this holiday could, and should, be embraced by academic institutions and libraries as well. After all, colleges and universities:

- are training tomorrow's teachers
- care passionately about literacy — for adults as well as children
- emphasize outreach and community service
- have students who are parents, or may soon be

In 1999, the presidents of a number of institutions signed the *Presidents' Declaration on the Civic Responsibility of Higher Education,* which began:

> As presidents of colleges and universities, both private and public, large and small, two-year and four-year, we challenge higher education to re-examine its public purposes and its commitments to the democratic ideal. We also challenge higher education to become engaged, through actions and teaching, with its communities. Celebrating El día meshes well with these ideals and programs.

Possible Activities

There are two types of activities that can be considered in celebrating Día on campus: activities for children and programs for adults.

Activities for Children

Kids are so easy to entertain, and adults can and do enjoy themselves! At New Mexico State University we've invited local school children to our library to see puppet shows (a big hit with all), read aloud bilingual books, and listen to stories. We always display bilingual and multicultural children's books and hold drawings and contests for book posters signed by their authors and illustrators. Other libraries let children make their own books or piñatas and invite folk dancers or musicians.

Children enjoy taking home something colorful to remember the celebration, so have some giveaways on hand. There are inexpensive giveaways available from ALA. They include:

- Activity books
- Bookmarks
- Book publicity posters

There are lots of resources to help you celebrate Día on the Web, replete with ideas and examples of programs. They include:

- Pat Mora (www.patmora.com/dia.htm)
- American Library Association (www.ala.org/dia)
- Reforma (http://reforma.org)
- Texas Library Association (www.texasdia.org)

Programs for Adults

University students, local parents and teachers might find a panel discussion informative. Education students and faculty addressing literacy, multicultural, and diversity issues in their coursework; creative writers and book illustrators interested in reaching children; and social work students studying cultural and family problems all are potential participants. Below is an excerpt from the University of Southern Florida Library's Día press kit.

Practical Benefits of Día de los libros ~ Día de los Niños

Students: The Día de los Niños ~ Día de los Libros festivities provide students with an enjoyable, educational, literacy-themed event that emphasizes the importance of literacy and reading through a variety of activities.

Educators: Día de los Niños ~ Día de los Libros will introduce creative ways for educators to promote literacy and reading comprehension through enhanced lesson plans.

Local Coordinators: Día de los Niños ~ Día de los Libros is a wonderful opportunity for organizations and associations to volunteer their efforts for a child-centered program designed to encourage reading, improve self-esteem, and ensure inclusiveness.

Parents: Día de los Niños ~ Día de los Libros can provide parents with the necessary tools to encourage their children's reading skills and allow parents to openly communicate with their children about the importance of reading and literacy.[1]

Possible Presenters

Inviting children's book authors and illustrators to your event will draw young people and adults alike. Our public and school library counterparts have much to teach us in how to best approach such a visit. Librarian Jo Ellen Misakian and author Fran Lantz have the following wisdom to share:

> Contacting Authors/Illustrators: Authors may be contacted through their publishers, [our research suggests this is best approach to take in most situations] or through their own websites.

> Honorariums: Authors and illustrators should be adequately compensated for their time. Those who have few books to their credit, are not so well known, or who are local will anticipate smaller honorariums than their more famous counterparts.

> Clear Expectations: Both the library and the visiting author should be clear on exactly what is expected, and libraries need to be prepared to stick to what they contracted for. Event outlines and appearance contracts should be made in writing.

Authors and illustrators are not the only individuals that can add to events. Here are some other ideas:

- students in the education, theater, or library-science programs who are taking classes in storytelling
- faculty with expertise in literacy, bilingual education, child development, or children's literature
- local educators with first hand experiences regarding how language barriers impact student literacy

Possible Event Venues

Multiple locations are available to the academic library looking for an event venue appropriate for children. The following are just a few of the possibilities:

- the university library
- the university student union
- the campus day-care center or laboratory school
- the public library
- a local public school or day-care center

All locations have advantages or disadvantages which need to be carefully weighed when making a final selection. Here are a few things to take into account:

- Ownership: Introducing children at a young age to the campus, and in particular the campus library, may have benefits down the road. The more exposure children have to the campus, the more ownership they will feel in the college community. This in turn may lead to a greater interest in college as they age.
- Child friendliness: Bringing children into the college library is a great way to introduce them to campus, but it is also important to keep in mind that academic environments are not designed for children. Care should be taken to have an adequate ratio of adults to children at the event for proper supervision. Additionally, children may not feel at home in the more subdued atmosphere of an academic setting. Public libraries and

school classrooms are alternate venues that provide established, colorful environments inviting to children.

• Accessibility: As literacy is not just a concern for children, but a goal impacting the entire family, events that include parents will have a greater impact. Is there adequate room, parking, or public transportation available to invite everyone who might like to attend?

Conclusion

We have listed for you here just a few of the many possibilities for hosting an El día de los niños/ El día de los libros event. This discussion is intended only as a starting point. Use your creativity to develop something uniquely your own.

Notes

1. www.lib.usf.edu/diversity/DIA.pdf, retrieved 10/5/06.
2. Lantz, F. and Misakian, J.E. (2002). Authors as celebrities. *Book Report*, 21(3), 20–23.

The Librarian as Marketing Director for a Small Press Publisher

PAULA M. STORM

Librarians are special customers of publishers. They court us at conferences and use us for feedback on their products. We read their literature and attend their demonstrations and workshops. It was because of this insight into the publishing industry that I came to manage marketing for a small press publisher.

St. Joseph Media is located in Wayne, Michigan, with three titles in print. It has been in existence since 1994. I had come to help work on the second book that St. Joseph Media published by building a bibliography of literally thousands of books and other sources used in its writing. I used other bibliographies, did citation searches, and ordered the books and articles through interlibrary loan. This was an obvious use of my skills as an academic librarian. This book, *Tumultuous Times,* was finally published in 2004, the first book on the ecumenical councils of the Catholic Church to be published in nearly 50 years.

Once published, though, it had to sell and to sell it had to be marketed. The subject of the book and the library binding of its over 600 pages meant that the market was small and had to be specially targeted. Though not as obvious a match to my professional skills as the bibliographer, marketing of the book became something in which I was highly interested. Father Francisco Radecki, the coauthor of the book and founder of St. Joseph Media, agreed that I would be the best person for the job. As a not-for-profit publisher, St. Joseph Media had a small marketing budget, so I had to use my professional knowledge and creativity instead of dollars to get publicity for *Tumultuous Times.*

As a librarian, I knew how to find out what I didn't know, and I began to research how to market and publicize a new book. The first thing that needed to be done was to set a price for the book. I researched the prices of comparable books that were currently in print using *Books in Print* and Amazon. We set the price at $29.95. I then began looking for a distributor using *Literary Market Place* and calling each possible distributor to determine the best arrangement. I soon found out that many distributors are reluctant to work with such a small press. Success finally came, however, and the first shipment of books was sent to our distributor.

Soon, *Tumultuous Times* received an ISBN from R.R. Bowker, the exclusive U.S. source of publisher prefixes and accompanying ranges of ISBN numbers. Copies were then sent to the Library of Congress and to some of the main book-review publications such as *Midwest Book Review* and *Choice*. Shortly thereafter, *Tumultuous Times* was listed in *Books in Print* and was selling through Amazon and Barnes & Noble. I asked those who purchased the book to write reviews for Amazon, because I knew that I read the Amazon reviews when contemplating the purchase of a new title.

Throughout this process I kept thinking about how publishers get me to buy their books. What catches my eye? How do I hear of new titles? Why do I purchase the literally tens of thousands of dollars worth of books that I do? As a librarian, I am inundated with publishers' catalogs, flyers, e-mails, and telephone calls. I began to look at these tactics with the eye of a marketer instead of a customer.

I began designing flyers, keeping in mind what I had learned from my study of the publishers' marketing tools. To produce a targeted marketing list I used *Encyclopedia of Associations* and *The American Library Directory*. I found a reliable, reasonable, local printer to produce the flyers. They were placed in envelopes, and off they went! I also sent hundreds of flyers electronically as well.

In my research of possible professional associations that might benefit St. Joseph Media, I came across the Publishers Marketing Association (PMA), and we became a member. PMA proved to be helpful in giving advice and strategies on how to market books. I later found out that the new book market is one of the most highly competitive markets that exist!

My expertise as a Web designer and searcher came into play when St. Joseph Media debuted on the Internet. Registering our domain name, linking to other related Web sites, and having our site linked to others helped to gain publicity that was practically free. The Web was perfect for the niche marketing I needed to do. By using my librarian's skills for research I found:

- names and contact information for potential customers (professors of history and religion, clergy, schools)
- book review sites
- online bookstores that have targeted markets
- online literary reviews
- book discussion lists
- contact information for media outlets
- associations for Catholicism, religion, history
- online radio programs
- book fairs, workshops and expositions

From the media contact information I obtained interviews for Father Radecki discussing *Tumultuous Times* on radio, television, Web broadcasts, and in newspapers. I used my librarian colleague contacts and arranged speaking engagements at local libraries. I added our title to book discussion lists, sent complimentary copies to book review sites, such as H-Net.org; online bookstores specializing in Catholic, religious, or historical literature; and some history and religious studies faculty.

In my capacity as librarian at Eastern Michigan University I am a reviewer for *Choice* and a couple of online book review sites, and I used that expertise in writing my own book reviews for *Tumultuous Times*, sending it to both online and print book review sources for publication. Not only did I get publicity from my published review, but I also got a publication that counts toward my tenure as well!

In 2005 St. Joseph Media published its third title, *The Family Catechism*, a children's catechism, which I helped edit. Though the market for the two books overlapped somewhat, the children's book market was something of which I had very little knowledge. I began the process of researching the children's book market and interviewed many children's librarians and children's bookstore owners. I used the knowledge of book promotion I had gained while marketing *Tumultuous Times* and added what I learned about the children's book market.

Gradually, I had come to realize how many of my skills were quite marketable. Not only did they make me a good librarian, but they were also valuable in other venues as well. Some of these skills are listed here:

- research skills
- finding information on a variety of subjects
- creativity
- writing reviews
- Web design
- collection development resources
- knowledge of books and publishing as a buyer
- design of instructional materials
- cost consciousness
- ingenuity
- communication skills

Though I volunteer my time and receive no monetary compensation, the experience of working as marketing director for a small publisher has been exciting, rewarding, and educational. A librarian's knowledge and experience makes her particularly suited to work in the development and marketing of books, Web sites, databases, or other media. There are many such positions to be found if a librarian is looking for an alternative career path. I encourage all librarians to take an inventory of their expertise and consider branching out to other fields outside the library world.

Why Publishing Is Good Both for You and the Profession

JUDITH A. SIESS

You, of course, are a librarian, but you can be a writer too. If you don't feel comfortable writing by yourself, find another librarian to coauthor a paper. A great idea is to cowrite a paper with one of your customers. How about getting a doctor to write a paper with you for publication in the *Journal of the American Medical Association* about the value of a librarian in finding medical information. Of course, *you* will do most of the writing, but the physician's name will get it published. The same goes for a law librarian, a lawyer, and the *ABA Journal*. Or, writing with your boss for *Fortune, Business Week*, the *Economist*, or another business journal. These articles will do the profession a lot more good than an article in a library journal telling us how wonderful we are. Other possible topics are a profile of another librarian, an author, or a customer or a book review.

What Should You Write?

One of the best ways to give back is by writing about your own experiences. Every librarian likes to read articles on "what I did good in my library." So, write about your successes. However, of even more value, perhaps, are articles about your failures. No one likes to tell what he or she did wrong, and this is exactly why these articles are valuable. We all can learn from our mistakes — and from the mistakes of others. Knowing what *not* to do can save valuable resources and the respect of others.

When Should You Write?

You should write whenever you have something to say, whenever you're asked, and whenever you have time.

Why Should You Write?

An important part of being a professional is the obligation to give back to the profession. You learned from and were helped by others and should do the same for those who follow. Getting published also lets others know about you; it raises your profile with your peers, your management, and your customers. It can be a subtle form of publicity. Other benefits of writing are that it improves your self-confidence, it is useful for analyzing and evaluating your own work, and you can earn money — not a lot, mind you, but there's no thrill like the one you get when you receive your first check. You probably won't get paid for the first articles you write (unless you write for my newsletter, the *One-Person Library*), but that's not why you're writing.

Where Can You Get Published?

You can get published by starting newsletters put out by local chapters or subject divisions of your professional association. I've never met a newsletter editor who wasn't actively (maybe even desperately) looking for material. Then there are the specialty publications, like the *One-Person Library, MLS: Marketing Library Services,* or *Searcher;* electronic newsletters, like *Ex Libris: An E-Zine for Librarians and Other Information Junkies* or *LIScareer.com;* and large-format "newspapers" like *Information Today* or *Information World Review.* To reach a wider audience there are the library association journals, like *American Libraries, Information Outlook, InCite* (Australia), or *Library and Information Update* (United Kingdom). If you have done a study of some aspect of librarianship, you can submit a research article to one of the more scholarly journals, such as *Library Trends,* the *Australian Library Journal, Law Library Journal, Aslib Proceedings,* or any of the Haworth Press journals (*Journal of Hospital Librarianship,* for instance). These are good if you are in a tenure track position in higher education. Finally, you can write a book.

How Do You Get Published?

Now to the nitty-gritty details of how to get published.

I won't write anything until I have a commitment from a publisher. Contact the editor and see if he or she would be interested in an article on your proposed topic. Ask for a copy of the publication's style sheet; it tells you how to format the article (spacing, length, type of footnotes, etc.). It is critical that you follow all the publisher's rules — if you don't, your work most likely won't be accepted. Find out the editor's deadline and meet it (even better, get your article in early).

After you submit your article, you may or may not get back an edited version. Some publications work on such a tight schedule that they don't have time to let you approve their changes — and nearly all editors will make some changes. I edit articles to conform to my newsletter's house style for things such as punctuation, use of bold and italics, and to correct obvious grammatical and spelling errors.

If you're submitting a research article to a scholarly journal, it most likely will be submitted to a peer review process. The paper will be sent to several reviewers who will first tell the editor if the article should be published at all. If it is accepted, the reviewers will make comments and ask for revisions. These will be sent to you. You can, of course, refuse to make the revisions, but it may result in the manuscript being rejected. Nearly always the revisions are reasonable and will improve your paper.

After you make the revisions, the editor and/or the reviewers will look over the paper again before final publication. This whole process can take months and the journal may have a backlog of articles, so it may be a year or more before your article appears. Therefore, make sure that the article will still be timely and make sense far into the future.

After your article is published, you may get a few complimentary copies of the journal for your own use. Sometimes you have to pay for the reprints. (This is a rotten publishing model, but it is a fact of life, so live with it.)

Finally, enjoy your success, but start thinking about your next article. This is an ongoing process and the more you write, the easier it gets and the more you will be asked to write.

Beyond the Blue Carpet

Simulating Reference Desk Activities in an Academic Library

JOHN H. HEINRICHS *and* NANCY CZECH

Academic libraries have traditionally provided their users with access to a variety of static, existing information sources, but the vision for the future library is changing to an active, energizing location supporting a learning community. To achieve that vision, discrete event simulation modeling represents an innovative method to understand and improve library processes. In the past, simulation models were regarded as too complex to be useful to librarians and were rarely used as a decision-making tool for libraries.[1] However, the new generation of librarians is comfortable with computer technology and the concepts behind simulation modeling. This new generation, which grew up with games such as SimCity, can easily transfer these gaming concepts beyond simple ideas, such as selecting the color of carpeting, to complicated decision support models aimed at improving staff productivity. Simulation models help focus the librarians on service-oriented thinking and can be used to clarify the tradeoff between customer satisfaction and service delivery. Students can benefit from simulation models by preparing them to make better decisions in their libraries through developing their critical-thinking capabilities.

The Library and Information Science Program (LISP) at Wayne State University (WSU) in Detroit, Michigan, offers a Competitive Intelligence course where students have the opportunity to simulate real-life library operations with real data. In fall 2006, WSU LISP students undertook an ambitious project to simulate the library processes used at the reference desks of three of the university libraries: Purdy/Kresge Graduate Library, David Adamany Undergraduate Library, and Science and Engineering Library. The reference desks at these libraries were selected because the Academic Research Libraries (ARL) statistics for directional, brief, and extended questions were readily available (see figure 1). The ARL statistics made the simulation project possible since students would not have had the opportunity to collect this volume of information in a timely manner. Students in this course were provided both the ARL statistics for November 2005 and the current staffing schedules for each library. To enhance the simulation model, additional time statistics for the directional, brief, and extended questions were gathered by the student groups. The students created their final simulation models using Arena, a discrete event simulation software productivity tool. In addition, each group was required to augment their models using one of the following unique aspects of simulation modeling:

- Training: How simulation models can be used to train library professionals in decision making.
- Optimal resource allocation: How an optimization tool is integrated with simulation models to enhance resource management decisions.
- 3-D animation: How 3-D animation is used to visualize results.

Science & Engineering	10/01/06			10/02/06			10/03/06			10/04/06			10/05/06			10/06/06		
	Dir.	Brief	Ext	Dir.	Brief	Ext	Dir.	Brief	Ext	Dir.	Brief	Ext	Dir.	Brief	Ext	Dir.	Brief	Ext
8:00-8:59																		
9:00-9:59																		
10:00-10:59				2	2	1	1	3		2	2	1			1	2		
11:00-11:59				1	2		9	3		1	3	2	3	1	3	1	3	
12:00-12:59				2	4	2	2	4	2	1	1	2		1	1	1		
1:00-1:59	2	1	1	2	2	3	6	6		3	6		2	6		3	2	
2:00-2:59	1	2		5	1	4		7	1	4	3	1	1			1		
3:00-3:59		11	1	2	1	1	2	3		1		2						2
4:00-4:59	1		3	2	2	1	6	1	1	2	2					3		
5:00-5:59	2	1	1	2	3	2	2	1	3	1	3		1	1				
6:00-6:59		2	1	1	1		2	7	2	1					2	3	3	1
7:00-7:59																		
8:00-8:59																		
9:00-9:59																		
10:00-10:59																		
Total	6	17	7	19	18	14	28	34	12	16	20	10	10	12	6	11	7	0
Overall Total			30			51			74			46			28			18

Figure 1: ARL Statistics.

Basic Model

Simulation is the process of designing a model of a real library system and manipulating the information collected to build a model in order to enhance the understanding of the behavior of processes and/or evaluate various strategies for improving library services.[2] Student groups each built a basic 2-D model of the reference desk they observed (see figure 2). The students used the captured data — types of questions, length of time to answer questions, number of staff, hours of operation, staffing schedules, and number of questions asked — to create models that represented the various reference desks. They flow-charted the model from the point a question was asked to the point in which it was answered. The model tracked patrons as they asked the question of the student library assistant at the reference desk. The assistant determined whether the question was directional, brief, or extended or required the professional services of the librarian on call. Once the question was answered, the statistics were captured and recorded.

Training

Group number 1 was in charge of enhancing a model for training library professionals. They created a simple user interface using a Microsoft Access database form that allowed what-if questions to be asked of the model. Therefore, the library professional could cre-

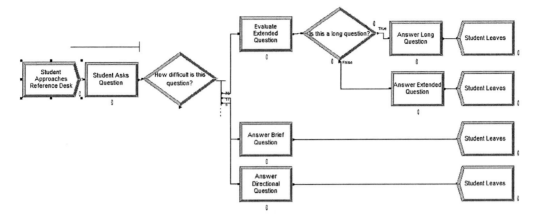

Figure 2: Process Model.

	Select	Control	Lower Bound	Suggested Value	Upper Bound	Type	Category
►	☑	Acquisition Librarian	2	3	4	Discrete (1) ▾	Resource
	☑	Intern	1	1	2	Discrete (1) ▾	Resource
	☐	Subject Specialist Librarian	1	1	2	Discrete (1) ▾	Resource
	☐	Requests Approved	0	0	0	Continuous ▾	Variable
	☐	Requests Denied	0	0	0	Continuous ▾	Variable
	☐	Requests in System	0	0	0	Continuous ▾	Variable

Control Selection: Select controls and set bounds.

Objective and Requirement Selection: Select an objective and any requirements (reqs. must have a bound).

	Select	Response	Lower Bound	Upper Bound	Value
	No ▾	Intern.NumberBusy			Average
	No ▾	Intern.NumberScheduled			Average
	No ▾	Intern.NumberSeized			Final
	No ▾	Intern.ScheduledUtilization			Final
	No ▾	Intern.Utilization			Average
	No ▾	Requests Approved Value			Average
►	Maximize Objective ▾	Requests Approved			Final
	No ▾	Requests Denied Value			Average
	No ▾	Requests Denied			Final

Figure 3: Example of Training Statistics Used.

ate various scenarios and receive customized feedback. For example, the interface allowed the librarian to change the number of available student assistants, the number of students asking questions, and/or types of questions asked directly in the Microsoft Access form. The simulation model was then run based on the questions asked by the librarian and the output was created into a Microsoft Excel worksheet (see figure 3). The professional thus would gain a greater understanding of the operation of the reference desk and how alterations in the process affect the overall productivity of the reference desk.

Optimal Resource Allocation

The students in group number 2 used their simulation model to assist library management in determining the optimal way to allocate scarce resources while maintaining the standard of service delivery. Using OptQuest for Arena, this group defined the project objectives and set the boundaries for the resources (see figure 4). The group sought to min-

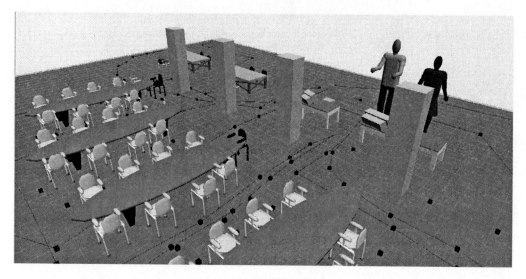

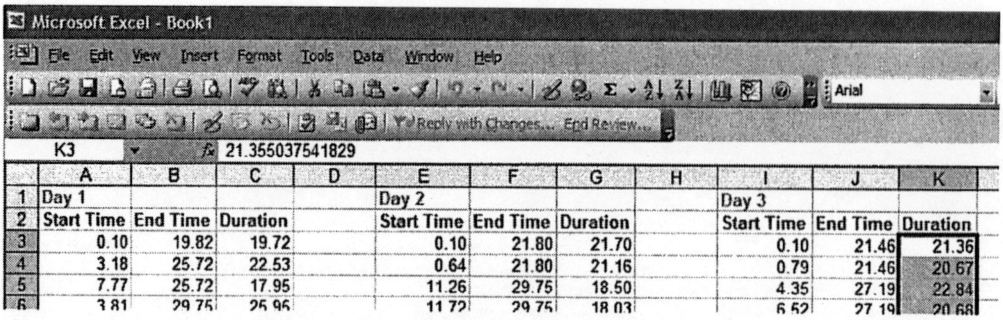

Figure 4: Project Objectives and Boundaries for Resources.

| | | | Day 1 | | | | Day 2 | | | | Day 3 | |

	A	B	C	D	E	F	G	H	I	J	K
1	Day 1				Day 2				Day 3		
2	Start Time	End Time	Duration		Start Time	End Time	Duration		Start Time	End Time	Duration
3	0.10	19.82	19.72		0.10	21.80	21.70		0.10	21.46	21.36
4	3.18	25.72	22.53		0.64	21.80	21.16		0.79	21.46	20.67
5	7.77	25.72	17.95		11.26	29.75	18.50		4.35	27.19	22.84
6	3.81	29.75	25.95		11.72	29.75	18.03		6.52	27.19	20.68

(K3 = 21.355037541829)

Figure 5: 3D Animation Model of Reference Desk.

imize the financial burden while maximizing the number of questions answered in a defined time period. They specified the least and greatest number of staff members who could be allocated to the reference desk. The model, given the restrictions, yielded the most economical and efficient mix for the allocation of staff.

3-D Animation

The students in group number 3 designed a 3-D animation of their process to provide library management with a realistic representation of activity around the reference desk (see figure 5). This group utilized Arena 3DPlayer to build an animation model depicting the entire reference area. The students included computer stations, reference desks, reference staff, various paths taken by the patrons, and physical constraints, such as building columns and bookshelves, in their animation layout. The library management team could pivot, pan, and zoom in on the model to explore activity from various perspectives. A 3-D animation model could be used to facilitate patron access and improve the aesthetics of the reference area. Furniture and equipment could be moved, and the color schemes of the carpet and walls could be modified. As the simulation model ran, patrons could be seen moving through the reference area as they asked their questions and had them answered.

Conclusion

This simulation exercise required students to propose innovative situations that would enhance the reference desk service. Students honed their critical-thinking skills by becoming familiar with every aspect of the service-delivery process. Resource allocation, design, and implementation decisions were facilitated by the various models. For example, the 3-D animation model highlighted the obstructed view created by the building columns which led group 3 to suggest that the librarians stand at the desk in order to be seen. The students also found that the simulation facilitated the decision-making process. Group 2 concluded that allocating an additional student assistant during peak hours would reduce the amount of time patrons waited to have their questions answered.

While conventional classes require students to read about data collection, data interpretation methods, and decision-making theory, LISP challenges students to build and manipulate a decision-making system from discovered data. Each year, students take existing statistics and gather additional information to examine a different library function. These simulation models enable these future library professionals to immediately see the impact of their proposed decisions and to "experiment and explore the cause-and-effect relationships between operating decisions and outcomes without facing real-world consequences."[3] Thus, these students, having dissected a real-life library operation, are prepared to confront the challenges they will encounter as they navigate their careers.

Notes

1. Linda Main. 1987. Computer Simulation and Library Management. *Journal of Information Science*, 13: 285–296.

2. W. David Kelton, Randall P. Sadowski and David T. Sturrock. 2004. *Simulation with Arena*. New York: McGraw-Hill.

3. Sarah Boehle. 2005. Simulations: The Next Generation of E-Learning. Training Mag.com, www.bluelinesimulations.com/pdf_docs/Simulearn/SimulationsJan_2005.pdf. Accessed March 15, 2007.

College Information Literacy Assignments

How to Move Your Lessons Out of the Box

Sandra E. Riggs

On many campuses, librarians have taken the lead in the development of information literacy programs. Librarians now have opportunities to teach classes within the general curriculum. While we have done a good job of convincing faculty that teaching basic information skills will serve students throughout the curriculum, our assignments work against the goal of integrating information mastery into students' life-long learning.

We unwittingly encourage students to compartmentalize their information seeking by using BI standbys, such as doing Boolean searching exercises in our subscription databases and creating annotated bibliographies. By focusing on traditional work in the campus library, or with library online resources, students come to believe that college research is a different process from what they'll need in the workplace.

We can solve this problem by focusing on information mastery assignments with new activities and stressing their value for workplace life. When planning creative assignments, I begin with three basic principles: 1) get the students talking; 2) show them that what they are learning is relevant in the real world; and 3) let them make mistakes.

Get Them Talking

College students often don't know their classmates and moan when they hear "group project." Despite such reactions, it is vitally important that students learn to talk to each other, negotiate divisions of labor, and have a circle of fellow experts for sharing information. These communication skills are as much a part of mastering information in daily life as accessing information. Make their information literacy class the one class in which they know everyone in the room. Encourage online communication when appropriate.

Show Them It's Relevant

Relate workplace expectations to the classroom as much as possible. Use and explain current buzzwords and business concepts, such as "knowledge management" and "assessment standards." Help them to see the information that they are learning in your class as a resource that they can tap in future classes and future work.

Let Them Make Mistakes

Most students feel that they are already information literate, which is a big obstacle to helping them achieve true information mastery! If a person thinks that he already knows all the answers, a mistake is his only path to learning. It is sometimes necessary to let them solve problems the way they want. If we really have ways of finding better information, then we should be able to compare our results to theirs and show them how to improve.

Sample Assignments

Given our guiding principles to assignment planning, let's take a look at some sample assignments and the goals and objectives that they could fulfill.

Sample Assignment #1

Goal: Identify information needs
Objectives:

- Help students to identify current information needs.
- Imagine and anticipate future information needs, such as in other classes or the workplace.

Problem: Students believe that once they are past college, they will not really be doing research.
Assignment: People Project
This can be assigned to groups or individuals. Have half the students pick a TV/movie character, while the others choose someone from a list of local community persons to interview. Make sure that you present the idea to all the potential interviewees ahead of time, so they can make time for appointments with students during the week of the assignment. Students should ask questions about information use or research the series/movie for answers and examples and present their persons to the class.

Examples of fictional people:

- Catherine Willows from *CSI*
- Jack McCoy from *Law & Order*
- Harry Potter
- Buffy/Giles/Willow from *Buffy:TVS*
- Gandalf from *LOTR*

Examples of local people:

- a dentist
- a university development officer
- a local small business owner
- a fire/rescue team member
- a graphic artist
- a hospital administrator

Examples of questions:

- Briefly, who is this person and what are his/her goals?
- What kind of information does s/he need? What are the consequences of not getting information?
- How does s/he get information? Give several examples.
- Are his/her methods of getting information successful?
- Does it require budgeting money or subscribing to services?
- How much time does the person spend in research? Using books? Using a computer? Using other means?
- Does misinformation ever play a role in problems? Is it intended misinformation (from a bad guy on a TV show) or accidental (misinterpreting a report or conversation in real life)?

Have a discussion about the differences between real information needs and fantasy needs. Students may be surprised by the information needs; indeed, some of the interviewees may be surprised by their own answers.

Sample Assignment #2

Goal: Access information using best practices.
Objectives:

- Have basic understanding of the technologies behind data access.
- Identify types and formats of information sources (scholarly, popular, trade, primary/ secondary, etc.).
- Learn search strategies.

Problem: Students don't understand the concept of controlled language and find databases cumbersome. Also, students don't realize that databases can contain any kind of information — not just journal articles.

Assignment: You Make the Database

Instead of starting students out searching databases, have them create databases. Divide the students into groups. Each group gets five to ten objects, hidden from the other students in a bag or box. This assignment can be as simple or complex as you like, depending on the choice and number of objects. Resist the urge to give the students library books or journal articles, which usually have clear-cut author/title categories. Photographs, artwork, business letters and other more archival-type items require students to think outside the box.

For homework, the goal is to make it easy for someone to find each item by coming up with a set of descriptions and rules for answering a search query. Each group must give themselves a database name and must describe their objects. They must decide what fields to use (author, keyword, etc.). They must also make a list of all their rules and features. This will help introduce them to the concepts of description, with controlled language a possibility for solving some disputes.

Next class, give a representative from each team a set of questions to answer or objects to find. Students can take turns "searching" the other groups. With each query, a database team must announce the number of "hits" for that search. Each team must follow its own rules. If there are no rules that cover a problem, that search gets zero hits. For example, if you don't have a rule for Boolean searching, the searcher can't use it.

After several searching sessions, have each team discuss some of their decisions.

Sample Assignment #3

Goal: Evaluate information and understand legal and ethical issues related to information and information seeking.

Objectives:

- Describe and assess works in terms of authority, coverage, scope, accuracy, and objectivity.
- Understand the concepts of bias, balance and neutrality.
- Work collaboratively in an online environment according to the netiquette of the environment.

Problem: Students don't know how to evaluate information resources.

Assignment One: Fact check

Find articles that contain several pieces of information given without citation. Ask students to verify facts and track down sources. For example, students would find the name and citation information of at least one study for the statement, "Studies indicate that eating dairy products helps dieters loose weight."

Assignment Two: What's a neutral point of view (NPOV)?

Rather than avoid Wikipedia, have students create individual Wikipedia accounts and select several NPOV projects to edit from the Wikipedia to do list. The students will have to become well versed in Wikipedia's policies regarding defining NPOV and netiquette. Have students participate in online discussions with other Wikipedians, saving copies of the comments, and creating a report to you on the editing process.

Professional Service and Rewards of Book Reviewing

KATHY PIEHL

Perhaps my elementary school teachers could have predicted that I'd spend hours of my adult life as a book reviewer. After all, I never complained about producing book reports to share with my classmates. Although the book reviews I write as a professional librarian have to adhere to more stringent requirements than those imposed by my teachers, they are based on the same basic premise of sharing opinions with others about books worth reading (or not).

When I finished library school 25 years ago, I contacted library journals to find out how I could review books. Knowing how important reviews are for librarians who select materials, I wanted to contribute professionally by providing those evaluations. As Dana Watson notes, "volunteer reviewers can serve the profession by dedicating some of their time and energy to ensure that reviews are available, that their quality is high, and that they reflect the needs of their colleagues" (19–20).

Yet, even librarians who use reviews regularly may lack a clear idea about what the reviewing process requires, what rewards reviewing offers, and how to get involved. Among those who have provided suggestions for potential reviewers is Steve McKinzie, who insists that "librarians ought to write reviews as often as they can and as many as they can get away with" (92). Anyone who wants to review should keep in mind the following:

Read the book carefully and fairly. Remember the amount of effort required to create a book. No one sets out to write a bad novel or inaccurate nonfiction. If you have a conflict of interest or know that you cannot be objective about a book, notify the editor as soon as possible. For example, when I realized how intensely I disliked a certain illustrator's style, I asked not to review any more picture books by that artist. Don't agree to review a book if you can't fit a complete reading into your schedule.

- Remember the audience for the book and the review. I review dozens of children's books, and the books themselves must be judged in terms of the knowledge, reading level, and maturity of the child reader. Yet, those who read most of my reviews are librarians selecting books for a school or public library. They are concerned about how the book compares with similar titles or fits into the curriculum. Another audience is parents, who may be interested in a book's entertainment or literary value. Depending on your background, assigned book, and review journal, you may review a university press book for other scholars in your academic field or provide information about a new thriller for a popular fiction selector in a public library.

- Follow the publication's guidelines. Sometimes a journal only reviews books that it recommends. When you receive a book, you must decide quickly if you agree with that positive assessment and notify the editors if you don't so that they can reconsider or reassign the title. Other journals emphasize the need to compare the book you are reviewing with similar titles or with earlier works by the same author. Sometimes you may have to follow a checklist to cover certain points.
- Write clearly and concisely. Reviews are usually brief. Yet, that doesn't mean the writing has to be flat or stilted. If you can inject some personality or humor into your evaluations, your readers will be grateful. Remember that someone may have to decide about purchasing a book based on your review. Provide enough information so readers know what the book is about and how it might meet their needs. For example, a review of a picture book that doesn't mention the illustrations ignores an essential component. Reviews of nonfiction need to take into account documentation provided.
- Provide a clear evaluation. Describing a book's content is usually fairly easy. It can be tempting to stop with a description and avoid evaluation. While a clear summary may be enough for a librarian trying to fill a subject gap, in most cases, the reader expects guidance about purchasing the book for a specific person or library collection. Reviewers of children's books may face dilemmas about whether or not to mention controversial language or subject matter. The line between informing and censoring is sometimes murky. For a variety of perspectives, see "Reviewers as Censors," in *School Library Journal*.
- Submit the review on time. Obvious but essential.

Most reviewers are unpaid. Librarians receive advance reading copies and/or finished books for their reviews. Scholarly journals sometimes provide copies of the journal issue in which the review itself appears in addition to the book. Keep in mind that the reviewing process can help you:

- Hone your writing and analytical skills. You'll learn to identify the important aspects of a piece of writing and make your points succinctly.
- Increase your knowledge of a variety of topics. As a reference librarian, I'm continually amazed at how often the research and reading I've done related to nonfiction for children and historical novels for adults provides insights for approaching a college student's topic.
- Improve your chances for professional involvement. When you want to tackle a longer article or make a conference presentation, your reviewing demonstrates that you can write and think clearly and meet deadlines. My reviewing led directly to offers to contribute to reference books about authors. The ability to read, analyze, and evaluate quickly has served me well on book award selection committees.

Once you've decided to try reviewing, you'll want to peruse articles such as the ones mentioned above. If you plan to review children's books, you should also read Kathleen Horning's book, *From Cover to Cover*, which offers in-depth guidance for evaluating various genres and for writing clear reviews. Then you're ready to take the following steps to get your reviews into print:

- Identify what kinds of books you want to review. Think about your reading interests, your subject background, and areas of expertise. Perhaps you can't wait to read the latest mystery. Maybe you're an avid birdwatcher or traveler. If you want to review for library publications, consider your expertise in areas such as reference, acquisitions, or instruction.

- Find publications that include reviews of those books. You probably read many journals yourself. Study the reviews in the ones that you find valuable. Determine if they use volunteer reviewers.
- Follow the instructions to apply to review. That information may be part general publication guidelines, near the reviews themselves, or on the publication's Web site. You probably will need to submit information about your background and interests and perhaps sample reviews.
- Keep trying. Sometimes journals are looking for specialties that don't match your interests. Perhaps they aren't accepting new reviewers at the moment. Try again in a few months. If your library has a Web site, you might post reviews of current titles that you have enjoyed. Maybe some of your colleagues will contribute as well. In addition to providing valuable information for those who use your collection, you gain reviewing experience.

When I applied to review, I never imagined that I'd write almost a thousand. Although there have been some books that I disliked intensely, even flawed books have provided insights and information that I might not have sought on my own. Whenever a large envelope arrives at my door, I still can't wait to see what review books have come my way.

References

Horning, Kathleen T. *From Cover to Cover*. New York: HarperCollins, 1997.
McKinzie, Steve. "The Noble Art of Reviewing: Challenges, Rewards, and Tricks of the Trade." *College and Undergraduate Libraries* 3.2 (1996): 91–99.
"Reviewers as Censors." *School Library Journal* Sept. 1990: 155–162.
Watson, Dana. "Reviewing: A Strategic Service." *A Service Profession, a Service Commitment*. Eds. Connie Van Fleet and Danny P. Wallace. Metuchen, NJ: Scarecrow, 1992. 19–41.

Tips for Reviewing Educational Media

Lori Widzinski

Reviewing educational films, audio books, and computer programs is a good way to start writing for publication and contributing to the profession. Reviews are usually brief, yet don't be fooled into thinking that means *easy*. Creating a critical, informative, succinct review is often more challenging than writing a longer piece.

Start with a Synopsis

Focus on the main points to emphasize in the review. It is important to describe content yet not recreate a tedious, blow-by-blow account of the story or action. Refrain from allowing the synopsis to take over the entire review, leaving out the valuable critical analysis. The synopsis should also include:

- The reason the piece was created (documentary film with a political message, instructional how-to, corporate training film, collection of experimental videos).
- Background information about the program creators. Mention other works by the same director, or producer, or works in the same genre.
- Any accompanying materials and their formats (workbooks, teacher guides, manuals, Web sites, supplemental works).
- The style and tone of the piece (news program, cinema-verité film, animation, recorded lecture, print material on CD, audiobook).

Write a Critical Analysis

The critical analysis should include a critique of the piece together with the essential elements necessary for librarians to make an informed purchase decision. Avoid expounding on personal feelings about an actor or a music selection, but rather describe how the individual elements of a piece contribute to the overall effectiveness of a program as an instructional aid or in meeting the director's goals.

151

If the program rates a negative review, it can be achieved without being overly harsh or personal. In fact, negative comments will be taken more seriously if written with sensitivity in a professional manner and supported by facts. Strive for a fair assessment, even with a negative review. For the critical analysis, assess the following:

- The strengths and weaknesses of the piece — where it succeeds and where it doesn't. Will it work for classroom use and be a valuable addition to a library collection?
- The technical elements (video and audio quality, editing, ease of use, special features included on DVDs) and whether they work to the advantage of the program.
- The quality of any accompanying material.
- The sets, costumes, acting, narration, navigational menus, animation, music, and lighting and how integral they are to the work.
- The tone, mood, and pacing.
- Any bias that may be prevalent. Documentaries may be nonfiction, but that doesn't mean nonbiased. Bias can be clearly stated or more subtle, which is sometimes difficult to determine, but an important part of evaluating a program.
- How the piece compares with other well-known works in the field or those by a certain director or actor, or perhaps commonly held knowledge on a particular topic or films from a certain distributor. Be specific and avoid sweeping generalizations.

Value for Library Collections

Specificity is the key to writing successful recommendations for library collections. To indicate value:

- Use the rating system of the publication (stars or other icon), and back up value statements with concrete reasoning.
- Identify the intended audience and the type of library, collection, and classroom situations best served by the program.
- Compare it to other works of the same type.
- State how successful the producer or the director is in achieving the main objective of the work.
- Evaluate the contribution of the work to the field(s).

Put It All Together

The integral parts described above work best when organized creatively around the main thesis of the review. Start by:

- Maintaining a central point or thesis and stating it where appropriate for the style of the review.
- Mixing the three main components of a review for interesting reading.
- Watching for hackneyed and conversational descriptive words such as *awesome, definitely, excellent, great, important,* or *interesting.*
- Using the thesaurus judiciously. Carefully watch for esoteric words and always check the exact meaning of a word.
- Staying in the present tense. Writing in the past tense deadens the feel of the writing.
- Using good grammar.

Reading Reviews

To get an idea of review construction and vocabulary, read professionally written film and computer program reviews from professional journals and large newspapers. Think about the type of information you find valuable in reviews. These Web sites offer media reviews for the library community:

- Internet Library for Librarians. Acquisitions (www.itcompany.com/inforetriever/ acq_r_md.htm) This Web site is a portal designed for librarians.
- Library Journal (http://www.libraryjournal.com/community/891/Reviews/42795.html)
- Educational Media Reviews Online (http://libweb.lib.buffalo.edu/emro/search.asp) This Web site offers a free database of reviews of media materials from major educational and documentary distributors and independent filmmakers. The reviews are aimed at an educational audience, primarily academic librarians.
- Video Librarian Online (http://www.videolibrarian.com) This Web site is the online version of Video Librarian, a "video review magazine for public, school, academic, and special libraries, as well as video fans who are interested in a wider variety of titles than what's found in the average video store."

Review Examples

Some reviewers start with their opinion statement, others with a description. Consider this excerpt from a review by Oksana Dykyj of *Hindle Wakes*. She includes the director's goal as well as several value-laden statements about the film in her opening paragraph:

> This second of four film adaptations of Stanley Houghton's 1912 play is groundbreaking on a number of levels: The play itself initially caused quite a stir in that it dealt with a modern attitude toward the sexual double standard. The film molds this narrative into one that additionally addresses issues of class and infuses it with spectacular location cinematography. *Hindle Wakes* is undoubtedly one of the most important films from the British silent period.

A fine example of combining description with critical analysis comes from Jane Sloan's review of *The Nightingale's Prayer*:

> Dialog and events address issues such as the Europeanization of the middle class via colonialization, the harsher codes of the countryside compared to the city, and the moral responsibility of individuals who take advantage of their position in society. Along side the fascinating lead actress, the script sketches many interesting characters who are distinct types, and who function in surprising ways. Fine acting and a sophisticated flashback narrative make the story consistently compelling.

Adding specificity to a description together with opinion can be achieved with simpler elements as well, for example it's easy to see which of the following is more engaging:

"The program includes a teacher's guide."

or

"Included is a well-researched teacher's guide offering quizzes, essay questions, and valuable class discussion points."

Wrapping up a review brings the entire work to a nice finish. Continue to be specific and use descriptive writing. Compare these two concluding statements and it's obvious which one will help readers make a more informed decision:

"This video is recommended for libraries with nonprint collections in biology."

or

"With its quirky characters and convoluted plot, *Stolen* sometimes plays more like a Hollywood thriller than a documentary, but that's one of its charms. An entertaining mix of art appreciation and whodunit with broad appeal, *Stolen* is recommended for school, public, and academic library collections." (From the review of *Stolen* by Mike Boedicker.)

References

Baumann, James F. and Dale D. Johnson, ed. *Writing for Publication in Reading and Language Arts*. Newark: International Reading Association. 1991.

Accessibility Beyond Our Walls

Using Web 2.0 and Podcasting to Teach Off Campus

STEPHANIE A. THOMAS

Web 2.0 technologies are transforming the ways in which people share, disseminate, and learn information. Social networking products are enabling people to be in charge of their own publishing and networking. With Web 2.0 tools, people are customizing everything they do online; creating personal and professional blogs and wikis, social bookmarking, creating avatars, and clipping and pasting text into their virtual "notebooks" for later. In the K–12 realm, teachers and librarians are using course management software tools like Moodle to create their courses online. They moderate and maintain blogs with their students to discuss content and assignments. They form Web pages on WordPress so that they can easily post slideshows, book reviews, videos, schedules, and assignments. They use podcasting to publicize author events, student-generated book reviews, and events at their schools and libraries.

At Parkrose High School in Portland, Oregon, we are using many of these Web 2.0 tools to teach in new ways. As the teacher librarian, I have noticed firsthand the hordes of students viewing and adding videos to YouTube. I started thinking about podcasting and thought that if I created a video podcast, I could use it as a tutorial. I have given instructional presentations to classes about using the library's resources and found that long-term they could only retain a small amount of the information. I also found that many students were using the library's resources from home or at the public library. I thought podcasting would be a great way to reach students off campus, and give them on-the-go information that they could view anywhere. I created the first audio and video podcast of the library's resources, and saved it in both .mp3 and .mp4 format so students could download the podcast to any MP3-enabled device, as well as video iPods capable of .mp4 files.

To create an audio/video podcast tutorial:

- I used Smart Board's Smart Recorder to record both audio and video. You can also use Screen Record from www.miensoftware.com. It's $20 and has both Mac and PC versions. Your file will end with an extension like .wma or .mov. Next, use a converter to convert the file into .mp3 or .mp4 format. I used DeskShare Digital Media Converter version 2.6. You may also use SnagIt from techsmith.com, Audacity, or XI Soft iPod Video Converter.

- You'll need either a built-in or external microphone or headphones with a built-in microphone.
- Open a blogger account. (www.blogger.com). I use the blogger account to host the files on the Web for free.
- Open a FeedBurner account. (www.feedburner.com). You will use FeedBurner to link to the blogger site. FeedBurner creates an RSS feed so that people can subscribe to your blog feed and your podcasts.
- Post your recordings on your blogger page. The easiest way to do this is to copy a "podcast logo" clipart to your computer, and in your blog post, insert the podcast image. Click on the image and in the link tab, copy and paste the link of the file.
- Once your file is uploaded on blogger, publish. Copy the URL of this blogger page. This is the URL that you will then paste into your FeedBurner account. Click on "Set up new Feed now" and paste that URL. Don't forget to check the box "I'm a podcaster!"
- Your podcasts should appear on your FeedBurner page. To see what your FeedBurner page is, click on the little xml logo next to the FeedBurner page name that you created. This will be the page that you want people to subscribe to.
- Go to your blogger page and insert a "subscribe" widget that will tell the people at the blog site to subscribe to your FeedBurner page and thus have access to downloading the podcasts.
- Since many people use iTunes for podcast downloading, set up an Apple account and submit your podcasts to the iTunes store. Users can conduct a keyword search and pull up your podcasts for downloading. This is free. It takes Apple a bit to authorize your FeedBurner page, so give it a day before telling people to search.
- On your library page, put a link to your FeedBurner site and insert text that says something like "subscribe to the library podcasts." Make sure to include the standard recognized rss/xml icon.

If you are using a Mac, it is much easier to produce and publish a podcast. Use Garageband and iMovie to produce the podcast. Use the internal microphone and iSight to create audio and video podcasts. Then use iMovie to put it together and post on your iWeb space, or burn to a DVD for later use.

Audio-only podcasts are much easier to create. They are great for sharing book reviews, instructions, and news events. Soon we will have audio-only podcasts up on our library page. The kids will be sharing book reviews with other students!

If your audio podcast is less than two minutes, you can use the Sound Recorder under the accessories tab on a PC. You can use Audacity if longer. Use Garageband if on a Mac. You might want to also store your podcast files on your school's server for safekeeping and/or linking to your library's Web site. Contact your IT department for assistance.

Now that the first podcast is up on the Parkrose High School Library Web page (www.parkrosehighschool.com/Academics/Library%20page/tutorial/tutorial1_page.htm), I am excited about doing more. Some of my ideas for future podcasts include using Big6 Skills, a Dewey Decimal Primer, and a "Tour of Parkrose High School" for new Parkrose students. Remember to keep your podcasts to about eight minutes or less. That way, you can post them to YouTube as well. You can find my podcast on YouTube by searching "Parkrose." It had to be split into three parts because I made my first podcast 20 minutes long. Think of your end user and their needs. Splitting the podcasts into individual topics is best.

Blogger has also been a useful tool for creating quick webliographies for class visits to the library. Is the Parkrose High School Library Blog that I have been using for two years is located at www.parkroselibraryblog.blogspot.com.

I created linked Wordpress pages for our teachers so that they could be in control of adding and updating their own content. Each is linked to the main Parkrose High School site (www.parkrosehighschool.com/gen_staff_directory/teacherwebpages.htm). Wordpress allows for slideshow and video uploading.

Web 2.0 technologies and podcasting has opened up a whole new world of access. Librarians will continue to embrace and use these new forms of technology as a way to market our services, communicate among our peers and our clients, and to provide on-the-go access. Libraries have always been the center of the community and the school, and we intend to keep it that way. Utilizing these technologies as we see fit will ensure our relevance in the present and future. It doesn't hurt to maintain the cool factor as well.

Librarians as Indexers

Taking the Arkansas Publications Index from State Periodical Index in Card Files to Online Database

ELIZABETH CHADBOURN MCKEE *and* MARY A. WALKER

Hidden in what the public now regards as antiquated card catalogs are the beloved indexing projects of librarians, historians, genealogists and other eccentrics of the bibliographic world. No doubt numerous institutions, especially public and academic libraries, have little-known files similar to those created at the University of Arkansas (U of A) Libraries over the past century or more. We retain card file records that represent literally decades of work by dedicated librarians, who enhanced their traditional services to researchers by creating their own local indexing files. Just at the U of A, for example, librarians and their assistants created card file indexes for articles on university faculty and students, for biographical information in books on the state and its people, for newspapers, for county history journals, and for state and regional magazines. No commercial publishers covered the state-level books and periodicals, especially for a less populous state like Arkansas. Librarians understood that economic incentives were required to produce national publications such as the Wilson indexes and they evidenced their sense of history and regional devotion by applying similar techniques to indexing their own regional publications. Arkansas is not unique, but at least exemplary, in this respect.

The Arkansas Experience

The Arkansas Publications Index began with card files initiated by Georgia Clark, head reference librarian at U of A's main campus in Fayetteville for nearly 40 years. We believe that work began on the various files during the early part of the 20th century, but it soon included retrospective indexing into the late 1800s. Clark collaborated with other librarians in special collections to establish a variety of separate files to aid researchers, covering names and events connected to the state and written about in the state's newspapers, periodicals, books, and other publications.

Work continued on the various files until the 1980s when computerization began to make significant changes in library work. The capacity to retrieve expanding amounts of research rapidly enhanced libraries' ability to produce resources, but the technology increased workloads in other ways. Time to index and produce card files began decreasing at the same time the technical ability to produce databases was increasing.

In the mid–1980s U of A purchased Inmagic's bibliographic text file software, and two librarians, Elizabeth Chadbourn McKee and Andrea Cantrell, designed the data structure, wrote indexing policies, and developed subject headings for the Arkansas Periodical Index. The software was excellent and brought database design and searching capabilities rivaling the commercial giants into the hands of librarian indexers. A grant from the Arkansas Humanities Council and the National Endowment for the Humanities partly supported the publication of a printed volume covering 1981 to 1985, produced from the Inmagic database. The project won the 1991 Gale Research Award for Excellence in Reference and Adult Library Services. Work continued piecemeal on the indexing for another decade and a half. But ask any librarian involved in similar projects where those hours come from and you'll see the secret knowing and smug smiles of stereotypical eccentrics.

Innovative Choices

As an Inmagic database, the file was only accessible in the library by one user at a time, since the U of A Libraries had not invested in the multiuser license. It also could not be accessed via the Web or remotely. Therefore, in 2004 a proposal was submitted from an in-house committee called the Web Development Group to make the database available via the Internet. Four options were examined:

1. To convert the current Inmagic DB/Textworks files to DB/Text Web Publisher Pro
2. To build an in-house database
3. To use OCLC's ContentDM
4. To convert the current files to a reference database using Innovative Interfaces (III) software

In the end the Innovative Interfaces platform was the recommendation of the group. Our reasons were that it appeared to be the quickest route to placing the files online, it seemed to be less costly, and it was a platform that many of our local staff were already familiar with. The local indexing slot was one we had previously used for files purchased through III, so the space was available for another index.

Web Access Accomplished

The Arkansas Publications Index (http://arkindex.uark.edu) was released April 15, 2005. The database can be accessed for free and incorporates:

- all of the records from the original print volume, covering 55 regional periodicals
- more than 80 books with biographical content on the state's residents, historical and recent compilations
- some newspaper citations test records, with a file of some 35,000 currently being edited

The prototype, still actively a work in progress, contains over 55,000 records. The libraries plan to load an additional 90,000 records in the coming months. Coverage ranges from the 1880s to 2000, with current indexing to be brought up-to-date as rapidly as possible.

1. Linda Main. 1987. Computer Simulation and Library Management. Journal of Information Science, 13: 285-296.
2. W. David Kelton, Randall P. Sadowski & David T. Sturrock. 2004. Simulation with Arena. New York, NY: McGraw-Hill Companies.
3. Sarah Boehle. 2005. Simulations: The Next Generation of E-Learning. Training Mag.com, http://www.bluelinesimulations.com/pdf_docs/Simulearn/SimulationsJan_2005.pdf Accessed March 15, 2007.

Data Structure

Since previous files held simple citations to various kinds of publications and the Inmagic database had only been periodical indexing, we were faced with the need to create a database that could accommodate multiple formats. We wanted to convert citations from books as well as periodicals and newspapers, and we even considered the possible addition in the future of other formats, for example, oral history interviews. We decided to expand our original periodical data structure to accommodate both journal citations and book content citations in the same database, similar to the various formats contained in databases such as Psychological Abstracts and the Modern Language Association Bibliography. We developed the following database structure, which we mapped to MARC fields. This allowed us to enter data from various card files and combine the citations into one database. We developed load tables, tested sample records, and began to upload records from one software program to the other. Data entry and editing is still being conducted on some files in Inmagic, but all new indexing and ongoing work can now be done with III.

Field Label	Fields	Content
AN	Accession number	Record # in database
TI	Title	Title of article
AB	Abstract	Abstract or annotation, any additional inform1-tion, phrases, keywords, or brief explanations about the article
AE	Author entry	Author's name, last name first; compilers; editors; or reviewers
IL	Illustrations	Abbreviations for photographs, bibliography, maps, diagrams, color
JN	Journal	Full title of periodical
COL	Collation	Volume (issue number), paging of article
DT	Date	Month, quarter, day
YR	Year of publication	Year of citation
CT	Check tags	Demographic information for ethnic group or gender: African American, Asian, Hispanic, Native American, Women, Caucasian

Field Label	Fields	Content
GL	Geographic location	If not used as an identifier, can include county, city, or states here
CC	Category codes	Two to three broad subject categories indicate general content of article and enhance searchability
SH	Subject headings	Based on Library of Congress subject headings, plus some local ones
ID	Identifiers	Additional index terms, proper nouns such as families, locales, companies, associations, etc.
URL	Online locator	Address for journal if online
BKCHAE	Book chapter author	Author of chapter or contribution, last name first
BKCHTI	Book chapter title	Title of the chapter or section if applicable
PUB	Publisher	Publisher of book
PL	Place	Place of publication
BKYR	Book year	Year book was published
ISSN	Serial standard number	International serial number
ISBN	Book standard number	International book number
CATLINKU	URL for link	Universal resource locator for link to catalog
CATLINKZ	Catalog link words	Wording for display in record
OLINKU	URL for other link	Universal resource locator for other links, such as association Web site
OLINKZ	Other link words	Wording for other link to display in record
NT	Notes	Messages or questions for editors if needed
IN	Indexer's initials	Name and date, optional

Other State Indexes

Two other online databases in Arkansas provide indexing to some of the state periodicals. They are Arkansas Legal Index (http://themis.law.ualr.edu:81) and Fort Smith Regional Index (http://libcat.uafortsmith.edu:81/screens/opacmenu.html).

Other states are also creating indexes. We apologize to those we are not aware of yet and look forward to hearing about them. Here are ones currently on the Internet:

- Alaska and Polar Periodical Index (http://goldmine.uaf.edu/uhtbin/cgisirsi.exe/x/0/0/55/1181/X)
- Louisiana's Bayou State Periodical Index (http://www.libris.ca/bayou)
- Hawaii Pacific Journal Index (http://libweb.hawaii.edu/uhmlib/databases/hpji.html)
- Index to Texas Magazines and Documents (http://vcuhvlibrary.uhv.edu/Txindex/home.htm)
- Minnesota Legal Periodical Index (www.lawmoose.com/index.cfm?Action=MLPI.ShowArticleFinder)
- North Carolina Periodicals Index (www.ecu.edu/lib/ncc/scope.cfm)

- Oklahoma Periodicals Index (www.library.okstate.edu/database/perindex.htm)
- Washington's Pacific Northwest Regional Newspaper and Periodical Index (http://db.lib.washington.edu/pnw)
- Historical Newspapers in Washington (www.secstate.wa.gov/history/newspapers.aspx)

Reading Programs with 21st Century Know-How

McKinley Sielaff

There is more treasure in books than in all the pirate's loot on Treasure Island.
                                                                    — *Walt Disney*

Enhancing reading programs with Web 2.0 technologies is now easier than ever. Some libraries are taking advantage of blogging, wikis, and other software to create their own unique services and by using other add-on products. Just what are libraries and other related organizations doing? How can a library benefit from these products and services?

Matching traditional services with modern advances in technology can be very efficient and effective for libraries, helping to enhance services, automate and thus streamline workflow, expand public relations, and meet the users where they are. Story hours, reader's advisories and reading programs are well-known. These programs share certain traits: They are highly social and interactive — two features that the Internet is also really good at providing. Let's look at these services in their traditional and modern applications.

Story Hour

To arouse and stimulate a love for the best reading is then the real object of the story hour.
                                            — *Alice I. Hazeltine, Library Work*

Many libraries have a slew of sessions aimed at introducing children to the world of reading. Along with hosting these sessions, libraries are creating online spaces also. Two examples are Kid Space at the Internet Public Library (www.ipl.org/div/kidspace/storyhour), which offers text-only and illustrated books for kids, and BookHive (www.bookhive.org), from the Public Library of Charlotte–Mecklenburg County (Charlotte, NC), which offers stories and activities, reading lists, recommendations and reviews along with files to hear books read aloud for children (birth to 12), their parents, teachers and anyone else interested in children's books.

There are many sites where children can watch, listen and play with books. Libraries are not the only ones using the Internet to provide such services. The Screen Actors Guild Foundation streams famous people reading children's books aloud (www.storylineonline. net). Even companies like Lego are getting into the act (www.lego.com/eng/preschool/ games/games.asp?id=17). Many sites offer materials in multiple languages and for a variety of age groups and skill levels. Librarians can easily set up Web pages or handouts hosted by their institutions which link to the best resources already posted online. This is also true for reader's advisories.

Reader's Advisory

Show me the books he loves and I shall know the man far better than through mortal friends.

— Dawn Adams

Reader's advisory is the practice of suggesting additional reading to a reader based on preferences and shared characteristics of literary material. Reader's advisory services is a specialty in many public libraries. In addition to library staff, there are many books, online subscription databases, and Web sites dedicated to this type of service. Books include the What Do I Read Next? series of reference books (from Thomson Gale), the Genreflecting series (from Libraries Unlimited), and the Reader's Advisory Guides (from ALA Editions). Again, libraries can easily create the means to add to this service by generating the content themselves, linking to services provided by others, pushing information to the user, or using social software such as blogs. Here are examples of each:

- Morton Grove's Public Library's Webrary (www.webrary.org/rs/rsmenu.html) includes bibliographies, book reviews, genre-oriented Web sites, and discussion guides.
- Inland Library System's Reader's Advisory Services (www.inlandlib.org/Reference/readers.htm) provides an annotated list of reader's advisory services on the Internet.
- Salt Lake County Library's Sites for Book Lovers (www.slco.lib.ut.us/booksnmore/index.htm) offers many different kinds of lists. Sign up for one or more of their newsletters to receive monthly updates on new materials with links to reviews.
- Bookends: Book Reviews from Tutt Library (library.coloradocollege.edu/bookends) offers reviews written by librarians.

Amazon.com is well-known for reviews. Other Web sites worth looking at are:

- Reader's Robot (www.tnrdlib.bc.ca/rr.html) matches your tastes with books in its database(s).
- Allreaders.com (www.allreaders.com) searches for books by characteristics of plot, theme, setting, and structure.
- Book Muse (www.bookmuse.com) features popular discussion group books, helpful to individual readers wishing to reflect on their reading. The site also offers discussion groups, brief plot summaries, discussion questions, literary analysis, and author biographies.

Reading Programs

When I got [my] library card, that was when my life began.

— *Rita Mae Brown*

There are many benefits to reading programs for youngsters; they help children strengthen their reading skills and vocabularies, connect them to other children, and introduce them to the larger world. Most programs allow children to self-select a specific number of books to read in a given time frame. Use the Web to highlight this program: Set up an online registration form, post announcements and winners, upload suggested books, etc. For more ideas look at library pages online as well as for other programs to participate in or borrow ideas from; here are a few starting places:

- Read Across America, a nationwide initiative of the National Education Association (www.nea.org/readacross) that promotes reading every day of the year.
- International Children's Book Day (www.ibby.org)
- Young Peoples Poetry Week (www.cbcbooks.org/html/poetry_week.html)
- National Poetry Month (www.poets.org)
- Annual Read-In and Reading Is Fun Week (www.readin.org)
- Library Card Sign-Up Month (www.ala.org/pio/librarycard)
- Teen Read Week (www.ala.org/teenread)
- Start Early, Finish Strong: How to Help Every Child Become a Reader, a publication of the U.S. Department of Education (www.ed.gov/pubs/startearly) that offers the latest research and recommendations to help all children succeed in reading.
- Dinner and a Book, a reading program of Idaho's Education Department (www.sde.state.id.us/DinnerandaBook) that helps parents get involved with their children's education.

Reading programs are not only for young children and teens. According to a recent study one out of every three adults in the United States reads a book daily (U.S. Department of Education [2006]. *The Condition of Education 2006*. Washington, DC: U.S. Government Printing Office). Many libraries have such programming for adults and nonnative English speakers. Some examples include:

- One Book (www.loc.gov/loc/cfbook/one-book.html), a community-wide reading programs initiated by the Washington Center for the Book in 1998, is worldwide.
- Everyone's Reading (www.metronet.lib.mi.us/BLFD/Adult_Services/everyones_reading.html) is a community-wide reading program sponsored by Metro Detroit public libraries that promotes community dialogue through the shared experience of reading and discussing the same book.
- Reader's Passport, a program offered by R.R. Bowker and Pikes Peak Library District (www.ppld.org), promotes literacy by encouraging the community to share its love of reading with others. Participants read six books and receive a free book for themselves and one that is donated to a nonprofit agency of their choice.
- Navy Professional Reading Program (www.navyreading.navy.mil) was developed by the U.S. Navy "to encourage a life-long habit of reading and learning among all Sailors."

Ideas

Reading is to the mind what exercise is to the body.

— *Joseph Addison*

Suggestions for Motivating Reading:

• Use local newspapers to encourage reading and discussion of interesting topics.
• Create displays of reading materials using current television and radio topics.
• Designate a special time in the day to "Drop Everything and Read!"
• Hold a read-a-thon.
• Give awards for reading achievement.
• Create a literary map.
• Have staff dress up as their favorite literary character.
• Start your own book award that lets your patrons vote on the winners (see www.nutmegaward.org).

Suggestions for Community Involvement:

• Invite local authors and personalities to speak on how reading influenced their lives.
• Learn about and support local literacy projects. Better yet, partner with such programs.
• Offer the community chances to sponsor library programs.
• Have a booth at local events offering library cards.
• Have book sales.
• Design "Read" posters (from ALA) featuring patrons.

Whatever the program, remember that outreach and advertising are key elements to drawing in participants, especially new ones, and in holding a successful event.

The Story of an Athenaeum Spider

CAROLYN DAVIS

How would you like to be the reference librarian to help link the Internet to a particular historical setting? That was the task that I was given at the beginning of 1997 at the Providence Athenaeum in Rhode Island amid controversy.

The athenaeum is housed in a small building near the heart of the campuses of Brown University and the Rhode Island School of Design (RISD). Its charm is based on its emphasis on the past: historic documents of local and national interest and out-of-print books, as well as collections that were and are specific to that athenaeum, such as a significant Audubon collection. To some, modern technology is as out of place in the Providence Athenaeum as a Jacuzzi in a medieval monastery.

"Computers in the Athenaeum? Oh, I hope not," was the expressed wish of one of the part-time librarians. The membership was somewhat divided too, but the director and assistant director forged ahead. The director reminded the board of trustees that the founders had been people of progress, and that if computers had existed in 1753 when the athenaeum's parent, Providence Library Company, began, they would have been all for the technology's installation. The attitude of some of the die-hards seemed to change slightly after that from that part-time librarian's "Oh, I hope not!" to "Well, we've got to keep up with the times to be competitive, I guess, but isn't it *sad*!" Attracting new members and retaining older ones is a challenge for the Providence Athenaeum. The library staff and volunteers knew that Internet service was attractive to patrons with families who otherwise would have access to it at any of the public libraries in the state, as well as at home, and those patrons would expect Internet technology at the athenaeum in addition to access to its vintage hard-copy collections.

The "New Librarian" Gets Rolling

I had worked at the Providence Athenaeum in 1994 as an intern, cataloguing the library's archives, but my role in 1997 was considerably different. I was no longer chronicling the past but applying modern technology in the present. My niche became "Internet reference," which was made available to patrons and staff. There appeared at first to be an age distinction in the patrons' use of the service: Students and parents of small children were the most interested, so it was quite a *coup* when one of the older patrons came in to the Internet room and began not only asking questions but also providing answers regarding the use of computers.

In addition to providing Internet service, I was responsible for the development and publication of the athenaeum's first Web page. This, in concurrence with the library's networking their computers, proved to be an unexpectedly complicated task, involving consultation with an Internet specialist from Boston as well as two or three consultations with a Web specialist whom I contacted through the Customer Support Department at Microsoft. The latter were conducted for the price of one phone call, since the Microsoft specialist considered ours an ongoing situation, and did not charge us repeatedly.

The day that the page was finally loaded successfully was a triumphant one, although it would be awhile before all the text could be loaded, since it had been collected in Microsoft Word format. A successor to that initial page is located at www.providenceathenaeum.org. My commendations to its current webmaster, for the current page is considerably more sophisticated than its ancestor of ten years past. Links include "Services/Collections," "Member Community" and "Programs and Events." There are directions to the library, as well as a small illustration of the building on the home page.

My role initially, like the machinery that I piloted, was not welcomed by everyone, but through the jokes, "*You* brought this in!" and the like, to which I responded truthfully that I was responding to a demand from the library director, with the agreement of the board of trustees (a majority, anyway), the general feeling appeared to be that the change was the result of Modern Times.

The Providence Athenaeum Remains "Tech"

The athenaeum's computer networking was made possible by a substantial grant. Networking allowed significant upgrades to the hardware and software, thus easing the facilitation to multiple Internet users and web page editing and updates. I left the athenaeum in June 1997 to prepare for a move to Jamaica and the upgrading and improvements continued. In the six months that I worked on incorporating the new technology, I also helped to introduce a different philosophy into an established structure. A significant component of the Athenaeum is its subscribers' good will, which translates into continued membership. This obliges this particular type of library to be somewhat more sensitive to each patron's input than public libraries, with their tax-supported memberships of thousands of patrons, need to be, although responsive staffs and directors in public libraries make strong, significant efforts to attend to individuals' needs, requests and concerns.

Was the Change Handled Well?

I believe that the director handled the transition to computerization appropriately. He identified and responded to the demand by presenting it to the Providence Athenaeum Board of Trustees as a project that required initiation. Then with the board's knowledge, he hired staff and identified and applied for funding.

The director and staff sought to reassure patrons by addressing their concerns directly. They explained the athenaeum's need to remain not only progressive, but also competitive to ensure its continued existence. This argument won over all but the die-hards.

My regret concerning myself was that the position of the Providence Athenaeum's Internet reference librarian was my first professional position as a librarian, and I remember mistakes that I made and glitches that occurred because of my inexperience. Technology was changing quickly then (and even more quickly now), so those of us who were fresh from library school, although relatively inexperienced, were in some ways the most technology savvy. Then, as now, the director who hires competent professional staff members and leaves them to learn, teach and advise in and about their assigned specialties is to be praised.

Another commendation for the director and assistant director is that they included the rest of the athenaeum staff and volunteers in the library's technology transition, but did not force anyone who resisted to participate. This strategy minimized resentment and enabled the staff to become acquainted with the transition as they wanted to. Another factor that helped was that no one felt that the technology was a threat to anyone's job, unlike the situation in the movie *Desk Set*, in which by order of the CEO, the librarians of the Reference Department are kept in relative ignorance and fear the worst.

In summary, this project was handled and integrated into a small, specialized setting with considerable success. I recommend these methods of integration to those who are planning to initiate new systems into older settings.

Using Technology to Reach Teens

ALEXANDRA TYLE

Are you wondering how to improve your teen services? Do teens often tell you they would like to participate in your program but are too busy? It's time to take your teen services online! This is an exciting time for teen services, and many libraries have jumped at the chance to start blogging, creating MySpace accounts, instant message, and use other Web 2.0 technologies. Not only will you be able to reach teens unable to attend your programs, but you'll also be offering a service that meets the technology needs and wants of teens.

There are many different technology services that your library can implement. If you have a teen advisory group, get their input on what services to initiate. You may even want to create a special teen group that focuses specifically on the creation, design, and implementation of your technology projects. The Homer Township Public Library in Homer Glen, Illinois, has the Teen Techies, a group that focuses on technology. The Teen Techies helped with the creation of the library's teen Web page, blogs, and social bookmarking site. A core group can tell you what projects will be successful with teens, what would be cool but probably fail, and what will have teens thinking "why is the library using this?" These teens can also help promote your new projects to teachers, students, and friends. Ask teens their opinions. Remember, what works for one library does not work for others. When I mentioned MySpace to our techies, many of the teens asked why and found the idea strange. However, many other libraries have successful MySpace accounts with many teenagers on the library's MySpace buddy list. Teens can help implement the technologies and keep you informed about new ones.

To creating your own Teen Techies, consider the following:

- To find members for the group, talk to teens who attend other programs, contact local high school technology and fine arts departments, and distribute press releases and flyers.
- Teens do not need to have a lot of computer experience, just a willingness to give input!
- Incorporate the group into your volunteer or intern program.
- Be prepared to teach AND learn!
- Have a flexible agenda for each meeting. Teens often want to show cool sites they've

found. We often have lengthy discussions about what we do and do not like about each site.

- Show teens other library teen sites. It's important to remember that what works at some libraries may not work at others! Let your group tell you what will work for your community and what will not.

Not sure what technology is out there? Or maybe you don't know how that technology can be used in the library world? Commonly used Web 2.0 technologies in the library world along include blogs, bookmarking sites, social networking sites, instant messaging, wikis, and photo and video sharing sites.

Blogs

Use blogs to keep teens informed about upcoming events and/or new library items. The Homer Township Public Library manipulated the template of their Teen Reviews Blog, allowing teens to post their book reviews based on genres. Try using a blog for an online book discussion.

Example Sites

- blogger.com
- livejournal.com
- wordpress.com

Library Examples

- Library Book Discussion (http://librarybookdiscussion.blogspot.com)
- HTPLD Teen Reviews (http://homerlibrary.org/teenreviews.asp)
- HTPLD Teen Events (www.homerlibrary.org/teenevents.asp)

Bookmarking Sites

If you're a librarian without access to the library server, this is a great way to keep your teen site updated with links to teen and homework sites. Instead of having to update the Web page and then uploading it to the library server, create links to your del.icio.us account. Del.icio.us also provides the HTML code to create tag badges. Have your teens help select sites entered into your bookmarking account. This is a great opportunity to teach teens how to evaluate Web sites.

Example Sites

- del.icio.us
- furl.net

Library Examples

- Homer Township Public Library (http://del.icio.us/homrteens)
- Brookfield Public Library Young Adults (http://del.icio.us/bfya)
- Osceola Library System (http://del.icio.us/osceolareference)

Social Networking Sites

MySpace allows you to show pictures (log-in required) and blog. While MySpace allows you to show pictures, you may want to add another photo site so that patrons without log-ins can view your pictures.

Having trouble designing your MySpace page? Try free MySpace layouts and generators. Remember, if you use a generator and layout page, the generators logo will appear on your site.

Example Sites

- MySpace.com
- facebook.com
- youtube.com

Library Examples

- ImaginOn (www.myspace.com/libraryloft)
- Carnegie Library of Pittsburgh, Carrick Branch (http://www.myspace.com/carrick_teens)
- Brookfield Public Library (http://www.myspace.com/bfya)

Instant Messaging

Instant messaging (IM) is a great way to communicate with patrons. If you step away from the computer, be sure to pull up the away message. This keeps IM patrons from wondering why you are ignoring their instant message. Also, be aware that there are patrons that will misuse the service. Create a policy on how to handle misuse, such as using inappropriate language or harassing the librarian. Also try sites such as Meebo.com and software such as Trillian that allow you to sign on to more than one IM service at a time. These sites allow you to reach more patrons since not all patrons use the same instant messaging service.

Example Sites

- AOL IM
- YAHOO! Messenger
- GTALK
- MSN Messenger

Library Examples

- Homer Township Public Library (www.homerlibrary.org/ask.asp)
- Hinsdale Public Library (www.hinsdalelibrary.info/ask/askhpl.htm)
- Champaign Public Library (www.champaign.org/find_answers/ask_a_librarian.html)

Wikis

A wiki is a Web site that can be edited. It can be used for meeting notes, projects, journaling, and personal portfolios. Most wikis keep a revision history showing previous page versions. If for some reason a user deletes or maliciously manipulates the content, you can revert to the original data.

Example Sites

- pbwiki.com
- wetpaint.com
- schtuff.com

Library Examples

- Teen Tech Week (http://teentechweek.wikispaces.com)
- Library Success (http://libsuccess.org)

Photo Sharing Sites

Providing pictures of events and programs allows you to show patrons the types of programs you have to offer. This is also a great way to advertise upcoming programs with pictures of your flyers and advertisements.

Example Sites

- Flickr.com
- snapfish.com
- webshot.com

Library Examples

- HTPLD (www.flickr.com/photos/homerlibrary)
- Public Library of Charlotte and Mecklenburg County (www.flickr.com/photos/library loft)
- Skokie Public Library (www.flickr.com/photos/skokiepl)

Video Sharing Sites

Example Sites

- Youtube.com
- vimeo.com

Library Examples

- Arlington Heights Memorial Library (www.youtube.com/profile?user=LibVlog)

If you are going to implement a Web 2.0 resource, make sure you keep it updated! If it's something that patrons have the capability to update and they have stopped updating it, promote the program again. Remember, there may be teens who do not know that the library has a teen Web page! You may want to keep track of the number of times your site has been viewed. Statcounter.com allows you to keep a visible or invisible counter on your site. The counter will keep track of the number of times the page was viewed, the number of returning users, and a variety of other data. While you're adding new online resources, think about incorporating some programming. This is a great opportunity to teach teens some basic HTML and also promote Internet safety.

If nobody is using the site after months of marketing, it may be time to stop and reevaluate the service. Try asking your Teen Techie group why people are not using the service. You may want to consider ending the service, or temporarily suspending it. If you want to keep the service running, invite other libraries to participate. The site will be advertised to more teens and the chance of teen participation increases.

Providing teen services online is not only a great way to attract teen participation but it also is a fun way for you, as a librarian, to become tech savvy.

Community Partnerships

ELIZABETH M. TIMMINS

I am blessed to work in a small and active community so it has been reasonably easy to accomplish the goal of creating community partnerships. Every person I meet affords me the opportunity to promote our great library!

I know that some of the following connections will resonate with you, the reader. Perhaps they will ignite you to try similar new strategies in your neighborhood!

- I made a bridge with the local paper, the *Times-Press*. I write a weekly column, "Mulling It Over at the Muehl Public Library."
- We are a member of the chamber of commerce. We report at monthly meetings about what is happening at the library.
- Our system, OWLS (Outagamie Waupaca Library System), participates in Legislative Day at the state level that is sponsored by WLA (Wisconsin Library Association). I have attended this twice so far. We talk to our local representatives.
- We have a strong, goal-oriented Friends group called the Friends of the Muehl Public Library (FMPL). They have an annual fall fundraiser — a wine, beer, and cheese-tasting event with silent auction. Our silent auction baskets are literary baskets, containing a book and items representing the theme of the book. The local golf course lets us use their restaurant and bar, gratis, for this event and the entire community donates items and services for this event. Proceeds benefit the library and positive publicity is generated for the businesses and services.
- We have very successful partnerships with other educational institutions in our community. (I think it helps that I was a teacher in a past life!) These include the public school district, the Catholic grade school, Hand in Hand day care, Seymour Headstart, Seymour Family Resource Center, and Good Shepherd day care (housed in the Good Shepherd nursing home — innovative because they are linking youth with seniors).
- I sit on the board of Home of the Hamburger. We have an annual community festival the first Saturday in August. The library has benefited from the contacts that this organization has created for us. We meet at the library and we have a Home of the Hamburger information phone at the library.
- I sit on a community committee for Alcohol and Other Drug Abuse Prevention. We plan family and youth-friendly activities. One of the Seymour City Council members (our governing body) also sits on this board.
- My governing board, the library board, has among its members a local city councilman as well as a school district representative. I inform the members about how great libraries are and the challenges that we face.

- I attend Public Property Committee meetings because the library is a public property. I have been hugely educated by attending these meetings and I advocate for the library at each meeting.
- I make it a point to know all city council members. I occasionally attend meetings as an interested citizen (although I do not live in this municipality which has been hugely advantageous for me — I am always advocating for the library but whomever I am speaking with cannot earn my vote!). I also did a presentation about the library at a city council meeting last year which was purely informational. They loved it! I want the council to be proud of our library. It is an extraordinary library for a community of this size. Also, I want to be visible to the council year-round, not just at budget request time.

It is a delight for me to "show and tell" our library. Occasionally civic groups will request a presentation and tour of the library or they will ask me to come visit their group and discuss the library. I love these invitations because I can merge my creativity and my passion for libraries. One Valentine's Day, I was invited to a home to talk about the library. I used the following exercise to educate my audience:

Trivia Questions about the Muehl Public Library   2.14.2006

1 — How many square feet is the library?

| E) 6,000 | V) 7,200 | L) 6,688 | O) 7,176 |

2 — How many hours is the library open in winter?

| V) 51 | L) 48 | O) 52 | E) 50 |

3 — How many hours is the library open in summer?

| O) 49 | E) 51 | V) 47 | L) 50 |

4 — How many items does our library own?

| L) 24,444 | O) 25,488 | E) 28,715 | V) 25,012 |

5 — How many total circulation transactions did we have last year? (this is defined as the total number of items both checked in and checked out)

| Y) 75,470 | U) 72,760 | R) 70,435 | O) 62,537 |

6 — How many Internet stations are available to the public at our library?

| O) 8 | Y) 4 | U) 6 | R) 9 |

7 — How many fulltime staff members work at our library?

| U) 1 | R) 2 | O) 3 | Y) 4 |

8 — How many part-time staff members work at out library?

| R) 5 | O) 4 | Y) 2 | U) 0 |

9 — Putting a reserve on an item is called a

| I) renewal | L) hold | B) checkout | A) check in |

10 — The number one source for reference questions is

| B) gardening | I) consumer questions | A) parenting | R) car repair |

11 — The number one priority for choosing books is

Y) reviews   B) patron requests   R) vendors   I)librarian favorites

12 — Which of these is offered twice weekly?

L) book group   R) story time   Y) computer class   A) author visit

13 — How many magazine subscriptions do we have at the library?

I) 60   A) 95   R) 105   B) 72

14 — Which ways can you find out about what's happening at the library?

L) ask a librarian   R) all of these   Y) check the website   A) look in the paper

15 — In which ways do we serve as a community service?

I) tax forms   Y) all of these   I) meeting space   R) energy assistance

We had so much fun with this because each question generated much discussion about what the public does not know about the library! For example, learning about reserves and that you can place a hold on any of the over 1 million items that are shared in our consortium was enlightening to this group! They did not know that we were connected to so many other libraries. They weren't aware that with their library cards they could check out materials from any of the locations and return materials to any of the locations.

It is amazing how you can talk and talk and talk about the library but there are all these well-kept secrets about the great customer service that we offer. We just have to keep getting the word out!

When all the correct answers are selected in the exercise, they spell out "LOVE YOUR LIBRARY." Perfect for Valentine's Day and perfect for any day! I am grateful to have such variety in my career all the time. Small successes, such as this exercise, make my day!

Finding Funding in
Your Own Backyard

PAM NUTT

Things that are tight: a new face lift, your new shoes, my pants, and of course your local school budget. So, how to you expand your spending without fear of losing your job? Writing a grant is not the most mysterious thing to do, in fact, once you have one on file, you can dust it off, change a few dates and amounts and use it over again.

The First Step: Identify a Need

All right, how about exercise equipment for the school? You've checked out the equipment in the gym and found out that all that is available are a few flat soccer balls and raveled jump ropes. You explain your idea of obtaining exercise equipment to the physical education instructor and ask for his opinion on what is needed for a good workout, what to buy and where. Surprisingly, he has a list of things for a program he would like to start with his class, but does not have the money in his budget. You ask if he would like to collaborate on obtaining the equipment by writing a grant. His enthusiasm quickly fades as he tells you how much he would like to help, but just doesn't have the time. Refusing to let him off the hook, you ask him to prioritize the list of equipment. You also ask him for catalogues to purchase the materials or better yet, does he have a funding source that you could approach?

Remember to Collaborate in Your Search

You have completed more research by working with the physical education coach than by doing it all yourself. Remember, there is no "I" in teamwork and your coworkers will resent a one-person show, even if they will reap the rewards of your work. It is so important to spread the workload around and ask for input. The coach suggests you contact his buddy Bruiser at the Big and Buff Sporting Goods Store. You go and talk to Bruiser, but quickly find out that his prices are extremely high even after he gives you a discount. You thank him for his time and move on. Where do you look now?

Let Your Fingers Do the Walking

Search the telephone book for companies in your area. I called several large companies in my area and asked if they had grants for education. EcoLab, one of the world's largest producers of cleaning supplies, is located in my hometown. I called the public relations director and asked if they had education grants for public schools. The director said they did and told me how to access their Web site for information regarding the application process. My school has received over $15,000 from EcoLab to purchase books for the media center and obtain classroom sets of books for the instructors. Many companies, especially those just getting started, are just waiting for you to ask for their help. But be warned, be careful about allowing companies to advertise in your schools or accepting expensive gifts. Check your school's policy manual for policies and procedures on gifts and donations. Also beware of accepting gifts from vendors that sell to your school or from parents who have companies that want to do business with you. Again, check your policies and procedures before accepting any gifts, especially if they are over a certain amount of money.

Search Cyberspace

The Internet is a wonderful tool for locating information. Search for "grants for physical education equipment" and see what happens. Are you surprised at just how much money is out there for education? According to the *Annual Register of Grant Support*, over $31 billion in educational grants was made available in 2002 with over 37,500 grant-making foundations in the United States alone. Even though you could use $31 billion, you only need what is on the budget sheet from the coach and what you can legitimately account for in spending. Keep in mind what you want to achieve and then read the grants carefully. Yes, this is going to take some time, but anything worth doing is worth doing right. Some grants will fund certain things, like they will fund gym equipment, but not the setup of the equipment. Others will pay for software, but not computers. Don't waste your time writing to a company for computers when their grant application clearly states that they will fund books but not computers. Big companies often fund large, highly visible projects. For example, Coca-Cola usually does not fund individual schools, but they would fund a regional library. Just think of the number of requests they would receive if they funded every school that asked for help. Check a company's Web page for the details. Also, if the Web site provides a contact person, don't be afraid to reach out and talk to him or her. Making a personal contact gives the grantor a better sense of what you are trying to accomplish.

Ask Locally

Don't be afraid to go to your local civic clubs and ask for support. Many of these organizations look for projects to complete each year, so you might as well be their project. The Spalding County Kiwanis Club built a 12-foot tree house for my media center and then donated books for my students. I found that the Kiwanis Club sets aside money for community projects, whether it is in the form of a grant, a one time donation, or a request. It behooves you to ask your community leaders if they have money available for special projects. When you approach the clubs, take a one-page proposal of what you want to accomplish. Have plenty of copies available and be very upbeat and prepared to answer lots of questions. If they don't ask questions, you should. The one-page proposal should include:

- an explanation of why what you want (gym equipment, books) is needed
- who it will benefit
- the projected budget
- when the project (if applicable) will begin

Where Is the Money?

One more place to look for grant money is your local banks. Banks are the keepers of the trusts and foundations and the marketing director or vice president can tell you which grants are available to suit your special needs. For example, I have been very privileged to receive the Agnes B. Hunt Foundation Grant for several years. The Hunt family wanted to help low-income students in my hometown. In order to receive the grant, I have to send the application to the board of trustees at the Wachovia Bank.

Now that you have your funding source at hand and you know how much money you need, all you have to do is write the grant. You have done the hard work by finding the grant, so what is left should be as easy as 20 deep-knee bends. If you do not know how to write a grant, there are several good books that can guide you through the process. The Internet has thousands of sites that are free and are full of information on achieving your goal.

You can do this. Oh, and one more thing, send everyone a thank you note for taking time out of their busy schedule to talk to you. Believe me, making the request more personal helps people see your need. Good luck!

Modern Mobilization

Creating a New Library Community

MELISSA AHO *and* ERIKA BENNETT

As changing times lead to changing jobs, obscure branches of librarianship are gaining ground. One professional aspect that has remained the same throughout the years is the librarians' tendency to collaborate.

Although shrinking budgets may be creating more solo positions or one-person library departments, social networking technology can help librarians meet our urge to collaborate. Librarians must be proactive! We cannot wait for other like-minded individuals to waltz along. Instead, we can use grassroots tactics to help foster new librarian communities.

Modern times provide modern solutions. In 2004, Minnesota career college librarians banded together, using both digital and classic social-gathering tools, to create our own professional group—the Career College Libraries of Minnesota (CCLM). It has been a rocky road, but we are still going strong. We would like to share our experiences on creating a modern, professional librarian network that serves a very specialized librarian community.

Social Transformation— Drowning or Swimming

Career or for-profit colleges are one of the fastest growing educational sectors in the world. Since many career colleges need MLIS-holding librarians for accreditation purposes, career college librarianship is also rapidly growing. While some career college libraries are small, others are large and networked, and all fall neatly (or messily) between ACRL and SLA. We may share comparative duties and customers with each other, but very few of our peers have the same combination of official professional memberships. This disparity thwarts dialogue, since we were traveling in separate circles.

So how do you create a library organization? Especially among competing companies? Here is a list of tips that we hope will help anyone attempting a similar collaboration in this rapidly transforming library world.

Preplanning:

- Conduct a needs analysis. What precise need(s) are you trying to fill and how will creating a new organization help with it?
- Explore existing professional organizations. Make sure your purposes aren't being served elsewhere, and if they are, consider contributing to leadership there.
- Check existing protocols. Are there organizational barriers to your collaboration attempt? This is extremely important because if you are going to be affiliated via your place of work, you should run your ideas by your supervisor. In other words, avoid complications later on by talking about it now.
- Find or start an informal group on the Web. This will help build interest and momentum.

People:

- Collect a list of prospective members and contact other librarians. The fastest way is through e-mail. (Specialized blogs and electronic mailing lists can also provide leads.) Also don't forget to send out an old-fashioned letter to those librarians or libraries you were not able to contact electronically.
- Gauge interest. Is anyone else interested in your idea or organization? If so, are they genuinely interested enough to contribute long-term time and effort to mutual goals?
- Note what skills are needed and available. Is there someone with a knack for Web design? A marketing specialist? A natural motivator? Look for any gaps in the skill pool that might compel specialized recruiting.
- To save time, set up an online forum to informally brainstorm in advance of your first gathering. Briefly mention the ideas for committees, officers, mission, goals, and meeting frequency to those you contact in order to get feedback and establish the importance of collaboration from the get-go.
- Don't be shy to announce that collaboration is a main group priority. Jumping straight into hierarchical governance, just because you are starting the thing, would be a mistake. Establishing group rule will take some time upfront, but it will save you enormous effort in the long run. If everyone feels valued, there should be fewer conflicts and less political griping.

First Meeting:

- Find a neutral place to meet on a day and time when the majority of people can attend (on a slow library day, perhaps). Pick a central location with food that is not too expensive. Be flexible. Remember it's not about accommodating everyone, which cannot be done, but about accommodating as many people as possible. Advertise by clearly stating what benefits your group will offer.
- Make it fun! Try to be sure that your first gathering is organized enough to be professional, but informal enough to be a good time. Announce that there will be time for banter after the official business is done.
- Set the tone of the group. Are decisions going to be made as a team or hierarchically? Much of your responsibility designations will depend on the leadership capabilities and personalities in the group. During our first year of operation, we were very informal. It was only in the second year that we set up bylaws and elected officers.
- Which decisions will be made by the group? Designating a charter committee can be a great way to ensure that the nitty-gritty gets decided without taking up valuable group time. Discuss formally the ideas for committees, offices, missions, goals, and meeting frequency. Our group ratified the charter by posting it on the forum and voting electronically.
- Designate future meeting hosts. Everyone loves the idea of getting together, but few want to host. In the beginning you could have everyone take a turn, but later you might want

to find a restaurant, café, or coffee shop that will welcome a group of wild and crazy librarians.

Tips for Continuing:

- After that first meeting, seriously, solemnly, and objectively consider whether the need for the group outweighs the effort involved in maintaining it.
- Use electronic media to decrease the burden of time commitments for your members. New Web 2.0 tools are tailor-made for social networks like these. Get your own Web site and discussion list.
- Don't panic if you see membership rapidly decrease. While every group innovator wants to see their membership skyrocket, be realistic that people will come and go. Some will only be able to attend sporadically and others will be content to lurk on the message boards.
- We encourage a light-hearted approach, but too much fluff in the leadership will make it hard to remain productive. Designate leaders. Write bylaws and elect a president and/or chair.
- Hold bimonthly or quarterly meetings.
- Invite speakers. Invite knowledgeable, prominent, and interesting librarians to speak to your group. We found that even the most famous librarians are willing to acknowledge invitations if you are polite and professional.

Our biggest obstacle to date has been communicating the positive nature of our mission to our administration. Many of our parent schools were happy in the beginning with our idea to work together in a new organization — as long as a school executive team had immediate oversight. Later, some expressed discomfort with the idea of employees from competing career colleges working so closely together. A few supervisors expressed concern that we were attempting to unionize. In the end we decided to break away from any school affiliation, meet outside of work hours, and change our name to CCLM.

Conclusion

So do you have a good idea for a new librarian organization in your area? Do you see a library niche that needs to be filled? Remember there are probably other librarians out there thinking the same way. They may be scanning the professional horizon for an organization filled with like-minded librarians. So give it a try. Give in to that primal librarian need. Collaborate!

School and Public Librarians Unite!

A Case Study Showcasing Collaborative Programming between Parkrose High School and Multnomah County Library

STEPHANIE A. THOMAS, RUTH B. ALLEN,
SARAH NELSEN *and* SARA RYAN

Librarians are always looking for ways to stretch their budgets. They try to find ways to cut costs by obtaining sponsored or free programming. They might share an author visit with other schools to save money or recruit community volunteers willing to present for free. School and public librarians often serve the same clientele — especially when the public library is close to the school — and are aware of each other's roles and services. It seems natural, then, for the two to form a partnership and benefit equally from shared resources.

Parkrose High School and the Multnomah County Library in Portland, Oregon, have found multiple ways to work together over a number of years. The partnership began when Parkrose High School was remodeled as a school/community center with a range of services open to the public, including a library envisioned to serve students during school hours and neighborhood residents when school was not in session. Eventually, operational and budget constraints made it impossible to continue operating the library as a joint school and public library location, and both organizations remained strongly committed to exploring new strategies for collaboration. The three projects described below highlight the ongoing partnership.

Author Lecture and Assembly

In 2006, Multnomah County Library and Parkrose High School embarked on a partnership to bring author Jacqueline Woodson to Portland for Multnomah County Library's fifth annual Teen Author Lecture. The Parkrose High School library media specialist joined four Multnomah County Library youth librarians, and the committee worked together for ten months to plan and present two events: the Teen Author Lecture and the Teen Author Assembly.

Prior to 2006, Multnomah County Library arranged for partner schools to bring anywhere from 60 to several hundred students to the annual lecture. But the demand always exceeded the number of student spaces because the library also sold tickets to the general public. Due to this demand and teachers' comments about the difficulty of getting students to an evening lecture, the committee decided for 2006 to host an additional event for students to connect with Woodson: a weekday morning assembly.

The committee chose ten schools from the 19 applications teachers submitted to be partner educators and participate in the assembly. Four hundred and fifty-one students from these schools attended the assembly and an even greater number read at least one of Woodson's books. Collectively, these classes spent over 100 hours preparing for their time with Woodson. How did the students get ready for the assembly and the lecture? They listened to booktalks; read Woodson's books either on their own or aloud in class; discussed the books; researched and talked about the author; created questions to ask Woodson; watched the movie based on her book, *Miracle's Boys*; and wrote poems.

The partnership made possible both the assembly and the lecture. In exchange for a block of seats for Parkrose High School and Parkrose Middle School students at the assembly, Parkrose High School provided the venue for both events free of charge. The media specialist dealt with all facility details in a timely manner and publicized the events in the community surrounding the school. The partnership also offered volunteer opportunities for Parkrose High School students. Students made signs and ushered at both events. Most exciting, two Parkrose students wrote and gave author introductions at the programs. The assembly was so successful that the committee recommended that the partnership continue for the 2007 Teen Author Assembly with author Laurie Halse Anderson.

Book Delivery

After Parkrose Cooperative Library at Parkrose High School returned to being exclusively a high school library, Multnomah County Library arranged implementation of a unique book delivery agreement with Parkrose students and faculty. The agreement allowed staff and students to select books from a computer in the high school library dedicated to the Multnomah County Library catalog, place the books on hold, and have them delivered to the high school library by county library courier. Knowing that this would cause an increase in circulation and overhead costs, the Parkrose High School media specialist maintained initial statistical data on usage. The book delivery service makes it possible to fill requests for materials that are not available at the school and proves very useful to Parkrose students.

After School Teen Programs

Two public library branches located near Parkrose High were experimenting with locations for hosting activities and proposed that the Parkrose High School Media Center host some of their teen programs. The school media specialist and public librarians agreed that

Parkrose students could benefit from the convenience of having the programs right at the high school. The first program offered through this partnership featured a cartoonist, who provided a two-session graphic novel/cartooning workshop. Many of the school's animation program students attended.

There is increasing interest nationwide in developing positive activities for teens during out-of-school hours. However, transportation is often a barrier for teens interested in participating in the programs. This kind of programming partnership opens windows of opportunity for local youth.

School Corps

Another way that Multnomah County Library librarians collaborate with Parkrose High School staff is through School Corps. Multnomah County Library School Corps connects students and educators in Multnomah County with the information resources of the public library. The goal of School Corps is to increase the information literacy of Multnomah County students by working in partnership with local schools. School Corps, staffed by three librarians, offers the following services to all Multnomah County K–12 schools:

- online research tools presentations
- Multnomah County Library catalog instruction
- Multnomah County Library databases instruction
- introduction to search engines and how to evaluate Web sites
- live homework help (tutor.com) demonstration
- "Think Before You Click" presentation on Internet safety and etiquette
- books and literacy presentations
- "Feasting on Forbidden Fruit" presentation on censorship
- customized booktalks
- curriculum Support
- bucket of books, which are tubs of 24 to 30 books on a topic, a teacher's guide with an annotated list of age-appropriate Web sites, and a pathfinder for doing research on the topic at Multnomah County Library
- customized book lists, webliographies, and pathfinders
- School Corps Quarterly (www.multcolib.org/schoolcorps/scq), a newsletter designed to assist educators in integrating public library resources with the curriculum. Articles give concrete examples of how teachers can use a service/resource or what benefits they and their students would derive from attending an event.

Parkrose staff stay informed about the public library through *School Corps Quarterly*, use buckets of books to add value to the book delivery service, and schedule presentations that reinforce and support the work of the school media specialist. Read more about Multnomah County Library's School Corps at (www.multcolib.org/schoolcorps). Schools outside of Multnomah County may find their local public library happy to provide similar services. It is always worthwhile for school library staff and educators to contact their local public libraries to discuss possible collaboration and information sharing.

As demands for our shrinking budgets increase, it becomes even more important for librarians from school and public libraries to share resources in order to provide the best service to our communities. Contact your colleagues and get creative with your services!

Authors R Us

RICK WALTER, EILEEN O'CONNELL *and* KATHY BARCO

The Taylor Ranch Branch of the Albuquerque/Bernalillo County Library System is unusual in that all three of its staff librarians are successful authors. Two have published in such intriguing areas as New Mexico breakfast eateries and historical science fiction, while the third is an award-winning poet. They presented a roundtable discussion at the library on how to get started, get published, and get paid. This essay is based on their presentation.

Rick Walter: Found in Translation

Rick Walter, adult services librarian at the Taylor Ranch Library, is cotranslator and coeditor of Jules Verne's novel *The Meteor Hunt*, previously unavailable in English, finally published in 2006. Walter has been a fan of Jules Verne ever since he read *20,000 Leagues Under the Sea* as a boy. That book would eventually lead Walter into his career as a translator.

Boyhood Bafflement

"When I was a 10-year-old," Walter recalls, "I read *20,000 Leagues Under the Sea* for the first time — I loved it, had dreams about it. But parts of the story baffled me — for instance, the characters started a campfire with 'a lentil' or loosened bolts with 'an English key.' Well, years later I read Verne's original French — these were idiotic mistranslations of *lentille* (lens) and *clef anglaise* (monkey wrench). I'd studied French in high school and college, so I decided to produce some accurate translations of these terrific 19th century yarns."

Walter discovered that his years in public relations and his experience as a scriptwriter were a big help in communicating Verne's theatrical, humorous style to American readers. His efforts enjoyed some commercial success: Before *The Meteor Hunt*, he collaborated on annotated translations of Verne's *20,000 Leagues Under the Sea* (offered by Book-of-the-Month Club in the mid–1990s) and *The Mighty Orinoco* (another English-language first). In fact, he's becoming nationally known as a go-to guy for Verne.

Networking Payoff

Walter credits his reputation to his networking efforts: "My objective is to be famil-iar as a Verne specialist in the U.S. publishing and academic scene. This way, I'm contacted when projects arise, plus I have clout in pitching a project of my own." To polish his approach, Walter gladly consults books on salesmanship. He suggests Keith Ferrazzi's *Never Eat Alone*, Joe Vitale's *Meet and Grow Rich,* and Jeffrey Gitomer's *Little Black Book of Connections.*

He's even comfortable with cold-calling: "I've phoned complete strangers (publish-ers, academics, other Vernians), just so we're acquainted." Walter's networking efforts also include:

- keeping up contacts through correspondence and exchanges of favors and assistance
- participating in listservs, such as the worldwide Jules Verne Forum
- joining organizations, such as the North American Jules Verne Society
- publishing in newsletters and presenting at conferences
- hosting events, such as the June 2007 NAJVS conference at the Albuquerque Museum of Art

What's the payoff of it all? "I've been repeatedly phoned out of the blue," Walter says, "resulting in four book jobs and a movie option!"

Eileen O'Connell: Verse-Atility

Eileen O'Connell, general services librarian at the Taylor Ranch Library, is a published poet and has twice been featured in the *Albuquerque Tribune*'s poetry contest. "Why poetry?" you might ask.

Self-Discovery

"Poetry is a great medium for obsessive people with limited time," O'Connell explains. "The shorter format lets me play with words and ideas. I value the opportunity to inten-sively craft and polish my work — to get each word right and in the right place. In the process I surprise myself. I keep running into things in my poems that I didn't know I knew."

Triple the Research

"There are three components to the research I do: one as a reader, one as a writer, and one as I try to place the work for publication," says O'Connell. She goes on to explain that

as a teenager, I used the library to track down a John Donne poem, "The Triple Fool," that Mary Stewart quotes in *Nine Coaches Waiting*. Stewart quotes the poem only in part, and I wanted to read the whole thing. Finding and enjoying other poets' work is refreshing as a writer as well as a reader.

As a writer, once I have an idea, I explore why it interests me and then work to communi-cate that interest with verve and precision. I research to find the right words, keep my ideas fresh, and get the details right. Any resource that sharpens my understanding sharpens the poem.

This brings me to the third component: researching how to get the work to a reader! *Literary Marketplace*, *Writer's Digest* and *Writer's Market* publications identify publishers, magazines, and journals that accept poems and what kind of poems they prefer. The acknowledgment pages (lists of where the poems appeared first) in books by poets whose audience is similar to the audience I seek also help me target where to send completed poems. Research, persistence, and confidence that the poems are as good as I can make them are my best allies in sharing finished poems with an audience.

Kathy Barco: It's Delicious

Kathy Barco, children's librarian at the Taylor Ranch Library, is the coauthor (with Valerie Nye) of *Breakfast Santa Fe Style: A Guide to Fancy, Funky, and Family Friendly Restaurants*, published in 2006.

Menu for Success

"Our book is innovative and has popular appeal," Barco points out. "Although there are lots of books that describe places to eat in Santa Fe, we limited ourselves to restaurants that serve breakfast. And, since we're both librarians, we include 'Recommended Reading' with each review. The booklist at the back of *Breakfast* lists over 60 books with a New Mexico flavor for kids, teens, and adults: history, mystery, guidebooks, cookbooks, photos, essays, poetry, classics, and biography."

Surprise Ingredient

When asked about the most unexpected result of becoming an author, Barco replied, "Marketing this book has turned out to be a huge job that requires creativity, persistence, and imagination. Morphing from librarian into blatant self-promoter has been an adventure."

"Although I seldom prepare food myself, I love to watch the Food Network!" jokes Barco. "If I had to whip up a breakfast burrito of marketing tips, it would contain the following:

- Cook up a marketing plan and be prepared to spend a lot of time following it.
- Devour books on marketing such as *Jump Start your Book Sales* by Marilyn and Tom Ross or *Publicize your Book* by Jacqueline Deval.
- Develop a website (such as www.breakfastsantafestyle.com) and keep it simmering.
- Have some 'gimmicks' to whet appetites (We have postcards of our book cover that add spice to our mailings. Speaking of the cover, we had it made into a 'photo tapestry' to display at all our book signings and library visits. It's huge, and we refer to it as the 'large print version').
- Participate in a support group (Although you may think I'm referring here to Overeaters Anonymous, I mean something like the New Mexico Book Coop or Southwest Writers).
- No matter how delectable it sounds to become a writer, don't give up your day job!"

Future Plans

What does the future have store for this trio?

Walter: "I've got some new Jules Verne thrillers for Americans to enjoy ... one of these days."

O'Connell: "Of course I'll pen and publish more poetry — plus maybe I'll try coming up with a murder mystery."

Barco: "I'm looking forward to marketing my second book *READiscover New Mexico — A Tri-Lingual Adventure in Literacy*."

Being Your Own Publisher

Judith A. Siess

I did not start the *One-Person Library: A Newsletter for Librarians and Management*. That brave step was taken by Guy St. Clair and Andrew Berner in 1984. However, in the fall of 1997, St. Clair asked me if I wanted to purchase the newsletter. I had quit my job as a corporate librarian and was looking for something else to do, so I said, "yes." After some lengthy negotiations, I became the publisher and editor of the *One-Person Library* (OPL) in May 1998. Now I only had to write or find enough words to fill eight pages per month and have the newsletters printed and mailed out to about 500 subscribers. *Only* indeed. It isn't quite that simple.

Publishing a Newsletter

The first thing I do is decide on a theme for the issue. I've used medical librarianship, continuing professional education, conference reports, blogging, and keeping current. Sometimes I don't have a theme and just use up articles I've accumulated.

Then I choose article that I wrote that fits the theme. Most of these articles are adaptations of things I found on the web or in a blog, but some I've written especially for OPL on subjects that I think are important. However, I usually confine my original writing to my editorial, "Thinking About...," which I usually write last.

I find I spend a great deal of time formatting the issue. I could have used a program like Microsoft Publisher which would do much of this for me, but I couldn't get it to work for me. So I use Microsoft Word and spend time making sure articles fit into 12 pages, deciding where column and page breaks go, and correcting text to conform to my house style (dashes, bold, italics, etc.). This usually takes about a week.

Then I have to get permission from all the people I quote. I'm very careful about this because a reader in Australia threatened to sue me for quoting her e-mail without permission. So I contact everyone who is quoted and get written permission. If permission isn't granted (either because they don't want to be quoted or I can't find the person), I paraphrase the quote or delete it. I keep all permissions forever. This process can take one to two weeks.

After the issue is finished, I send it via e-mail to my proofreader, John Welford, who lives in England. I usually get the proofed copy in about two to three days.

I print out the issue, using high-quality format, and take it to my printer. I print my own address labels, even though my printer could do them, because I want them to be as up-to-date as possible. My database is in askSam, so I have to export the data, and then import it into Word to print the labels. This takes about an hour.

One-Person Library is published on the first of the month, so I try to get the copy to the printer by the 23rd of the month or so. Sometimes I'm late, but I have a wonderful printer who sometimes works miracles and turns an issue around in a day or two. He also folds it, stuffs it in envelopes, seals and stamps the envelopes, and mails the issue for me. I build these charges into the subscription cost. That's why the electronic version is 30 percent cheaper than the paper version and the cost of a paper subscription outside of the USA and Canada is 15 percent higher. (If everyone subscribed to the electronic version I could double my profit.)

The last thing I do is send the electronic file with the issue to my webmaster for posting on the Web for those who subscribe electronically. He also extracts all the electronic links in the issue and posts them elsewhere on the site.

An ongoing part of being a publisher is maintaining the subscription database. It is much more work than I had imagined. Half of my subscriptions come through subscription services (and two-thirds of those are from Ebsco) and arrive with all the customer information and a check. The rest come individually, via the form on my Web page, e-mail, or post. Credit cards have to be processed and checks deposited. Sometimes I have to contact the subscriber for more information (e-mail address, billing address, etc.). Changes to addresses are common, as are questions about the status of a subscription. All this takes time.

Then there are the claims. Every publisher hates claims. I know that I sent the issue to the address the subscriber gave me, but some issues go astray. I have *no* idea why. Some subscribers have even claimed every issue. (When that happens, I suggest an electronic subscription. If they refuse, I sometimes tell them I can't send any more issues.) My policy is to fill claims with a paper copy if I have one, or with electronic if I do not. I fill claims only once. These are very expensive to provide and also very time-consuming.

Also time-consuming is the renewal process. I send out a renewal reminder postcard when there are about two months left on the subscription, another a month or so later, and another when the subscription expires. I don't remove people from the database until two months after the subscription expired. Why am I so generous? The reason I publish OPL is to get the information to people, not to make money. Your reasons and policies may differ.

What Works

When I took over OPL I kept the page size, print color, two-column format, and the regular departments and columns. I've added some columns and departments over the years and dropped others, but it was important to make the transition as smooth as possible. I kept St. Clair's policy of paying for articles and added payment for conference reports of the major library association meetings. I pay $100 for an article of 1000 words or more (about one column), $50 for shorter articles, and $25 per conference session for a two to three paragraph report. This policy makes it a lot easier to get people to write articles for me. The electronic-access-only version has saved me a lot of money and increased my bottom line, but not as many people have taken advantage of it as I expected, especially in the United States. Retaining subscribers has been a *big* problem. The number has dropped every year, to where it may not even be worth doing. But because I've priced the newsletter right, I'm still making money. Some people think I charge too little, but I think if I charged what they suggest ($300 or more per year), I could just close up shop.

What Doesn't Work

Looking back, buying back the Australasian edition of OPL wasn't such a great idea. I wanted all subscribers to get the same content, but I lost a lot of subscribers when they no longer got content specifically for their geographic area. Instead of St. Clair's editorial board, I appointed a board of correspondents, who were supposed to send me international news and articles, but I got very little from them and finally disbanded the group. Selling back issues didn't generate much money, so I quit charging and just sent people back issues and considered it advertising. Speaking of advertising, I've done some, but it's very expensive and since so many subscriptions come through services, it's very difficult to assess the success of an ad. I haven't done much advertising recently. Whether more advertising would have kept my subscriber list up, I don't know. I stand by my decision.

Is This for You?

Only you can answer that question, but if you like working for yourself, are disciplined, enjoy writing, have an eye for detail, have another source of income (at least at the beginning), and, most importantly, have something to say, go for it. I've certainly enjoyed being an editor and publisher.

Crafting a Cover Letter

Kathryn Yelinek

You're heading to a job interview. You've perfected your resumé, memorized your pitch, and pressed your suit. You're all set. It's cold outside, so you pull on an old overcoat that you wear while gardening and...

Wait a minute. It makes no sense to wear a dirty old overcoat to an interview. While it may not cost you the position, such carelessness will certainly make an employer hesitant about hiring you.

Just the same, it makes no sense to overlook your cover letter. After spending days, weeks, or even years perfecting your work, you want to put this finishing touch on your submission. It's the first thing an editor or agent sees, and it lets that person assess your professionalism with a quick glance. This essay shows you how to create a cover letter that demonstrates you mean business.

First, read the submission guidelines for your target publication. Most magazines and publishing houses maintain a Web site that includes tips for submitting your work to them. Read these guidelines carefully and *follow them exactly*. Here you'll learn if you should include any special information, such as a biography, in your cover letter. There's really no excuse not to follow the guidelines. It only annoys the editor and wastes your time.

Your Paper Cover Letter

Assuming the publication guidelines don't ask for anything weird, you'll write a paper cover letter in standard business format. This means you should:

- single space
- left justify
- insert blank lines between paragraphs (do not indent)

Note that this is different from standard manuscript format, which calls for double spacing and indented paragraphs.

At the top, type your contact information. You probably included this information on your manuscript. That's good. If your cover letter gets separated from your manuscript, the editor can still contact you.

After your contact information, skip a line and type the date. Skip another line and

194

type the editor or agent's name and contact information. Include the person's full name and position title.

Unless you know the editor or agent personally, don't use their first name in the salutation. Instead, write "Dear Ms. Jones" or "Dear Mr. Smith." If the person has a gender-neutral name, either do a little research to discover their gender or resort to "Dear Editor Miller." Include a colon after the name, not a comma. Your letter should look like this:

12345 Country Road
Hometown, PA 17000
(999) 555–2121
kyelinek@myemail.com

January 1, 2008

Editor's Full Name
Publication Name
Publication's Street Address
Big City, NY 10000

Dear Ms. Editor's Last Name:

Your pitch.

Sincerely,
Your name

Your E-mail Cover Letter

When you submit a piece by e-mail, the e-mail itself is your cover letter. Begin the e-mail with the editor's name as described above. Remember to use a colon after the person's name. Don't cut and paste from MS Word into your e-mail. Some e-mail programs have trouble reading Word documents. You don't want an editor to open your e-mail and see only gibberish! A cover letter is usually short enough to type directly in an e-mail program. If you do this, be sure to use spell-check. If you prefer to type the letter in Word, follow these directions to convert it into plain text:

- Use at least a 12-point font.
- Select all of the original text.
- Set the left and right margins to 1.5 inches.
- Go to File, then Save As. Under Save As Type, select Plain Text. This will give you a document with a .txt extension.
- If you receive a warning prompt about compatible features, select "Yes." Also, check the box that asks if you want to insert line breaks.
- Open the new document in WordPad or NotePad and read it carefully. If you weren't able to check the box to insert line breaks, insert them manually now. Be sure there is a blank line between each paragraph. Make changes, if necessary, since you have lost italics and bold formatting.

Cut and paste the plain text document into your e-mail. Include your contact information after you conclude your letter (not at the beginning). Your e-mail should look like this:

Dear Mr. Jones:

Your pitch in plain text.

Sincerely,

Your Name
12345 Country Road
Hometown, PA 17200
(999) 555–2121
kyelinek@myemail.com

Send the e-mail to yourself first as a test. Read it over carefully. Only once you're completely satisfied with the e-mail should you send it.

What to Write

Unless the publication guidelines say otherwise, your cover letter should be one page or less. At its core, your letter needs only three components: your contact information, an explanation of why you're contacting this person, and a thank you for the person's time. If you're submitting a short story, for example, you may only want to write: "Enclosed, please find my 3,400-word short story, "A Wonderful Story." I hope you'll use it in an upcoming issue of *Your Great Magazine*. Thank you for your time and consideration. I look forward to your response." Short and sweet.

Some other things you might consider:

- If the agent or editor requested your piece, or if you're being referred by a mutual friend, say so in your first sentence. For example: "I'm enclosing my short story, which you requested on such-and-such a date at the Important Writer's Conference."
- As a rule, your paper manuscript will only be returned if you include an envelope with sufficient return postage. You should state your preferences concerning the return of your manuscript and whether you've enclosed a return envelope.
- If you're including additional items such as photographs, mention them in your letter. Also state your preference concerning their return (include enough postage if you want them back).

One of the biggest questions about cover letters is what to include about yourself. Should you mention that you're unpublished? Or that you write for your local historical society? Of that your wife loved your article? In a word: No. Remember, your cover letter is a business letter between two professionals. You need to establish pertinent writing credentials.

So, what do you do when you're unpublished? If the piece is library related, stress relevant work experience and accomplishments. If the piece is about some other topic, again focus on work that you've done that is related to the topic. Or stress the expertise of anyone that you're interviewing for the piece.

You didn't write in your job application that you loved books or that your mother thought you'd be perfect for the position. You kept your application professional and stressed your related experience. If you were fresh out of an MLS program, you focused on your coursework, field placement experience, or volunteer work — any transferable skills that were relevant to the position. This is exactly what you need to do in your cover letter. Of course, if you have no or very little related experience, don't apologize or point this out in your letter. Simply stick to the basics as given above and let your writing speak for itself.

Take a deep breath. Writing a cover letter doesn't need to be difficult. Remain professional and give just enough information to make that editor or agent take a look at your piece. You've done the work. You've written your article or short story. Now you just need to put on the finishing touch before sending it out.

Newspaper Column

A Conversation Among Book Lovers

GABRIEL MORLEY

Writing a column about your library for the newspaper is a good way to keep patrons informed about library events. Your column will also alert potential visitors and remind loyal patrons about the services provided at the library. Most importantly, a regular column allows the library to establish an ongoing dialogue with the community it serves.

But before you rush down to the newsroom to sign up take a moment for some self-reflection. Newspaper editors are notoriously blunt. I was one for many years. Be prepared to outline specifically what you want to do. Do you want to write a monthly column? Twice monthly? Weekly? Will you be reviewing books (the paper may already have someone doing this) in your column? Or will your column focus on the library and its activities?

Do a Self-Assessment

Be honest with yourself. Are you capable of writing a weekly column that people will *want* to read? Newspaper columns are generally between 500 and 750 words. Each paper is different. Some run columns vertically, some horizontally.

Make sure you are willing to pay attention to the needs of the paper. You should take special care to learn about newspaper style. You don't want an editor dreading your column every month. Follow the prescribed column formula at your paper and you will have more success and a better relationship with your editor.

Two important things to remember about writing a column are: Have something to say; and make sure you can write a column before you approach an editor.

The first steps in the process are to convince an editor that your column is needed, that it will be read regularly and that you can write. A good editor is going to want to see a list of column ideas upon your initial meeting. Be prepared. If you're writing a monthly column, have at least 15 to 20 ideas with a brief three to five sentence abstract describing what you intend to do with each idea. If you're writing a weekly column, you will want to come up with 20 or 30 column topics. This list also helps with your own planning. Having a list of topics ahead of time makes it that much easier once you start writing.

Don't try to fool yourself by saying you will think of something to write about when the time comes. You might be able to do this a few times, but mostly you'll be staring at the computer screen wishing you had developed more ideas ahead of time. It takes practice to be a good columnist. The best have written thousands of columns and have become attuned to what makes good copy. They find ideas in their daily lives related to work or home life. They write about questions they have, or concerns. For your library column think about changes and peculiarities of your library system. But keep it interesting. No navel-gazing.

Columns Are More Than Just Ideas

In addition to having a list of ideas, take at least six fully written columns with you for the editor to review. Yes, at least six. Bring more if you plan to write a weekly column. I can't tell you how many times someone came into the newsroom brimming with enthusiasm to write a column about something, only to be foiled when they realized they couldn't actually do it or only had a few real ideas that could be developed into columns.

A doctor came into the newsroom once full of energy to write a weekly column. We made him submit two columns before we committed. He never submitted a third. A local investment broker was hot to write a weekly financial column. We asked him to submit two columns, as well. He called us before ever submitting anything to say it was harder than he thought and he couldn't come up with two ideas. (At least he called.) The reason newspapers are so particular about columns is because it is embarrassing to announce a new columnist only to have it fizzle a few weeks later. It makes the paper look bad. An editor wants to make sure you're committed, that you can write and that you have ideas.

By writing six columns prior to approaching an editor, you will have a head start if you are accepted as a columnist, and you will have a window of opportunity to work on subsequent columns without deadline pressure.

It is appropriate and often appreciated if you can recommend a headline or two for your column. If you're writing a regular column it will have a standing head such as, "Library Lagniappe" or "Book Talk" or "Book Ends." Then, each individual column will have a headline referring to something contained in the column.

A Column Is Not a News Story

A column is a little different from a regular newspaper article, which is written using an inverted pyramid model. (All the important information is put at the beginning of the story and then less important and background information fills in at the bottom.) A column is typically more conversational, as if you are relating a story to a friend.

When you're writing your columns keep these things in mind:

- Make sure your ideas appeal to a wide audience, not just regular library patrons.
- Remember to write economically, using short sentences. You are not writing a scholarly research paper. Your tone should be easy to understand and enjoyable to read. The goal is to communicate, not impress the reader with your vocabulary.
- Use specific examples and tell anecdotes that relate to your theme.

- Choose your topics carefully. Certain topics may generate backlash — be prepared.
- Writing should be crisp and concise. Take pains to be clear. Once the paper rolls off the press thousands of people are going to be reading what you wrote. If you think words aren't dangerous, wait until your first phone call from an irate reader.
- Strive to be unique, but not so esoteric that no one understands what you're writing about. Try to offer a new perspective on the topics you tackle.

As a columnist, you do not have to abide by the same stipulations as a reporter, which is to say you don't have to be impartial. One of the reasons people generally write columns is to offer their opinions and perspective. Make your examples relevant so the reader can identify with what you're saying. Don't forget the reader. Keep asking yourself why someone would read what you're writing. If you don't think this is important, think about all the newspaper columns you skip over in the paper every day.

For column ideas, start thinking of things to write about as you talk to people and read other interesting articles. Think of all the columns you've read that were about some ordinary aspect of life presented in a new way. Feel free to use "I" and "you" in order to become more intimate with the reader and to personalize your columns. End with a brief conclusion.

It is important to proofread your work and get someone else to look at it before you submit it to your editor. Your editor does not want to correct your grammar or fix your spelling errors.

Overall, a newspaper column is one of the easiest and best tools to reach out to library patrons in the community. Sometimes it can be drudgery if you aren't prepared and don't enjoy writing the column. The only way to know if it suits you is to sit down and try to write five or six columns. If you like the process and are pleased with your writing, visit your local newsroom.

The Poetry Sweepstakes

Beating the Odds of Getting Published

LISA A. FORREST

Sending off poetry submissions can feel a lot like entering a million-dollar sweepstakes contest. As the envelope disappears into the dark abyss of the mailbox, you are hopeful, yet simultaneously full of doubt. Being published *shouldn't* matter, but as any artist will confess, it feels *good* to be validated by the public. Why create art if not to share it with the world? Unfortunately for the sensitive soul, it can be a blow to the old self-esteem when you experience rejection (not unlike dating, but something keeps you trying anyway, doesn't it?).

Poetry has always guided the way that I view the world, so naturally, I carried my love of verse into my career as an academic librarian. One of the first things I did after taking my librarian position was to start the Rooftop Poetry Club (yes, we really do meet on the rooftop on the library). As leader of the club, I am frequently asked for editing and publishing advice. I often remind students that being a poet isn't *just* about getting published. While submitting your work is certainly a part of the equation, it's also important to establish yourself within a community of writers. With that said, here's my humble advice for getting your work out of those tattered notebooks and into the real world:

- Join a writing group or poetry club. Check your local literary organization for a listing of established writing groups that meet in your community. Local newspapers often carry listings as well. Writing groups provide opportunities for you to present your work and improve upon your poetic skills. If you can't find an established group, start your own! As a librarian, you're in a unique position of leadership. Use the library space itself to inspire creativity. The club that I founded meets on the rooftop of the library in the warm months and up near the poetry stacks in the cold months. Make up some flyers and buy some refreshments—you'll be surprised who shows up. Take down e-mail addresses and set up a MySpace page for your club. Your meetings don't have to be elaborately planned. They may be as simple as everyone sharing a poem or two with the group. Poets.org has some great poetry resources to get the conversation started. I would also highly recommend Bernadette Mayer's creative writing experiments at www.factoryschool.org/handbook/creative/experiments.html.

- Participate in local open-mic readings. Local newspapers often provide a calendar of open-mic reading events that are held at bookstores and coffee shops. Don't be shy. Put on your most flowing clothing, get out there, and meet other poets! You never know who might hear (and want to publish) your work.

- Join your local literary center. Never underestimate the power of community. There are a heck of a lot of independent poetry magazines out there — and *lots* of poets submitting *lots* of poems. Sometimes being noticed is just a matter of making the right connections with the right people. Established poets are often very involved with their local literary centers and have good advice to give on where to send your work. Participate in workshops, attend featured readings, and make friends with eccentric poets.

- Start small. Don't waste your time or money entering national poetry contests or sending off poems to the "big shots." Start by making a name for yourself in your very own community. Submit your work to local newspapers and magazines. If you're really motivated, start your own print or online poetry journal. Remember, as librarians, we are perfectly situated to become leaders in the writing community, including a poetry journal editor. If you are working in a public or academic library, chances are you already know patrons who write poetry and would be interested in contributing their work to your journal.

- Blog. The Web offers a variety of options for disseminating and archiving the written word. Blogs are one of the easiest to use self-publishing tools out there. Best of all, they're free. Think of your blog as an online writing portfolio. Blogs also allow a unique opportunity for networking with other poets by linking to their blogs or Web sites. Blogs, which allow readers to post responses to your postings, can also serve as a forum for constructive critique and discussion of poetry-related topics. I've had local editors contact me, asking if they could publish poetry they read on my writing blog. Trust me, it works.

- Create your own chapbook. We've all seen our artist friends barter their paintings, photos, or music. As poets, it can be hard enough to *give* away our work! Let's face it — words are cheap. But handmade chapbooks can provide tangible depth and meaning to the written word. Check out the bookmaking supplies at your local art supply store. Browse through the bookmaking section of your library for inspiration. Attend a workshop on handmade books. Poetry presented in creative ways is truly a work of art (and makes a thoughtful gift). Most chapbooks can be created economically with an ordinary computer printer and a little innovation. For added inspiration, try collaborating on projects with photographers, visual artists, graphic designers, or musicians.

- Think community. Publishing comes in many forms. At our library, I have organized group poetry projects to celebrate National Poetry Month. The campus community has been invited to write poems on obsolete catalog cards and old topographical maps. Our most recent project used discarded 35-millimeter art slides for poetic inspiration. We've held an online sonnet contest to celebrate Valentine's Day. Our club also hosts a variety of workshops run by student members (which they can then add to their resume of leadership experiences). What can you do to inspire community and creativity in your library?

- Browse the poetry magazines. Our neighborhood bookstore carries a wide variety of small press poetry publications that you just can't find anywhere else. Grab a latte, seat yourself in the magazine aisle, and page through the poetry magazines. It helps to maintain a journal of magazine titles and submission criteria, which can also be used to keep track of which poems you send out to each magazine.

- Submit to Web zines. Let go of the need to see your words only in hard-copy. There is an abundance of electronic poetry magazines (e-zines) just waiting for your submission. The Rooftop Poetry Club has compiled a list of electronic publications at www.buffalostate.edu/library/rooftop/resources/publications.htm.

- Use your library. You've got the knowledge and resources at your fingertips! Use reference sources, such as *Poet's Market,* to discover the right places to submit your work. Browse through poetry journals and electronic poetry magazines to check out submission criteria. Does your work fit? Use your library skills and do your research *before* you submit. Not only will it save you the effort of submitting to a journal inappropriate for your work, but it'll also spare the mailman from delivering another rejection letter to your door. You've got the research skills, so use them to help yourself succeed.

• You'll never know if you don't try. Yes, it can be overwhelming to put yourself out there into the literary world. Nobody likes to hear that they didn't make the cut, but remember that rejection isn't always about you. Pick yourself up, dust yourself off, and play the sweepstakes. No purchase is necessary and this time around, you might just be holding a winning ticket.

Publishing an Article
in a Scholarly Journal

Perry Bratcher

I've been the editor of the *Southeastern Librarian* since 2004. My interest in becoming an editor came naturally through my background as a cataloger. The detail-oriented work of a cataloger lends nicely to the work of an editor. Performing editorial duties also offers variety and fulfills duties required as a tenured faculty librarian. The *Southeastern Librarian* (SELn) is the official publication of the Southeastern Library Association (SELA). Two newsletter-style issues and two issues including juried articles are published yearly.

One publication venue sought by many librarians, particularly those in a tenure-track or other college/university position, is a scholarly journal. These publications abound in the library field, from newsletters to state, regional and national journals. Some are topic specific, related to a particular area of library service, while others are more generic, but perhaps tied more closely to a readership of a particular state or region. Whatever the case, there are common guidelines which the prospective author should consider prior to submission.

Before addressing issues specific to the article, it is important for the author to understand the publisher's perspective. This will help the author select appropriate journals for their article, saving both the author and publisher time and effort. Articles submitted to scholarly journals are generally reviewed by various individuals depending on the publication. Some publications follow a process of review by an editorial board, while others may also utilize peer reviewers. A double-blind process may be used, where neither the author nor the reviewer knows each other's identities. This is done in order to eliminate any possible bias. Peer reviewers may or may not have expertise in the subject area of the article. In these cases, reviewers consider readability, grammar and presentation of the subject. Many editors and reviewers are volunteers, not employees of the publisher, particularly for those journals published below the national level. These volunteers hold "real" jobs in addition to their duties as editors or reviewers. This means that the review process can be lengthy.

The steps involved in the publication process can vary, but include the following:

1. The author submits an article to a selected journal. Articles should be submitted to one journal at a time, not to several journals simultaneously. Many publishers state in their submission guidelines that articles are not to be considered elsewhere.

2. The editor acknowledges receipt of the article, solicits reviewers, and forwards articles to reviewers, removing the identity of the author in order to adhere to the double-blind process.
3. Reviewers return comments to the editor along with a recommendation.
4. Reviewer comments, recommendations, and the article are sent to the editorial board for review.
5. The editorial board and editor make a decision regarding publication.
6. The author is notified of the decision. If the article is accepted, reviewer comments are forwarded to the author for possible revisions, with the identification of the reviewer removed.
7. The author makes the requested revisions and sends the article back to the editor.
8. The editor reviews the revisions and holds article for compilation with other articles to form an issue.
9. The issue is compiled and formatted by the editor.
10. The issue is sent for typesetting.
11. The editor proofreads the issue.
12. The issue is printed and distributed.

The time frame for this process can stretch from several months to a year, depending on the publication schedule, the backlog of articles to be published, the time of year the submission is received, and other factors.

There are several things an author can do to increase the chances for publication as well as shorten the timeline above. These include:

- Know the audience of the journal. Do not submit an article foreign to the journal's focus. "Generic" articles will be given more favorable consideration if the topic is somehow tied to the journal's audience. A journal's audience can be determined by reading the author submission guidelines, reviewing articles published in recent issues, or investigating the conference Web site of the publication's organization.
- Pay attention to author submission guidelines, especially length of manuscript, how to submit attachments (photos, graphics, etc.), format for references and method of submission.
- How-to or "How we did it well in my library" articles are generally a tough sell. These articles are not considered "scholarly" or "research" by many editors and reviewers. Whether or not this is a valid viewpoint, there is still hope for consideration of these articles. The article may be strengthened by including results of a literature search or a comparison of similar methods used in the profession. The author could also contrast the method used with those used by other libraries or organizations. A little forethought and investigation can make a how-to article more acceptable for publication.
- Be patient, but feel free to contact an editor for an update. Editors consider several submissions simultaneously. This, coupled with performing their other job duties, means time may have slipped away from them in keeping in contact with authors.

As editor of the *Southeastern Librarian*, I have seen many reviewer comments regarding improving a manuscript and reasons for rejection. The most common suggestions for improvement are:

- expand or better focus the thesis or conclusion in order to lend more support to the topic being addressed.
- ensure consistency in writing style (need for use of active voice, third person, etc.)
- adhere to submission guidelines

These reviewer comments are sent to the author when a submission is provisionally accepted. They offer viewpoints which the author may not have considered or reflect ways to clarify and enhance the text. Most authors welcome these suggestions and incorporated them into their texts. Some viewpoints may not meet the intent of the author and are not used. When making revisions, the editor generally notifies the author of any changes, since even the most innocent change of a word or phrase may alter the meaning of the text in a way that does not reflect the author's intent.

The most common reasons given for rejection of an article include:

- The length of article does not meet submission guidelines.
- The topic discussed adds no new ideas to the profession or is so basic as to be general knowledge to the profession or audience.
- The topic is not discussed fully or in-depth. Specific examples or research of the literature are not included.
- The topic is inappropriate for the journal's audience.
- The article does not include any citations.
- Poor writing style. Even though an author may think he or she has expressed ideas clearly, it can be invaluable to have another colleague critique an article before submission. It may also be valuable for this colleague to be outside the specific area of expertise addressed in the article, so a determination can be made whether the article is readable and clearly conveys the author's intent.

A good submission can strengthen both author and journal reputations. One way for the profession to keep up-to-date is for its members to learn from one another through reading the professional literature. The opinions outlined above will help in the expression of ideas which will benefit both the author and the profession.

Showcase Your Writing with a Professional Portfolio

Gabriel Morley

One of the most important things you should have as a professional writer is a portfolio or clip file of your previously published writing. Your portfolio allows you to showcase your writing samples to potential editors. It doesn't need to be fancy, but it does need to look professional. This is your personal marketing tool kit. Make sure it is thorough and effectively displays your talents.

A portfolio or clip file should contain your best published work. At the beginning of your writing career, you want to have all your published clips at your disposal. As you grow as a writer and publish more, you will filter out subpar work and exhibit only your best clips.

The Proof Is in the Writing

Your clips serve as evidence you can write and that other editors have been able to work with you. Clips also mean you are familiar with the editorial process. It's alright to ask pertinent editorial questions, but repeated phone calls about when you're going to see your name in print is annoying and will not win you many friends in the publishing community.

You would be surprised by the number of aspiring writers who refuse to have their work edited or changed in any way. If you are not willing to work with an editor to make your writing as good as it can be and fit the publication's specifications, then don't bother submitting. Almost everyone's writing gets edited for one reason or another.

You should keep accurate records of all your published clips. I have an index of published clips for quick reference. Your records should contain:

- name of the publication in which the article appeared
- date the article ran in the publication
- editor's name, phone number and e-mail address
- how much you were paid (if anything)

(If you're an academic librarian it is important to have this information for your tenure review, too.)

It is a good idea to include a wide variety of your published work from book reviews to feature articles to scholarly work. The portfolio not only serves as a means for proving to editors that you can write and that you have been published in the past, but it also neatly categorizes your publishing history for your own purposes. If you need to refer to something you wrote in the past it will be easy to find of your clips are stored in an organized manner.

In the old days, writers used a folder to hold their published pieces. Many writers still do. I use an oversized manila envelope. I keep newspaper articles in one envelope, magazine and journal articles in another and fiction in a third. With the proliferation of computers and the Internet, many writers have begun keeping electronic files in addition to their hard-copy clips.

Many writers have recently made the leap to cyberspace by creating personal Web pages to promote themselves and their writing. This is a personal decision that requires careful consideration. What you put on the Internet is available for public viewing in most cases. Unless you password protect your site, you won't have much control over who sees your site. Potential editors may do an Internet search and turn up unfavorable information about you or your writing ability. If you do create a Web site to display your work, make sure you only put your best writing on the site and keep it professional. More and more editors are willing to go to your Web site to look at your clips.

I don't have a personal Web site, but I do have an electronic clip file of my published work that is ready to be e-mailed or printed at a moment's notice. As more and more magazines and journals begin accepting electronic submissions, it's important to be ready with some writing samples. You need to make sure these are easy to access and saved as either a Word or Adobe document. The key is to make the clip as easy to access and read as possible. Preferably, you should ask the editor how he or she would like to receive the writing sample. If you make this step difficult for editors, they might be hesitant to work with you.

As tempting as it is to throw out your hard-copy clip file, don't do it. Keep a hard copy of all your clips, even the ones published electronically. Your job is to make it as easy as possible for the editor. Often, the people who are easiest to work with get more work.

Maintain an Assortment of Clips

An important tip to remember is to have a mixture of writing styles available in your portfolio. You never know when an editor might ask to see something different. Perhaps you are interested in writing a feature article about a new book, but the editor just wants a review. You need to have something in your clips to show the editor you can write a feature and not just book reviews. Sometimes as deadlines approach, an editor may need something short to fill a hole. Be prepared to jump on any opportunities that come along.

If you're just starting out and don't have any clips to put in a portfolio, don't despair. Many publications will publish book reviews with your byline or small opinion pieces. Most writers and editors will tell you this is the easiest way to break into publishing. Not only do you get a byline, but you begin to form relationships with editors. If an editor knows you and knows you're interested in writing feature articles or a regular column, when the opportunity arises, the editor is more likely to call you.

To get published try some of these tips:

- Seek out lesser-known publications and publishing opportunities that veteran writers might pass up. Even if you have to write for free at first, your goal is to amass publishing credits and show professional development.
- Look at nontraditional library sources to build your portfolio, such as math journals or business publications. These areas often need books reviewed.
- Timing is key. If you are serious about getting published, you always have to be on the lookout for opportunities. Sometimes, it doesn't matter how much experience you have or what your credentials are, it's simply a matter of being first to the table. The week before I got this assignment, I e-mailed an editor who had posted a call for book reviewers on Beyond the Job. However, the editor had posted the call three days earlier and all the books had been promised to other reviewers who had responded the first day of the posting.

Don't be discouraged if you have some bumps in the road. Sometimes getting published is just a matter of timing. Improve your chances by making your portfolio and clips look as professional as possible. I used to think sending out clips to editors was easy until I saw someone who had prepared a whole book of color clips that looked fantastic. I knew if he had taken the time to prepare those clips he was probably a good reporter and writer. I would have hired him.

Basic Staffing Study

SIAN BRANNON

It started with a memo from the director of the libraries: "We all know and feel it at the end of the day that we are working harder. I want you to know that we are beginning a process to begin working smarter." The process would begin with a study conducted system wide to determine what cost savings and staff redistribution could occur among all library branches. The central library in particular was overdue for a reevaluation of its staffing levels and work processes. The results of the study would also be critical to the preparation for the expansion of the southern branch, which would be occurring without the addition of any new personnel. A caveat, however, was that the study needed to be done within a few months, before the new fiscal year began.

The goals of the study were simple enough:

- Determine how many library assistants, librarians, and clerks are truly needed at each of the three libraries in the system through a system of averages.

  Determine how many staff are needed in other departments, including Courier/Transit Services, Interlibrary Loan, Systems Administration, Technical Services, and Library Administration.

  Maximize everyone's performance with current staffing levels.

  Look for areas to streamline workloads and processes.

  Use statistics to justify the changes.

  Implement changes before new fiscal year started.

We gathered a team that included the director, the three branch managers, and a few representatives from various departments. The team decided to conduct the study in phases. We also determined what data we wanted to gather and communicated our intentions to the appropriate city departments. In each phase, the first step was to define job tasks for uniformity in data reporting.

Phase One: Technical Services

Luckily, before the staffing study officially began, the technical services staff had started creating a manual for their department, so they had been tracking the "what" and "how-to" of their operations already. What they focused on next was the quantity of items handled, the length of time these items spent in each area of the department, and the number of people needed to accomplish the tasks. It was essential to determine which processes could be outsourced. Because of this examination of day-to-day tasks, it was easy to see that certain mundane items, such as title cards and placing barcodes, were taking up too much staff time. Purchasing a product for electronic invoicing also helped free up time for cataloging and authority control.

Phase Two: Circulation Clerks and Library Assistants

A circulation clerk and a library assistant also served on the study team. They were included to provide their coworkers with instruction with regard to the study and to direct questions back to the management team. After identifying and defining the basic tasks of each group of workers, the tasks were put onto the library's Intranet for all to see. We utilized two forms to track the activities of workers:

1. a typical workday form, which divided the day into 15-minute increments
2. a daily summary sheet, which identified and tracked the numerical data that we wanted to gather, such as the number of checkout sessions, holds pulled, items shelved, library cards issued, and information questions answered

Staff used these forms to track one month's worth of work. Ideally, a study would cover a range of months, and ultimately months in different parts of the year, to get a better picture of actual workloads. However, due to our time constraints a month was the best we could do.

Phase Three: Data Compilation

The completed forms were forwarded to a designated "compiler." It took a considerable amount of time to transcribe each worker's form into summary spreadsheets with computed averages of time spent doing each task. The forms also needed to be summarized and compared. It was discovered that even though substantial time went into choosing and defining tasks to use, many staff made up their own tasks, tracked their numbers differently, and therefore had a difficult time filling in the forms.

Rough, basic comparisons were made between the amounts of time spent by workers on simple tasks. It was also evident that each branch had a distinct process of handling items in circulation, and utilized their library assistants for different tasks. Now was the time to create a more uniform job description for these assistants and identify the best methods of handing items.

Phase Four: Statistics

Aside from the input given by the workers themselves, there was raw data already gathered daily that was taken into consideration. We previously were tracking at each branch:

- hourly gate count and total library visits
- total circulation

- number of hours open
- daily overdue notices printed
- drive-through window transactions

These numbers over the course of the study, along with the knowledge of quantity of staff at each location, afforded us the opportunity to compare the number of visits per hour at each branch, the number of items handled at each branch, the average circulation per staff, the circulation per hour, and many other calculations. With the addition of salary figures, we could also ascertain the labor cost per customer and per circulation.

What We Accomplished

The director warned staff at the beginning of the study: "Please know that in all likelihood your current job duties and responsibilities will change." Staff were told that they may be transferred to another department or branch and that their job descriptions could be redefined. This was startling to some staff, but others took it in stride. It was widely known about the strict municipal budget and previous reductions in city employees, so most were assuaged by knowing that at least they were keeping their jobs.

Time was limited, so the study did not adequately assess the details of certain departments like Interlibrary Loan or Administration. A phase for librarians began, but was not completed because of discrepancies in the delineations of tasks. An agreement could not be reached on what constituted their tasks. These are in the works for next year.

Many cost-savings changes resulted from the study. It was obvious that too much circulation staff time was spent in the area of processing pulled holds for patrons. Not only were the hold shelves relocated to the public floor instead of behind the circulation desks, but a software program was also purchased to create preprinted hold labels. Another software program was installed to handle reservations and printing coordination for the public computers.

Staffing levels did change as a result of the study. Individual staff to staff comparisons were not the purpose of the study, which was discouraging to some staff who thought that because the data they collected was not used intensely, it was a waste of their time. On the contrary, it provided administration with data for job descriptions and new ideas for relocating some of the paraprofessional staff. In a few years when we are ready to start this whole process over again, hopefully at a time when we are planning to expand again, we will be sure to go slower and make sure everyone knows what it is that we are trying to accomplish. More planning, explanation, and spot checks during the data gathering will surely help.

Building the Dream Teen Space

JILL S. CARPENTER

For a few fortunate libraries, teen areas are already a dream come true. Most teen librarians, however, have only fantasized about creating the perfect teen space. At the Pikes Peak Library District (PPLD) in Colorado Springs, Colorado, the East Teen Center is quickly becoming a reality! For those of you who are still drooling over the *VOYA* "YA Spaces of your Dreams" articles, here are few helpful tips to get started on your dream teen space:

- Survey local schools. The response from students and teachers will be an overwhelming "YES!" and will let your administration know that local teens think a teen space in the library is important to the community.
- Survey your youth advisory council. This survey can be more in-depth than the school survey. Allow the students space to write their own arguments for a teen area. This lets your administration hear from vested teens in their own words.
- Scope out a space. Look around the library. Where is space being wasted? Is it that storage room? Is it that alcove? Can those magazines be moved to another area? Most likely any area that you spy for your teen area will not be empty. You will have to devise a plan for shifting books or containing storage items somewhere else. Make sure that you have that plan in hand before asking for the space.
- Suggest a space. Once you've singled out a possible area subtly begin suggesting the idea of carving out that space for teens. Never officially ask for the space without first giving the administration time to ruminate over the idea.

You Have a Space, Now What?

Throwing posters on the walls and reshelving the teen fiction isn't enough! Get a focus group! We included teens from our youth advisory council (YAC) as well as interested teens recruited with the school survey. We wanted ideas from our YAC as well as fresh ideas from other teens in the community. Focus groups allow you to direct all of that survey input into feasible designs. And with teen focus groups you will receive confirmation on what makes a "cool" teen area. Here are some tips for making the most out of your focus groups.

- Give the teens cameras to take pictures around town of designs that they like and ideas they would like to see in the teen area.
- Bring in design books to get their synapses sparking.

- Bring in color books so they can learn to pair color choices and make wise decisions about carpet and walls.
- Ask the teens what services the teen area should offer. Should it focus on entertainment, education or both? Should the space include patron computers, a reference desk or a college information center?
- When the teens know what they want the area to look like and what services the teen area will offer, have them speak to your board of directors. Hearing the design proposal straight from the teens is more convincing to the board and most definitely more impressive!

Architects?

If your teen area design is large enough to require an architect, make sure the architects and focus group meet! The architects need to know that you are serious about creating a teen-designed space. Here are a few tips for making the architect/teen meeting run smoothly:

- Make sure the teens know that their initial plans may change. The architect will have new ideas, new spins and a ton of design knowledge. Make sure the teens understand that they must be willing to make compromises with the architects.
- The resulting plan must be a mesh of teen and architect ideas. The teens have thought long and hard about what they want in a teen center, and their desires and ideas must be included in the final design.
- During the meeting be sure to remain neutral. Yes, your design ideas matter too, but be sure to keep everyone open-minded and ready to consider all ideas.

A Note About Grants

I didn't write any grants but the PPLD Foundation did. If you are writing your own grants, good luck! However, I did write a "case statement" that gave the PPLD Foundation all of the information needed to write grants. The case statement answered the following questions:

- Who benefits from a teen area?
- What is unique about your teen area? Why should your teen area get a grant over others?
- How does the teen area fit into the vision of your library?
- What is so great about your library and your teen services?
- Who are the teen staff?

Write this statement early, before you write any grant proposals. You can then use pieces of this statement to argue for your teen area or tailor it to specific proposals.

Reality

Where does the dream end? The sky! PPLD teen services, the focus group and the architects dreamed big. We put everything into the teen center plan that we wanted, with no thought to cost. Did we do it because PPLD had an unlimited budget? No! Like everyone else, PPLD had a very limited budget for the East Teen Center, but we were also counting on grant money and we didn't want to sell ourselves short. What if we got a huge grant and we had only created a plan that was worth the library's approved teen area budget? On the other hand, if we created a "sky's the limit" plan, and didn't get the money, we could always cut back later. You'd be surprised at how much you can actually get out of your dream plan on a limited budget. Yes, we still had to cut out a few luxury items, but we eventually found ways to get everything else! Here are a few tips for getting what you want:

- Get your IT Department on board with the project. Your IT staff will have really cool ideas for teen-oriented technology and they might even pay for some of that technology!
- Think Target, Wal-Mart and Ikea. You do not have to stick with conventional library furniture and supply companies!
- Repeat the phrase, "But it's what the teens want." When it comes time to begin trimming that dream plan, the easiest method is to simply not do something that the teens want. The difficult method is to get creative. Getting creative means more planning, more thinking and more effort but you'll be more satisfied with the results.
- Be prepared to work with all departments in your library. Creating a new teen space doesn't just affect teen services; it will affect your IT Department, Circulation and Shelving departments as well as Collection Development. However large or small your teen area, creating a new space for a specific user group within the library will affect everyone! Shelvers will have to know what books to shelve in the new area. Collection Development may need to create a new location code for the library catalog.

Patience is a virtue. PPLD has waited over two years to see construction begin on the East Teen Center but it's been worth every minute. After waiting this long, we can be certain that we are getting a space that teens will love. Patience will give you time to get what you and your teens want. And given enough time, all dreams can come true.

Connecting with Customers

RUTH A. BAREFOOT

"I love doing my job now!" says a longtime San José employee. In our bustling California Bay Area where millions of people are on the move each day, San José Public Libraries is coming up with creative ways to extend its most valuable resource: staff. We're very motivated to growing people for direct customer service because of our rapidly growing gate counts, more complex customer demand, and changing technology. We know our customers highly value what staff deliver: Customer service where and when it's needed without the customer having to ask. The key is assigning staff appropriately to deliver consistent high-quality service to more than 25,000 people daily. Could we be a victim of our own success? Oh yeah! We have surveyed our library users repeatedly to continually align our resources to what customers want. In this book the author's essay, "Customers in the Driver's Seat" has several points on why and how we changed as a service organization without changing our library's mission. What has changed is we are now seeing ourselves as partners and collaborators with our customers and their changing needs. Let's walk into one of our San José libraries.

Arrive at the door of a newly built San José library and drop your return materials straight into the backroom before entering the building. Why? We have staff dedicated to a streamlined check-in process, rather than in traditional libraries where check-in is shared on the floor for public to see: a codependent model. In the old model floor staff would be inundated with multiple, sometimes complex customer-service issues that continually arrest effective materials handling. In the new model staff perform materials handling behind the scenes, bringing relief for ongoing and ever-increasing materials processing. Fewer mistakes are made and we are providing something much more visible to the customer: face-to-face dedicated customer interaction.

Now that our clerks and pages are freed up from a streamlined check-in, they are moving out on the floor to accomplish a great deal more for the customer, such as teaching them how to be self-sufficient. In a traditional library most librarians are busy dealing with the majority of floor interaction. If you study the types of interactions going on, and San José did, we found that more than 80 percent was *not* librarian level interaction. Why would we place our most expensive staff out on the floor to deal with the majority of work that is not suited to their training? Were we placing our doctors in the waiting room? To turn this around we needed to address political and emotional change before beginning training. It was political because librarians have traditionally covered the floor while clerical staff covered the back room. Librarians felt that they were doing a fabulous job taking care of the customer. And they were, but how much of the professional level work was being put off to another day, month, or year? Worlds were clashing and a joint staff effort was needed to develop the tools for the new model. The primary principle of putting the customer first in all decisions helped devise the road map to clarify workloads, job descriptions, scheduling guidelines and even staff rebalancing. Task forces worked on specific areas that helped define changes needed for all staff to help customers:

- use self-check machines
- pay fines online
- reserve a computer or group study room
- look up a title in the catalog and reserve material 24/7
- explore library layout through tours and orientations in other languages
- use the display collections designed to "package" materials that minimize first level reference questions
- refer questions if necessary
- place holds
- issue cards, explain borrowing policy
- troubleshoot equipment, replace printer tapes
- accept undisputed fines, explain "blocks" on patron records, set items missing
- change customer PIN
- security stop
- locate information about library services on WebPac
- search catalog (and nearby library systems) using simple search, by author and title

For the clerks and pages to accomplish this they needed to be released from behind the desk and back rooms to teach customers on the floor. Customers are reducing the need for desk assistance because they prefer the self-directed service counterparts listed above. Staffing circulation desks seemed extravagant. Librarians who are quite comfortable out on the floor with customers were crucial in defining training and mentoring for this change. Enabling a wider range of our staff to deliver a larger number of services improved our customer interaction and ratings because customers perceive everyone as helpful. More customers were confident in the library and needed less repeated assistance. When you survey customers the one thing that really intimidates them is the desk. They dislike identifying themselves as needing help and nine out of ten don't ask in the retail world. Most customers want to be self-sufficient.

Librarians in our branches were balancing the floor work and doing a multitude of other things. How do we place the right staff to do the right work? Since most of our branches are 28,000 square feet or less, a practical step was to combine the various service points into one, thus forming one customer queue line and minimizing confusion. Doing this has improved crosstraining, teamwork, and communication.

One of our goals is to make certain that customers have a positive interaction with staff and are not caught in a loop of finding the "right" staff member for assistance.

Our San José Way Service Model has outlined basic services any staff can deliver in a seamless fashion from anywhere on the floor. Staff work from a hub or single service point where staff tools are located, but are assigned to focus on a service "zone" and rove farther afield to help customers. Such areas are the children's area, the adult area or the tech center. What is different in this model? We have a wider range of staff able to fill this need because it is more appropriately assigned now. Also, customers are not given the runaround or sent on scavenger hunts to find their favorite staff. Librarians are on call as needed, when it's most visible, which further maximizes their planning time.

These are some of the steps we've taken in San José to help our staff thrive working the floor and help customers connect up with resources, materials, and people. Staff has a more successful interaction with new customers because they have the time to help them now, wherever they are on the floor. What happened to other librarian staff savings? Librarians are now increasing programming and partnership programming with outside agencies, teaching online tools, training and mentoring other staff, working closely with central selectors, providing analysis on how well this is all working and coming up with ideas to improve the model.

Or, as one of our own says, "I spent years in the profession seeing the need for change and coming up against roadblocks, whether from levels above me, or from staff I supervised. Trying to be flexible and responsive to customer needs in a 'we've always done it this way' environment that got to be so frustrating, I left the profession! I'm glad I came back, because now I'm part of the San José Way and I love it!"

I Play Two Roles at My Library

Elizabeth M. Timmins

I play two roles at my library. I am the library director and the children's programmer. This has been fun for me! I draw upon my education for both positions.

My background in education has taught me to collaborate with others and to share resources. In the role of children's programmer, I teamed up with two other library directors whose libraries are in close proximity to ours. We wrote a system grant and had it funded so that we can take field trips to local nature preserves. This idea fit in with the summer reading program for this summer, Paws, Claws, Scales, and Tales. We call our bus the Magic Library Bus, and we pick up passengers at all three library locations. The trips are fun and educational. Also, because the field trips are fully funded by the grant, we are meeting the needs of families who might not otherwise be able to visit nature preservers on their own.

I wrote a little jingle that we sing on the Magic Library Bus and it is sung to the tune of "Take Me Out to the Ballgame."

> Take me out of the library
> Board the Magic Library Bus
> Look at us all in our fancy caps
> We don't care if we never come back
> For it's time to honor nature
> We love paws, claws, scales and tales
> For it's one, two, three
> Libraries that rock
> Black Creek, Shiocton and Seymour!

This is the schedule of trips for the Magic Library Bus:

Friday, June 16: Navarino Nature Center
Friday, June 30: 1,000 Island Environmental Center, Kaukauna
Friday, July 14: North Park with naturalist Randy Korb presenting Wisconsin Frogs at Black Creek at 11:00
Friday, July 21: Barkhausen Waterfowl Preserve
Friday, July 28: New Zoo in Green Bay
Thursday, August 3: Nature's niche naturalist Dino at Buboltz Nature Center
Friday, August 11: Mosquito Hill Nature Center

The system grant funds the cost of the bus for each field trip as well as fees for demonstrations and entrance fees. The Magic Library Bus takes reservations for up to 40 children and 20 adults (the capacity of the bus) and pick up children and adults at each of the three libraries. Bus service is provided by Conradt Bus Service of Shiocton, Wisconsin. I have the largest location so we have 30 slots on the bus and the other two locations (Black Creek and Shiocton) have 15 slots each.

Collection development has been one of the most challenging and inspirational responsibilities for me as a library director. For this task my educational background taught me to capitalize on talents and to be open to new ideas.

Collection development is an exciting endeavor. When we are creative with how we approach this task we find that our collection becomes stronger and our circulation goes up. Strategies that have been successful to our library have two characteristics. They are economical and give ownership of the library to the community that we serve. I hope that you will get a new idea or two by reading this essay. Most importantly, enjoy yourself! Librarianship is the greatest profession in the world!

As a brand-new library director in November 2002, I knew that collection development was going to be both fun and challenging. At one of our first staff meetings, I discussed with my staff what areas of the collection they felt they had strengths in and I assigned those areas to them for collection development. Capitalizing on my staff's talents improved our collection immediately. I am blessed with a small but diverse staff. One staff member knows all about gardening, breeding dogs, cooking and great adult reads. Another staff member knows gentle fiction, agriculture, medical reference, and herbs. A third staff member is great at the DVD and video collection as well as young adult books. My strengths are children's books, travel, and some adult nonfiction.

We revived our Friends of the Muehl Public Library (FMPL) in 2003. They began some very successful fundraising efforts. At each monthly Friends meeting, I am invited to make a request for spending funds for the library. We came to the agreement of having a collection development augmentation project. Each month the Friends pay $300 to boost a certain area. The chart below is an example of how I organized this.

January	*February*	*March*	*April*	*May*	*June*
CD-ROMs	Requests for purchase	Movies or graphic novels	Kids and summer reading program theme items	CCBC young adult	CCBC junior

July	*August*	*September*	*October*	*November*	*December*
Paperback of all genres	Classics	Reference	Accelerated reader titles	Best sellers	Reference

My next move was to give some ownership of the collection to the patrons. I did this in two ways. First, we developed a request for purchase form that is available at our counter and on our Web site. Patrons have come up with really good ideas for items to purchase. Second, a discount book store opened in Green Bay and a young adult patron said there were lots of great books for the young adult area. I talked it over with the Friends and they agreed to send the patron with $200 to purchase young adult books. She has done an outstanding job. She knows where there are holes for both young women and young men AND she is a bargain shopper.

Another great idea was when our library established a wish list with Amazon.com. Any library can do this. When people ask us what our wishes are for our library, we refer them to the link on our Web site. It is a terrific management tool for us because we can add to the list at any time. We can also delete items from the list as our wishes are filled. We have had wishes filled by anonymous donors. We have had some happy surprises from as far away as California!

Recently, I used the Barnes & Noble wish list for another terrific opportunity. The swim club in our community was doing a fundraiser through Barnes & Noble in Green Bay. They invited us to participate. For every book on the list purchased, the book came to the library and the proceeds of the sale went to the swim club. In other words, people were making two donations. We received ten new books as a result of this endeavor.

In conclusion, I would say that we need to keep libraries in the forefront of people's minds. Patrons will think about ways to help us with our collection which is the largest part of what we do. In addition, try to think in a new way and ponder about how your choices benefit your library. We are always presented with opportunities. We need to make a habit of taking advantage of them!

Teens as Library Employees

Thayla Wright

Staffing a library can be difficult. Working hours are not traditional, money is frequently a problem and finding people who can do the job is not as easy as some might think.

For over a decade the Arthur Johnson Memorial Library in Raton, New Mexico, has hired high school teenagers as part-time library aides as a solution to these problems. In 13 years we have not been without at least two teenage employees at a time. In the decade that I have been the director, I have found that the right teenager is quick to learn, consistent and reliable. An added bonus is that their presence tends to draw other teenagers to the library as patrons.

Hiring the Right Teenager

Just as every adult is not suited to library work, neither is every teen. But there are certain qualities to look for if you want to hire a teenage employee

- Involvement: A teen who is involved in school activities and organizations will be involved at work. School activities might create some scheduling challenges, but the benefits more than offset the occasional difficulties. Consider the compatibility of your scheduling needs with the teenager's schedule when hiring. Sports practice and games eliminate some potential employees for us, as our needs require that they work after school, every other Thursday evening, and every other Saturday. But we have hired students who are in organizations such as band, choir, student government, National Honor Society, Business Professionals of America, art club, theater club, Eagle Scouts, the Student Organization for Youth and tennis. The enthusiasm that leads a student to participate in such activities will carry right over onto the job.
- Ability: Good students learn quickly. We pay attention to an applicant's extracurricular activities as an indicator of mental quickness. Our applications require references, and I notice if a teacher or group sponsor is listed. Contacting these references will help determine how the students are perceived by adults who interact with them on a regular basis.

  Set up a test that relates to the job your teen is applying for. I administer a short test on the Dewey decimal system that requires them to place groups of Dewey numbers in order. I also ask them to write a brief response to a simple reference question. These tests help me assess the applicant's numeric and language skills.

Ask your current teen employees about who they feel could do the job. They usually know students who meet the criteria who are interested in working in the library. Your teens will not be involved in hiring, but their opinions can be a valuable resource.

- **Attitude:** Teenage attitude gets a lot of negative publicity, but many young people have the proper attitude for public service. You can spot this during an interview. Does the teen seem withdrawn or interested? Do they look you in the eye? Do they have reasons other than money for wanting the job? Do they carry a chip on their shoulder or do they display self-confidence? Often you will be interviewing someone who has never held a job before. If you set them at ease, you will get a much better sense of their personality and style. Look for a teenager who has a sense of humor. One young lady had a patron approach the desk and ask, "Do you have a yeast infection?" Our teen wondered if answering this was part of her job before the other shoe dropped and she realized the patron wanted to check out *The Yeast Connection*. She showed great professionalism by waiting until she had served the patron before coming into the office to laugh in private.

Training New Teenage Staff

As one of my new teenagers recently said, "I thought this job would be a piece of cake. Was I wrong!" Even though they are provided with a job description, our teens are still surprised at the amount and variety of work in the library. I recommend using the following simple techniques when training teens.

- Start with the jobs they will do every day. If the job is desk service, introduce new teens to the checkout system when the library is closed. Have them do practice work before they ever serve a patron. Keep an experienced employee with them for several days until you are satisfied they are comfortable with the procedures. Introduce your teens to shelving with a complete tour of the library and a shelving manual that meets your specific needs. Have teens shelve books on their side so the work is easily checked by an experienced staff member. Have them correct their own shelving errors.

- When they master one procedure, introduce them to another. Teenagers who do the same thing day after day are quickly bored. Learning a variety of jobs will keep them interested for the duration of their employment. The more they can do, the more valuable they will be to you as an employee.

- Teach them your policies, procedures, and what is good library practice. Teens are like any other employee. They need to know how you do things, why you do them, what is legal, and how best to interact with the public. Check to make sure they are doing things properly. We have occasional competitions in which the employee who wins gets a prize. The prize doesn't need to be expensive. Chocolate is a favorite and is usually passed around.

- Give them fun jobs. These might include participating in children's programs, computer work, or setting up visual displays. It depends on what your teen enjoys doing. One of our young men was such an expert on the Titanic that I had him create a display that included a scale model of the Titanic and handouts with all the esoteric facts he could find. He was in heaven. Because of this display, he later spoke to several community groups on the subject.

- Make sure they know you are there for them. Because teens are inexperienced, they may not realize they can come to you for a variety of reasons. Encourage them to approach you with problems, questions, ideas and desires. This will give them confidence in you as their supervisor, and you won't be left out of this amazing loop. Teen ideas here have resulted in tripled attendance at Summer Story Hour, an expanded youth section, an audio center, a yearly Banned Books display, a birthday party for Harry Potter, wearing crowns to work, kissing a pig and dyeing our hair purple (well, only one of us did that).

The tips I have listed are just that. There are no unbreakable rules for hiring the right teenager. Use your own judgment. I recently interviewed someone who answered the question, "Why do you want to work here?" with "I want to make money." But he looked me in the eye when he said it, and he is the top student in his class. I'm glad I hired him.

Your staff and patrons will come to know and love your teenagers. The generation gap does not seem to exist. Our teens interact with and enjoy (almost) everyone. Those graduating and going on have told us, "This is the best job ever." We have told them, "We're so glad you came here." For all of us, adults and teens, working together has been a positive experience.

Time Management Skills in Writing

LORIENE ROY *and* SARA ALBERT

You have found a topic to write about. Perhaps you are writing a thesis or a dissertation. Maybe you are preparing a contribution to a newsletter, a magazine, or a journal, or possibly you are writing a book review. You are excited about this opportunity but then reality sets in: You have work to complete and the deadline is already looming near. You are worried about writer's block. How do you organize your life so that you can complete this work? In this essay we introduce some time-management skills that might help you meet this—and future—writing responsibilities!

Review the Manuscript Submission Requirements

Read over the author instructions, paying special attention to the acceptable word length. You can estimate that each page of manuscript has around 250 words; divide the word length by 250 to determine the number of pages you will need. New writers often think that publishers want lengthy, heavily documented contributions. You may be surprised to learn that brief manuscripts are often preferred. This information makes the writing assignment feel doable.

Visualize Your Final Project

Find completed samples that were published in the same publication. This helps create a mental imprint of how much text is needed and the layout of the page. A visual check helps you equate the requested word count with a completed document. It also gives you a preview of what your writing will look like when it is published!

Set Reasonable Goals

Do not expect to do your best work at the last minute or without one or more revisions. Many writers have to write steadily over time. Unrealistic goals sometimes lead to discouragement which can cause missed deadlines and unfinished work. Also set intermediate goals with short-term deadlines. This will allow you to indicate to others (and yourself) that you are making good progress!

Create a Writing Game Plan

Imagine that your writing project will take 100 hours to complete and you have one month to complete the work. You will need to devote about three hours and 20 minutes a day to writing. Divide the daily three hours of writing into segments. Set aside the first five-minute segment for an intensive writing period. Then increase your writing segments by five minutes until you are productively working for up to an hour.

Write an Outline, Cartoon, or Storyboard

List the major divisions of the article. Then draft a map to accompany the outline. You may use flowcharting software to diagram the topics you plan to cover. Add predicted word-count limits to each section of the outline. If you are cowriting, assign segments to each writer. This map plus word count becomes your storyboard.

Avoid Last-Minute Tension

While many people claim to work well under pressure, you may be more productive if you stay on top of deadlines with a more measured writing pace. This avoids having to deal with last-minute stressors, such as unexpected visitors, the encroachment of other work responsibilities, illness, and technology glitches.

Read and Write

Except for dissertations or review articles, you usually do not have to read or summarize all key publications related to your topic, but you may need to read up on your topic before and during the writing process to be sure you are up-to-date. Alternate between writing and reading. Create your bibliography of related publications as you encounter these resources. If you wait to create your bibliography, you will end up rechecking citations and otherwise wasting time.

Summarize Your Topic

Can you summarize your ideas in one sentence? This will be the hook sentence for your work. You can then work to extend this sentence into 50 words, a paragraph, and then 100 words.

Recruit a Cowriter

It is useful to have a second pair of eyes to read over your work, contribute ideas, and help package your writing for submission. Acknowledge your writing weaknesses and preferences. Your writing partner may be more skilled at choosing catchy manuscript titles or at creating transitions or writing the summary. He or she may have special technical skills and be able to improve the overall appearance of the manuscript by creating tables or illustrations. Report to each other frequently and even daily.

Organize a Writing Space

One of my colleagues has a small book cart on which she organizes the supplies for her current writing project. Your writing space can be that small, or you could have an entire room to write. Whatever space you use, make sure that preparing your writing space is not an exercise in procrastination. Some people write best at home with a radio or television on. Others write in restaurants or other public spaces. Some people need a bland, quiet work setting, while others want noise and to be surrounded by people. Test one or more writing environments to determine what works best for *you*.

Avoid Working with a Blank Page or Screen

A blank page or screen can stifle your writing process. This may be a time to revert to three- by five-inch notecards. Jot down keywords, ideas, or phrases on each notecard and use them to construct sentences, which you can then type in.

Sneak Up on the Difficult Sections

Introductions and summaries are often the most difficult portions to write. You might write one of the other sections of the paper first. Generally, it is easiest to write about what action you took.

Know What You Will Do Next

Take breaks when you are at a point when you know exactly what you will do when you come back to your work. This reduces the recovery time needed to return to your writing frame of mind. For longer breaks or at the end of the day, create a "to do next" note to yourself. This way you know what needs to be done when you sit down again. This helps you avoid the feeling that you are starting at the beginning each time you come back to the assignment.

Defer Gratification and Set Up a Reward System

Consider what actions to take to reward yourself. Save that shopping trip, movie, or food treat as a reward for meeting an intermediate deadline. Add small incentives, such as playing a game of solitaire, as a reward for meeting your daily writing goal.

Reduce Interruptions

People often face numerous interruptions in the workplace. Consider working at home when you have a writing deadline. If this is not possible, let others know that you are writing under a tight deadline. Post a sign on your door asking others to send an e-mail or leave a note. Put your cell phone on vibrate.

Give Yourself a False Deadline

Plan to complete the article before the deadline. This tactic is especially helpful if you have two or more deadlines or important tasks due around the same time. Competing deadlines can lead to a logjam of thinking and stalled writing. On the other hand, completing even one task can help you make progress on other responsibilities.

Read Your Article Out Loud

Actually, read your draft out loud several times for content, for organization, and for grammar and writing style.

Take Notes

Carry around a notebook to jot down a good turn of phrase or idea for this — or the next — writing assignment.

Be Comfortable with Your Accomplishments

Do not let fear of not writing your best prevent you from finishing the work.

Finally, enjoy the writing experience! Having written is a great feeling that sometimes releases a positive artistic energy. We find that the best way to use that energy is to start another writing project!

New Distance Education Librarian

Tips and Tools from the Trenches

MELISSA AHO *and* SOMMER BERG-NEBEL

Distance education is one of the fastest growing areas in academia. If you are in a small community college, a career or for-profit college, or a large university, you must designate one staff member to help your students access and learn about the online library. Our particular story takes place in a career college in Minnesota. We hope that it helps you to strategically create or improve your own library's online services.

Once upon a time our college had only four campuses, four libraries, eight librarians and a few online classes. Today it has seven campuses, seven libraries, 14 full-time librarians, student workers, numerous online classes, online undergraduate programs, and a brand-new MBA online program. Things happened so fast that we went from one and a half librarians (who were not really offering any online services except an e-mail address) to one online librarian with 50 percent of her time allocated to online students.

Do You Need a Separate Online Librarian?

Why spend money on hiring someone new when you can have one of your current librarians add online responsibilities to her already overburdened work schedule? We tested this path the hard way. Our school started with one librarian kind of doing it and another librarian kind of following along and found that even with offering just a few online classes, this really did not work out. It ate up an incredible amount of time for the librarian, and the classes were not yet designed with online library instruction in mind.

When the college implemented online programs, our library was allowed to allocate 50 percent of one librarian's time for online and distance educational services. Next, our library attempted to clarify what services would be provided by the online librarian, and we embarked on an aggressive marketing campaign, ensuring accurate information was posted on the course management system (ours being Blackboard) and the library home page. We detailed the services the online librarian and online library offer and where to go for nonlibrary help.

How Do You Set Up as an Online Librarian?

What do you need besides a computer? We recommend creating a spreadsheet to track your queries and the amount of time spent devising an answer. This is your documentation to justify the existence of an online librarian or perhaps to show how you need to add hours, hire more staff, etc.

It is also important to make friends with your IT Department. This relationship can make or break your program. If you do not have a good line of communication with IT, it can create unbearable roadblocks.

Services to Offer Your Online Library Patrons

Create a separate Web page for your online library patrons with all the information they are going to need to succeed as online students. This could include links to the course management system, databases, handouts, and so forth.

Offering reference chat on a free messenger service is an excellent alternative if your school doesn't want to chip in for a virtual reference program. Try Trillian, a free instant chat download that supports multiple chat programs including MSN, Yahoo, and others.

Your library could also offer live online library information sessions for students and faculty. Offering a wide range of dates and times at the beginning of the quarter or semester is extremely helpful to your students who will not be able to participate in a residential library instruction session. We recommend separate sessions for students and faculty. Webinar software such as Microsoft's Live Meeting and WebEx are excellent platforms for delivering live instruction. A conference call can be set up through a conference call service to supply the audio portion if the interactive software does not support it.

No matter which online services your library offers, be sure to post the hours that you are available for e-mail and virtual reference with a disclaimer that the hours are subject to change.

Marketing Yourself and Your Services

It's helpful to have a list of the e-mail addresses for online students so you can send mass e-mails announcing new services and reference tools and products. Keeping in touch with students not only reminds them of your presence, but it also makes you more approachable and familiar.

Be sure to embed your contact information and services available in the course management system your institution uses. Make it as easy as possible for patrons to contact you and be aware of how you can help them.

What We Learned the Hard Way

Answering e-mail reference questions can be extremely time-consuming, so we figured out a way to be more efficient. We began saving the librarian's responses in a Word document, clearly marked by a sample question, so we could use them again. Information that needed to be modified in each response, such as suggested keywords and topic suggestions, was bolded in the document so that changes could be made quickly to match the query. Not only did turnaround time improve, but less time was spent writing each response, thus streamlining the online reference interview and answer delivery.

Unfortunately, the syllabi for online classes were the same ones that the residential classes used. This caused confusion as several of them stated that an hour of library instruction was required. Starting with the 2006 winter quarter, we offered live library instruction sessions. It turned out to be an excellent service. Online tutorials are also in the works for specific programs and basic library information.

Another obstacle was personnel changes in the Online Department. From the head of the program down to instructors, there was a constant turnover. This hampered us in coming up with a cohesive direction for the program and the online services. Thankfully this is no longer an issue.

The Future

Keep on the lookout for new technology, training sessions, and services that you can add to your library to better help your online library patrons. Podcasts and RSS (really simple syndication) feeds are gaining popularity and the possibilities for incorporating them into online library services are limitless. Book reviews, library announcements, and other information can be automatically downloaded to your patrons' aggregator.

As online programs expand, change, and adapt to new technology, the online librarian must be constantly looking toward the future. Try new things! Good Luck!

Online Resources

Trillian (www.ceruleanstudios.com)
Microsoft's Live Meeting (http://office.microsoft.com/livemeeting)
WebEx (www.webex.com)
Webinar tips and product information (www.charlwood.com/webinar_software.htm)
Conference call services (www.calleci.com) or (www.conferencecall.com)
Podcasting information and resources (http://en.wikipedia.org/wiki/Podcasting)
RSS information and resources [http://en.wikipedia.org/wiki/RSS_(protocol)]
RSS Feed Aggregators (www.newsonfeeds.com/faq/aggregators)
Tristana Reader/Aggregator (www.charlwood.com/tristana)

For Further Reading

"Guidelines for Implementing and Maintaining Virtual Reference Services." American Library Association. 2006. www.ala.org/ala/rusa/rusaprotools/referenceguide/virtrefguidelines.htm (accessed 05 May, 2006).
"Guidelines for Distance Learning Library Services." American Library Association. 2006. www.ala.org/acrl/resjune02.html (accessed 05 May, 2006).

"Developing Library and Information Services for Distance Education" www.col.org/knowledge/ks_libraryinfo.htm.

Cochrane, Todd. *Podcasting: The do-it-yourself guide.* Wiley, 2005.

Finkelstein, Ellen. *Syndicating Web Sites with RSS Feeds for Dummies.* Wiley, 2005.

Jones, Marie F. (Sept-Oct 2001). "Help! I'm the new distance librarian — where do I begin?" (Distance learning library services: The tenth off-campus library services conference; Part II). In *Journal of Library Administration*, 33, p397(13) (retrieved June 14, 2006, from *Expanded Academic ASAP* via Thomson Gale http://find.galegroup.com).

Nicholas, M. and Tomeo, M. (2005). "Can You Hear Me Now? Communicating Library Services to Distance Education Students and Faculty." *Online Journal of Distance Learning Administration, 8* (2). www.westga.edu/%7Edistance/ojdla/summer82/nicholas82.htm (retrieved June 14, 2002).

World Geography and WebCT

Victoria Lynn Packard

Being a librarian today is an exciting time with so many opportunities. No longer are librarians expected to stay in the library and wait for patrons to come to us. We are not only "allowed" but also expected to leave the building and form partnerships with other colleges on campus.

The paradigm of teaching is changing rapidly and so must we. Almost five years ago a new professor for world geography and I created a world geography distance education class. The World Geography 1303 level class was one of the first online classes. The original basic online class has grown to a multilevel WebCT class.

Universities are offering classes online to better accommodate their students, who can "attend" class and complete the assignments on their own schedules. Over time, the World Geography class has evolved from a basic online class to a WebCT module.

The World Geography WebCT class outline is as follows:

- Syllabus. The syllabus is a breakdown of the course with phone numbers, office hours, class description, and student learning objectives.
- Discussions. Students are able create study groups and discuss assignments.
- Calendar. The calendar lists beginning and closing dates and access times for tests and homework.
- E-mail. E-mail is used by class for discussion and class changes.
- Threaded News Groups (TNG). There are four geography-related topics. Students search the Internet and locate a Web site to answer each topic. They then post the URL to the class and state why it is a good site, using Web page evaluation criteria. Fellow students must respond to postings following the same criteria.
- Tests and Homework. Tests and homework are accessible during preset times.

Students learn how to maneuver within WebCT. They learn general Web usage and how to access the system, post messages, use threaded news groups, and e-mail.

The second part of the class deals with information literacy. Students learn to access the library from off campus. Many times this means reconfiguring their computers.

Distance education (DE) students need to know all the resources they have access to for their education. At Texas A&M University–Kingsville, students can sign up for a Texshare card. Texshare is a group of 697 libraries, including junior colleges, universities, and public and private libraries throughout Texas and western Oklahoma. Students applying for cards have check-out and in-house use privileges at participating libraries. This is a great bonus for students who travel while doing research or live far from the main campus.

Interlibrary loan (ILL) is a very important resource for students. DE students are able to complete forms online and send them directly to the ILL Department. When the requested material arrives at the library, it can then be sent directly to the student's home. For students with home faxes, material can be sent directly from the lending library.

Within the OASIS online catalog we cover keyword searching and how to limit using Boolean searching. Students can also limit by language, material type, publisher and year. They can search by subject for videos, theses or dissertations. Students learn how to use the Library of Congress subject headings online since many of them will not be able to come to the university to use paper versions. The title section contains book and periodical titles, CDs, DVDs, theses, government information and other research materials.

Most of the following Web sites are covered in the world geography class. They provide a broad area to choose from when students complete the threaded news groups assignment.

- Government information Web page (http://168.53.200.6/reference/docs/govinfo.htm)
- Geographic/cartographic Web sites (http://168.53.200.6/reference/docs/Geog_Carto2_Sites.htm)
- Geography and GIS (http://168.53.200.6/reference/docs/handouts/Geography-GIS.htm)

Students are shown the Jernigan Library electronic databases which offer a variety of full-text and index and abstract articles. If the information is not available through the databases, students can get it in-house or through interlibrary loan.

Some of the subject-specific databases are agriculture and scientific, such as agricola, nature journals, and wildlife and ecology studies worldwide. Government Web sites offer a great deal of information. For example, the Environmental Protection Agency, Science.gov, U.S. Fish & Wildlife, and the U.S. Geological Survey provide a wealth of geographical information. Government information can be in the form of reports, statistics, raw data, and current research. This type of information is easily merged with GIS programs.

Internet searching is the final section. A number of our students have not used WebCT for instruction or the Internet for educational research before. We offer many advanced Internet classes, such as Web Page Evaluation which enables students to evaluate the Web sites they use for various assignments.

In Web Page Evaluation we discuss:

- history of the Internet
- how to maneuver on the Web
- domain names (.gov, .edu, .net, .org, etc.)
- authorship (where to locate the author)
- purpose (does the site persuade, educate, etc.)
- design and stability (how does the site look)
- content (is the content trustworthy)
- Search engines
- General search engines (Google, Hot Bot)
- Directories (Yahoo, Alta Vista)
- Meta search engines (Metacrawler, Dogpile)
- Subject search engines (About.com, Ask)

By the end of class, students know what to expect. They can locate information using the OASIS online catalog, databases, Web sites and know how to evaluate information for assignments. If they require extra help, they can contact the professor or me by phone or e-mail, or come into the office and request group workshops.

Previously, the World Geography WebCT program changed each semester to accommodate problems, updates, and class changes. The class is now streamlined and changes are limited to technology updates.

Currently, we are working on streaming video to replace the presentation aspect of the program, which will allow the professor to monitor training through WebCT. Macromedia Captivate will teach students the OASIS online catalog, general database searching, and building search strategies.

It is exciting that technology can take teaching to any geographical location.

The Mobile Librarian

Carolyn Davis

Have you combined another discipline or two with your library science degree and experience? Doing so can be rewarding because it enables you to expand your intellectual, physical and geographic territories. Below are some examples from my career and some advice for entering another arena.

After obtaining a library degree the Providence Athenaeum in Rhode Island, I joined the Peace Corps in 1997. I was in the Youth at Risk sector, as it was then called, in Kingston, Jamaica, and was assigned first to Abilities Foundation, a vocational school for young adults, and was then transferred to the Jamaica Council for Persons with Disabilities, run by Ransford Wright. In the capacities of librarian and researcher I conducted a national survey which led to the development of the Jamaica Coalition on Disability. This work included public speaking, which at one point involved my being propelled in my wheelchair up a ramp angled at 70 degrees (see accessguidecardiff-online.blog.com). The people who designed the ramp, as well as those who expected my wheelchair to ascend it, had little knowledge of engineering or balance. They were truly surprised when I stopped the chair to insist, in what I've come to recognize as my "superpower voice" (that is, two parts Katharine Hepburn and one part Franklin Roosevelt), "Let's find an alternate route." This tone surprises some, but on more than one occasion, it has prevented me from becoming the late Carolyn Davis.

From Mediation to Library Science

In late 1992 and early 1993 I worked first as an intern in Conflict Management in Coleraine, Northern Ireland, then as an independent researcher in Stroke City, so-called because whether it was known by the designated name "Londonderry" or "Derry" depended on the Protestant or Catholic affiliation of the speaker.

After that, I decided to change from conflict to generic research. A practical way to make the change was to get a master's degree in library science. I looked at a few schools that offered a program: the University of North Carolina at Chapel Hill, the University of Rhode Island, and the Graduate School of Library and Information Science at Simmons College in Boston. As I recall, I applied to the programs at the University of Rhode Island and Simmons, citing access and my desire to work part-time as a particular need and interest, respectively. To my surprise, Simmons sent me many letters of detail regarding physical access and encouragement to attend. As a small private college, it had the staff and means to do this.

Deciding on Simmons, I moved into a dormitory (at age 34) and prepared yet again to be "Dorm Mom," the oldest one in the building. To my surprise and gratification I wasn't; a man in his late fifties was in the apartment across the hall.

He was a retired foreign service officer who had been ambassador to Somalia and Rwanda, respectively, some years previous. During one of our early meetings, I told him a little bit of my international relations background, while musing to myself about the irony of beginning a library course to qualify as a "generic" researcher, only to have an international relations specialist as my neighbor.

I became his research assistant and we began planning seminars, an average of one per month, for which invited guests who were specialists concerning or VIPs of particular countries or areas spoke and answered questions for approximately 90 minutes. Among the guests were diplomats and academics, of course, but also high-profile public-relations people, such as the president of Ireland.

Peace Corps, Jamaica

One meeting that the professor arranged for his undergraduate students featured a recruiter from the Boston Peace Corps Office and had an audience of three or four, including my neighbor and me. The woman presented the complete recruitment program and laughed as she said that in the past she had presented to an audience of as "few" as one. Within a week I called the local office.

The standard Peace Corps process for clearance and placement takes from nine to 18 months, and the stages generally comprise:

1. An interview with and subsequent nomination for a particular post by a Peace Corps recruitment officer. This may be done by telephone if the prospective candidate lives a considerable distance from a recruitment office.
2. FBI clearance.
3. Medical clearance by that particular Peace Corps department.
4. An invitation by the Peace Corps to join a particular group and country (for example, Group 68, Jamaica).
5. The candidate's acceptance, followed by the issuance of a Peace Corps passport. The Americans with Disabilities Act has made acceptance of people with disabilities easier, but a candidate's assertiveness and knowledge of the law are assets and were necessities in my own case.

Wales (2001–2006)

For those who have wondered about being a "foreign correspondent," I respond without hesitation that it can be edifying as well as fun. I went to Wales primarily to gather information about the relationships between the Principality of Wales and England in the 14th century, learn Welsh, and discern if particular conflict theories that were developed in the 20th century apply to certain situations and structures of the medieval period. On a previous trip, I had been asked to write an article for the journal *Technicalities* about an international graduate summer school in librarianship. When I returned, I was asked by its then-editor Sheila Intner to continue with a series to be called Tales from Wales. Additionally, I continued with library research for a dictionary that is becoming an encyclopedia and research about the West Indies as well as about access issues of Jamaica and Wales.

To share your expertise in a particular area of research, make contact with editors and publishers of journals in library science. If you are new to the field or adding an area of expertise, a good beginning can be to contact the professors in your GSLIS for references to publications or a direct publication submission if a particular professor is an editor or publisher of a journal.

For additional references to library publications, the Internet provides many references to professional journals, publication houses and literary agents. An excellent online source of publications concerning many topics of libraries and librarianship is the Wilson Library Literature and Information Science IndexSource. This database contains nearly a quarter of a million records in the form of bibliographic citations and more than 12,700 are added each year, according to its Web page.

Many of the publication houses and literary agents have particular specialties that are listed, and there are Web pages that provide recommendations and warnings for and about agents. One page that I've found particularly useful is "Predators and Editors" at www.invirtuo.cc/prededitors. This page has a number of subheadings, including one for the "Struggling Writer."

Above all, in coordinating different disciplines and getting published be assertive, develop skills in assessing your strengths and weaknesses in research and writing, stay positive and keep working to develop your particular niches!

A School Library Media Specialist in Australia

MELISSA ALLEN

A school library media center is the hub of any successful school, and media specialists are the facilitators who ensure the hub is functioning at its highest potential. As a school library media specialist in a public high school, I seek opportunities that will increase my knowledge base and skill level in order to positively influence the learning that takes place in my school. I recently returned from Exmouth, Australia, where I participated in an Earthwatch Institute expedition. I was able to participate in this wonderful opportunity through grant funding from the John Treworgy Fund, Georgia Southern University, and the Glynn County Public School System. During the expedition, I worked as a field research scientist on a research study of whale sharks at the Ningaloo Marine Park. Earthwatch's mission is to engage people worldwide in scientific field research and education to promote a sustainable environment. The project leader and lead biologist, Brad Norman, established that the natural skin pattern of whale sharks does not change over time and created a photo-identification process and library. Norman has also discovered a new species of copepod living on the skin of whale sharks and established the size of male whale sharks at maturity. Prior to the mid–1980s there were less than 350 confirmed sightings of whale sharks worldwide, thus Norman and his colleagues established a three-year study to address the conservation of this endangered species. Earthwatch is a world leader in the field of experiential education, providing opportunities in the field. There is no experience necessary to be involved and hundreds of teams worldwide are in need of support and volunteers. Visit www.earthwatch.org or call 800–776–0188 for more information.

My scientific research team worked to collect and process sighting data (including date, location, sex, size, etc.), took identification photographs for the database, measured each shark encountered, took biological field samples of plankton to identify the quality and quantity of whale shark food, recorded environmental variables, analyzed and photographed the fauna associated with each whale shark, and educated tourists about the whale sharks and their environment. Although there are still many unknowns about these great creatures, many facts about the whale shark exist because of research. Our research will bring about an improved understanding of whale shark movements, behaviors, numbers in the wild, growth rates, and habitat.

The data we collected is viewable by the general public and other scientists on the online whale shark photo-identification database at www.shepherdproject.org/overview.jsp. Over the next three years scientists will use the data to determine whether the whale sharks are showing signs of recovery in the wild and offer suggestions for their conservation. The data will show if and how whale shark numbers and behaviors are affected by ecotourism pressure and environmental conditions. This information can be used by other countries considering developing ecotourism to ensure the long-term conservation of this threatened species. If countries do not work toward the conservation of these creatures together, then there will be no ecotourism industry for any of them. In addition to conducting research, we received training, attended presentations, and listened to guest speakers. Guest speakers included several biologists and a Conservation and Land Management (CALM) ranger, who spoke about whale shark management and conservation as well as the whale shark ecotourism industry. A local aboriginal Thalanyji member also spoke with us about the aboriginal heritage.

I know one of the best ways I can utilize my experiences is by sharing them with teachers who work with an ever-changing population of students who are increasingly more diverse. I know from my previous professional experience in another country that I will use my experiences in my every day work environment. In addition to being a school library media specialist who finally found her true calling, I am also an ardent traveler who has visited numerous countries including Mexico, Canada, England, France, Italy, Germany, Austria, and Switzerland. Traveling is a passion of mine and I often take note of other countries' educational systems and teaching techniques. I even chose to complete my student teaching requirement by teaching for three months at Lynfield College, a public school consisting of grades six through twelve, in Auckland, New Zealand. I taught science to sixth through twelfth graders and worked under the school's science department head, who was a veteran teacher and a native Kiwi (New Zealander). I was inspired by the school's teaching methods which allowed students choice and individuality and empowered them to be responsible for their own learning and behavior. I incorporated these methods into my teaching upon returning to the United States.

I work collaboratively with all teachers in the school to create and coteach lessons, incorporate technology and print materials into the curriculum, and develop teaching aids and resources. I am continuously informed about the instructional program by reviewing courses of study, curriculum guides, textbooks, lesson plans, test data, and so forth in addition to attending departmental meetings. I give firsthand accounts of my research experience when I coteach units with science teachers and firsthand accounts of Australia when I coteach with social studies teachers. I also work with the other high school in my county to ensure all students are provided the same opportunity to utilize my experience to enhance their learning. I am also the webmaster of the school's Web site, and I link all the teaching aids and resources that I obtain and develop to the Web site. I also hope that the bonds that I formed with fellow colleagues in the program will result in extensive collaboration across country borders and state lines.

My firsthand experiences with science research and Australia help shape the curriculum at my school. The teachers, students, parents, and community members all benefit from my experience in this program by utilizing the resources I obtained and by my new expertise in science research, whale sharks, and Australia. I am able to provide students with a deeper learning experience by incorporating personal stories, pictures, and artifacts from Australia. Even Internet users around the world will benefit from the resources I post on the Web page.

Teaching Prospective Librarians as a Fulbright Scholar

ANN MARLOW RIEDLING

Since 1999, I have had the wonderful opportunities to teach and work with librarians in Bahrain, Yemen, Egypt, and Oman. How was that possible? I was awarded Fulbright Scholarships. (Please see http://us.fulbrightonline.org/home.html for more information regarding the Fulbright Foundation and the opportunities available.) In this essay, I focus on Egypt and Oman.

American Research Center, Cairo

While in Cairo, Egypt, I worked as a consultant for the American Research Center (ARCE). My purpose at ARCE was to serve as a consultant regarding the upcoming automation of the library collection. Ian Whitney, ARCE head librarian, and I discussed the current situation and possible solutions for the future. The collection was currently on cards; automation had not begun. We made the decision to begin the automation process by creating a database on the software program, Endnotes. We believed that by placing all important information in this database, two major purposes would be served: 1) creation of an up-to-date catalog with all pertinent information that will be searchable via computer (local online public access catalog or OPAC); and 2) placement of information in exportable form, such that it was part of a worldwide network. As of February 2000, over 500 records were entered in the database. Currently, they are all entered and they have purchased a much more elaborate automation system.

Our major obstacles were a lack of appropriate hardware and software and a lack of personnel to perform retrospective conversion of the collection. Additionally, more space for the resources was needed, as a portion of the collection remained in boxes or stacked on top of shelves. Our hope was to make all materials completely accessible to the patrons—a critically important rule of a properly functioning library.

My contributions included a wide variety of activities. In addition to individual consultations with Ian Whitney, I visited numerous people and institutions: Laila Mulgaokar at the Library of Congress at the American Embassy in Cairo; Shahira El-Sawy, dean of the

American University in Cairo (AUC) library; Ruth Monical, associate dean of the AUC library; Jayme Spencer, director of information literacy at AUC; Martha Plettner, director of information technology at AUC; and Ann Radwan with the Fulbright Commission in Cairo. My discussions with these people focused on ARCE's automation process and the upcoming training. I toured their facilities and provided information as requested. Additionally, several conversations regarding the ARCE library occurred with Everett Rowsom, vice president of ARCE. Recommendations for the American Research Center in Egypt included:

- Acquire appropriate, up-to-date hardware and software for proper library automation.
- Complete retrospective conversion for a local OPAC and a larger wide-area network (WAN). Additional personnel should be hired to perform this conversion.
- Expand the facility so that adequate space is available for all resources.

With the proper equipment and space, the ARCE library grew, flourished, and enhanced its reputation as the most accessible and comprehensive egyptological collections in Egypt.

Sultan Qaboos University, Oman

My teaching experience in Oman was one of the most exciting and memorable of my life. During my stay in Oman, I taught graduate students (who were previously in the field of science) about medical librarianship. Students at this university were chosen because they were in the top 5 percent of their high school graduating class.

My overall mission was to instruct and assist in the field of medical librarianship, medical classification and subject headings in particular. Medical librarianship is a unique field that requires knowledgeable instructors who are familiar with specific information, including databases, Internet sites, search strategies and tools, medical subject headings (MeSH), and the National Library of Medicine (NLM) Classification Scheme.

Using my knowledge of library and information science, I instructed and assisted students using a wide variety of teaching techniques and approaches. Hands-on, authentic instruction is essential in the field of medical librarianship. Learning and understanding medical librarianship requires diligence, attentiveness and tenacity, so I taught this information in a user-friendly manner, offering much support and guidance. Students learned about databases, such as PubMed, Medlineplus and Locatorplus; online references, such as the Directory of Information Resources Online (DIRLINE); books, such as Shelflisting Procedures for Monographs and Classed Serials; Internet sites, such as NLM Databases and Electronic Information Sources, and so forth. In addition, they gained knowledge of the National Library of Medicine Classification Scheme and medical subject headings.

Library and information science is vital to the success of individuals in today's global, technological society. Having worked in this field for over three decades, I wanted to share my knowledge and experiences and assist students in becoming well-versed in the field of library and information science, specifically, medical librarianship. Having instructed at the university level for over a decade (and in K–12 for over nine years), I acquired numerous creative and successful teaching tools and techniques.

Each of my students (there were 11 of them) were placed in various hospitals throughout Oman as medical librarians upon graduation. The top students received the top jobs so competition was fierce. The students were extremely bright, eager to learn, dedicated and polite.

A description of a medical library is provided below:

Sultan Qaboos University

Course: INFO 5230 and 5210 (Classification 2 and Subject Analysis)

Instructor: Dr. Ann Riedling, Fulbright Scholar, USA

E-mail address: ariedling@iglou.com

Texts and supplies: No textbook required; articles and Web sites provided.

Course description: Via this course, students learn about the use of the National Library of Medicine (NLM) Classification System, with an emphasis on the class QS-QZ and W-WZ, as related to medicine and other similar sciences. Students will also learn about controlled vocabulary as reflected by lists of subject headings such as the medical subject headings (MeSH). In addition, this course provides a practical introduction to a variety of printed and electronic sources used to locate information in medicine, consumer health, nursing and allied health; as well as discussions of the changing world of health sciences.

Objectives: Upon completion of this course, students will be able to:

- Identify and use a wide variety of medical information sources, including medical databases from the National Library of Medicine, the Internet, and so forth.
- Demonstrate an understanding of health professionals' use of information sources in the field of medicine and health sciences.
- Demonstrate knowledge of medical subject headings and associated issues.
- Discuss the important roles of the National Library of Medicine (and others) as sources of medical information.

Modes of Instruction: lecture, group and individual work, hands-on (including computer) experiences, class discussions

Expectations:

- Students will attend all classes (excused absences must be approved by instructor).
- Student will actively engage in discussions during class.
- Students will notify instructor immediately regarding any concerns/questions/issues.
- Students will work collaboratively in groups.
- Students will complete assigned midterm, assignments, and final examination.
- Students will ask questions!
- Students will learn and have fun!

Assignments: classroom discussion, assignments, midterm examination, final examination

Assessment:

    Classroom discussion = 15 points
    Midterm examination = 20 points
    Assignments = 45 points (15 assignments, each worth 3 points)
    Final examination = 20 points

Conclusion

These experiences were certainly beyond the circulation desk! I have been honored to teach and consult in other countries, as well as learn and enjoy people from all over the world. I remain in contact with many of my students and colleagues and hope to return to Egypt and Oman in the near future. I have been blessed and librarianship has a much deeper meaning for me now.

The Digital Doctorate in Library/Information Science

MARGARET LINCOLN

My career as a school library media specialist spans a 34-year period. Upon receiving my AMLS from the University of Michigan's School of Library Science in 1973, I took a position with the Lakeview Public Schools in Battle Creek, Michigan.

Keeping abreast of technological developments has been important for someone who entered the profession years before the microcomputer even existed! I have regularly attended professional development workshops, returned to Ann Arbor to take summer classes and gained educational technology certification from Michigan State University. Participation in the Library of Congress American Memory Fellowship Program and my work as a museum fellow with the United States Holocaust Memorial Museum (USHMM) provided further opportunity for professional growth.

But perhaps my most notable effort to stay current as a library professional came in 2004. At that point, my career moved decidedly beyond the circulation desk. As a true life-long learner, I embarked on a path to pursue a digital doctorate in library/information science.

A Program to Train 21st-Century Librarians

I remember the date: January 25, 2004. While catching up on reading professional articles and book reviews in that month's *School Library Journal*, I noticed an announcement about a new distance-independent PhD program at the University of North Texas (UNT) which aimed to do the following:

- Create a diverse cohort of doctoral students, easing or erasing monetary, cultural and geographic roadblocks.
- Develop a professorate needed to train capable, thoughtful, and caring 21st-century librarians.

With funding from the Institute of Museums and Libraries (IMLS), the UNT program proposed paying tuition for the coursework portion of the doctoral pursuits of ten students (five public librarians and five school librarians) over a two-year period. IMLS funds would cover broadband connectivity, providing a largely Web-based coursework and socializing experience. This model for a doctoral program went beyond the traditional brick-and-mortar setting by creating a blended learning environment of distance education and on-site interaction. Prospective participants were urged to send an e-mail or letter of inquiry to Dr. Brian O'Connor, coordinator of the Interdisciplinary PhD Program in the School of Library and Information Sciences (SLIS) at UNT in Denton.

A preliminary look at the UNT Web site convinced me to submit an application. Designated as a doctoral/research university extensive by the Carnegie Foundation, UNT ranks in the top 4 percent of U.S. colleges and universities. UNT had already achieved success with an online school media program and with the delivery of numerous Web-based graduate courses. In 2004, the SLIS faculty of 15 members had published 45 refereed articles and presented more than 200 papers at 50 international, national and state conferences.

An eight-page application, three letters of recommendation, writing samples and graduate record scores had to be submitted to UNT by February 24. Although I had just a few short weeks in which to gather the necessary materials and do some honest introspection as to whether I ought to apply, the opportunity to further my knowledge and broaden my experience in the library/information science field was the deciding factor. What did I have to lose and how much did I stand to gain!

The afternoon of Friday, March 12 brought a telephone call from Dr. O'Connor and favorable news. Ten librarians had been selected from 60 applicants based upon scholastic ability, potential for success in a rigorous graduate program of research study, and prior performance in the broad context of information science. The ten librarians represented the states of New York, Ohio, Pennsylvania, Texas, Illinois, Indiana, and Michigan. I had been admitted to the program!

Institutes in Denton

Following the initial excitement and sense of pride that I felt upon learning of my acceptance into the cohort (as the ten librarians would be called), I became acquainted with the other cohort members. As would be fitting for an online program, we introduced ourselves to one another through a rapid exchange of e-mail messages. Along with the feelings of elation that we shared, there was a fair amount of trepidation and anxiety. The program was built on the premise that we would all keep our full-time library positions while engaged in online coursework. Nonetheless, equipped with our new wireless laptop computers, we prepared for our first weekend in Denton.

The first institute was held on the UNT campus June 11–13, 2004. The IMLS grant covered travel expenses and lodging. Over the course of a typical weekend, we attended class from 9:00 A.M. until 5:00 P.M., breaking for lunch. Evenings were often spent again in class or we gathered at the home of a faculty member in a more informal setting. On Sundays, we departed Denton by 1:00 P.M.

Subsequent three-day institutes took place in Denton in August, October and December of 2004 and in January, June and October of 2005. For two years, the pattern was to begin coursework during the weekend institutes and then to return home and continue with follow-up assignments and participation in discussion forums through online communication. Many classes used the interface of WebCT or WebCT Vista, permitting instructors to post lectures and deliver instructional modules through distance education. In January 2006, our group convened in San Antonio and presented poster sessions about our developing research projects at the Association of Library and Information Science Education (ALISE) conference.

The preparation stage of our PhD program consisted of 48 credit hours. Included among the institute classes were such core curriculum requirements as Doctoral Seminar in Information Issues, Readings in Information Science, Research Methodology, Communication and Use of Information, Management of Digital Resources, and Electronic Databases and Online Services. I also chose such electives as Survey Methods Research, Educational Statistic, and Qualitative Analysis.

Completing the PhD

Was it a challenge to continue working as a high school library media specialist while pursuing this degree? Absolutely! I jokingly remarked that weekends, evenings and most time off from Lakeview High School were spent tethered to my laptop. But thanks to the wonderful support provided by my fellow cohort members and the guidance and mentoring offered by outstanding professors at UNT, I entered the final stages of the PhD program.

My research became connected to another fervent interest and project that took place in Battle Creek while I was involved in the UNT program. Through my position as a USHMM Mandel Fellow, I helped bring a traveling exhibition from the museum in Washington, D.C., to the local Battle Creek Art Center and organized an accompanying educational outreach program. The topic of my dissertation thus became the online and onsite Holocaust museum exhibition as an informational resource. In partial fulfillment of my qualifying experience, I presented a paper at the 2006 Museums and the Web Conference in Albuquerque, New Mexico (one of 35 presenters accepted from among 150 proposals). I successfully defended my dissertation in October and received my degree on December 16, 2006.

The PhD is concerned with the generation of new knowledge. It involves not only the learning of certain facts or processes but also the ability to think about issues, to engage in synthesis and analysis and to passionately pursue a significant new question. I am grateful to the University of North Texas for developing a distance model with broad application to doctoral level education in our field. I urge colleagues everywhere to pursue your own goals and aspirations of professional advancement and lifelong learning. The digital doctorate will hopefully be within the reach of more librarians in the 21st century.

Learning to Review, Reviewing to Learn

Darby Orcutt

Forget what you know about reviews. Forget your attitude toward reading them. I'm going to focus here on the act of reviewing. While reviews are helpful — and occasionally mandated — in many selection contexts, librarians usually find them useful in inverse relation to collection size or strength of budget. And, quite frankly, most reviews are neither very good nor very interesting.

So why write them?

One can argue that librarians have a responsibility to the field, and especially that those of us with strong analytic skills, writing ability, and/or subject expertise *ought* to contribute to the literature in this way. I know that my peers, particularly at smaller institutions, benefit from my reviews because they go out of their way to tell me so. I also know that the overall quality of published reviews will not improve unless those of us who can offer better actually do so.

Yet, whether I'm teaching reviewing to students, advising colleagues, or justifying to myself my own reviewing activities, I keep coming back to one selfish reason: I like free books. No, that's not it. Rather, the reason is this: I continually *learn* through reviewing.

The skills involved in reviewing, particularly the skills involved when a *librarian* reviews, develop evaluative abilities and perspective that transcend the work in hand. A strong review requires, among other things:

- close attention to detail
- knowledge of context
- consideration of format
- critical judgment

Let's consider each of these in turn:

Close Attention to Detail

Stereotypically not a problem for librarians, intense focus on the fine points of a work breeds the facility to readily spot distinguishing characteristics. In the language of visual perception, *figure ground* refers to a person's ability to cognitively separate objects from their surroundings, an ability that may be honed through practice. Figure ground serves as an apt metaphor for the reviewer's ability to notice that which is different in a work, whether an unfortunate typo or a unique method of presentation. Practiced reviewers usually find they have "accidentally" picked up strong editing skills and quickness in incisive analysis. Practiced readers of works make better "readers" of situations, people, images, and processes, as well as of texts.

Practicing this close attention to detail in reading also promotes closer attention to detail in one's own writing and other productions. Especially when the practiced critical eye is my own eye, I am indeed my own worst critic, and thus hold myself to a higher standard. Given that many publications severely restrict the number of words in reviews, the practice of self-editing develops a second nature of conciseness and frugality of expression that most of us can really use.

Knowledge of Context

Nothing exists in a vacuum. Every work fits into certain general, preconceived expectations on the part of its users or readers, and also into constellations of other works, ideas, genres, theories, attitudes, and so on. The reviewer must understand and articulate the place of the work in hand within this larger world.

Whether reviewing a mystery novel or a reference set on particle physics, the best reviewers know and comment upon what has been published or is already available, as well as the potential interest, use, audiences, and/or need for the new work. As a reviewer, you may already be an authority on these things in some cases, but in others, maybe not. If you do not know the context of a work completely (or at all!), who better to learn than you? As a librarian, you *are* an authority on finding information and especially on finding information about published materials!

Every instance of contextualized reviewing provokes some degree of subject-oriented learning. Every new work constitutes an addition to its field, even if a poor and unnecessary one. I strive to take each new work that I review as a call to update my knowledge of its genre, and to revisit my assumptions; that is to say, I take the act of reviewing as a call to learn about the world.

Consideration of Format

Librarians, above most others, generally appreciate the physicality of books. To be effective, librarians must consider books not simply as texts, but as objects—and especially, as objects that interact with human users through a physical interface. Not only is it "okay," as students have asked me, to comment on the physical quality and characteristics of the object of review, but it is also mandatory for a good review to consider these things and comment as appropriate. When I received a reference work that was literally falling apart at the seams, I felt obliged to comment on its poor binding. Mine may have been the only copy in such condition (though I suspect not), but potential buyers needed to know that the work might not survive even light use. In an ideal world, the intellectual content of a work may be the full story, but I know of no library not located in the *real* world.

Even electronic resources rely on some sort of physical interface with human users, and so require similar consideration. In reviewing an online bibliography, I at first found many apparent omissions; upon closer inspection, I discovered that the content was not at fault, but rather the searching functions; for example, searches returned results only for the first instance of a term on each Web page of the resource, which made its indexing only slightly better than useless.

Sometimes easily lulled into thinking of books and other library resources as intellectual rather than actual objects, we regain a balanced perspective through the act of reviewing. As importantly, however, we put ourselves in the shoes of our users and gain valuable insight into how they may interact with and perceive resources. As experienced librarians whose job requires it, we often know more than our users about their own reading and information-seeking habits, but we never know all, and the kinds of perspective taking necessary for reviewing fosters our deeper understanding of others and often humbles the reviewer in the face of new discovery.

Critical Judgment

As a service profession — and not an especially lucrative one, librarianship generally attracts people who focus on meeting the needs of others, and stereotypically, librarians do not relish quick decision making. Some of us go against type, of course. Esteemed *Guide to Reference Books* editor Bob Balay and I have frequently bantered about how we "reference" and "collections" types are simply wired differently. Yet, we find a connection in the act of reviewing.

The perspective taking involved in considering all aspects of a work from the standpoints of potential users may feel more natural to "reference" types, but such exercises prove fruitless without a weighing of evidence. A work may be useful, but to whom? How? More useful than what else? The most helpful judgments for readers of reviews are not wholesale evaluations of the work, but smaller and supported opinions which they may use in their own contextualized judgments (e.g., "if you enjoy the style of author *X*, you might enjoy this book," or "if your library leases *Y*, then this database would be largely redundant"). Well-done reviewing builds valuable critical-judgment skills by forcing the librarian to develop such reasoned stances, rooted in evidence gathered through keen observation and consideration from multiple perspectives and clearly expressed.

As a librarian, I am committed to the idea of fostering lifelong learning, both in others and in myself. Reviewing works many metaphorical muscles and serves as a constant source of learning and growing for me. That is why I review, and I encourage you to do likewise.

National Board Certification as a Professional Development Opportunity

Melissa Allen

The school library media specialist is an important partner in providing an integrated curriculum that prepares students to be lifelong learners. School library media specialists who excel in their field seek out opportunities to collaborate with all members of their learning community in order to grow professionally. The national board certification process is one such opportunity.

The National Board for Professional Teaching Standards (NBPTS) was created in 1987 as a way to try to professionalize teaching, bring effective educational practices to the classroom, and ultimately enhance student learning. The national board process is expected to add to the human capital of teachers. Thus, national board certified teachers are expected to be more effective teachers after they have gone through the assessment process. Having been an assessor for national board and having completed the process myself, I know that these experiences have improved my professional performance through reflection, analysis of my current practices, and increased involvement and collaboration in the learning community.

NBPTS provides a set of standards by which educators can measure their own performance. The standards give a basis to reflect on personal practices and activities while also providing ideas and goals for future professional growth. NBPTS's endeavors have raised the standards for teachers, strengthened their educational preparation through the standards, and created performance-based assessments that demonstrate accomplished application of the standards. The process should be a learning experience as well as a recognition for exemplary work.

National board certification is considered by most to be the highest credential in the teaching profession. Although most educators who seek national board certification are already active members of multiple learning communities, during the process many candidates join new learning communities that focus primarily on the certification process. These communities include other candidates, educators who have already been through the process, and online education networks. As a candidate two years ago, I believe that having participated with all three of these learning communities during the process led to my successful certification on my first attempt. Although many educators successfully certify by working through the process alone, there are so many opportunities to work with other candidates, experienced national board certified teachers, and NBPTS employees that there is no reason to be isolated during the process.

After three years of working as a media specialist and having adjusted to the transition from the classroom, I decided that I was prepared to accept the challenge of the process. I decided my first step would be to learn as much about the process as possible before beginning. On the NBPTS Web site I found job opportunities to assess the portfolio and assessment answers of candidates during the summer. I sent in an application and was accepted. I was assigned assessment #6, Knowledge of Literature, with four other library media specialist and one trainer. While my main purpose was to learn more about the process, I also formed bonds with the other media specialists and they were the beginning of my local group of candidates undertaking the process. NBPTS waived the application fee ($300) for any assessors who began the process themselves, so four out of the five assessors in my group alone applied for the following school year. NBPTS has since changed this to a partial fee waiver for assessors serving at least two years. The assessing process was a way to make money during the summer, earn a fee waiver, meet other library media specialists who wished to excel in their profession, and learn more about the national board process. I would recommend assessing to anyone who is interested in the process even if you have to travel to one of the scoring areas (Atlanta, GA; Baltimore, MD; Charleston, SC; Charlotte, NC; Chicago, IL; Cincinnati, OH; Dallas, TX; Denver, CO; Greenville-Spartanburg, SC; Henderson, NV; Jackson, MS; Miami, FL; Mobile, AL; Mt. Laurel, NJ; Oklahoma City, OK; Pittsburgh, PA; San Antonio, TX; Tampa, FL; Tulsa, OK; Washington, D.C.).

Many people served as inspirations and role models to me during the year that I worked through the national board portfolios and assessments. One such person was the choral teacher in my school, Kathy, who had just completed the national board process and was waiting for her results. She encouraged me to pursue this worthwhile endeavor and provided me with firsthand accounts of the organization and process that I needed to feel confident that I was ready to begin. While I was still in the beginning phases of the portfolio, Kathy was notified of her certification and officially became my mentor, a position she was not comfortable with until she was certain she had certified on her first attempt. Although I was seeking certification in the library media field and Kathy knew little about that area, she was very familiar with the process and was willing to study the standards for my certification field in order to assist further. Having someone else in the same building who understood the stress that often came with the certification process eased the anxiety that I felt.

I was also a member of a local support group composed of other candidates seeking certification in the library media field. Our group only met twice that year but we provided support through e-mail and phone conversations. The goals of the support group were to provide emotional support, a backboard for bouncing entry ideas around, peer editing for entries, assessment preparation, support for adherence to all NBPTS rules and policies, and comments on video quality. Only one member of our support group did not certify on the first attempt and the rest of the group supported her through this disappointment and encouraged her to continue as a candidate the following year. As a member of a national listserv (librarymedia@yahoo.com) that focuses on national board certification in the library media field, I am able to collaborate with NBCT and candidates all across the country. Yahoo groups has listservs for all the certification areas of national board. Anyone can subscribe to the library media group by sending an e-mail message to librarymedia-subscribe@yahoo groups.com with "subscribe" in the subject line. Through this listserv, I was also able to connect to local candidates by posting messages seeking other candidates within driving distance as well as to communicate through mail and e-mail with others around the nation. I continue to actively participate in this listserv to help others along their journey to certification.

As media specialists in schools, we can play a valuable role in candidates' certification by offering to assist with the video recording part of their portfolios. These videotaped entries are often the most stressful because there are so many things that can make a tape unacceptable — bad sound, poor lighting, an inexperienced cameraperson who does not focus on needed action, quality of the tape itself, etc. Media specialists with expertise with video and recording equipment and schedules that often allow time to assist with videotaping during a class period can ease anxiety by providing advice, equipment, and videotaping services to increase the possibility of obtaining a quality entry on the first attempt.

Sandynista

STEPHEN FESENMAIER

During the last ten years I have used the life, work, and career of Sanford "Sandy" Berman as a guide for some of my activities as a librarian. There are a group of others like me who are called "Sandynistas." Sandy was forced to retire in 1999 from the Hennepin County Library. Since then we have shared feelings of outrage and loss as well as energized each other to expand our library activities.

Library of Congress Subject Headings

During the summer of 2002, the trapped coal miners of Quecreek, Pennsylvania, were international news. During that summer, Sandy and I teamed up for the first time to create a new Library of Congress (LC) subject heading: "Mountaintop Removal Mining." Sandy is the only person in the world to create his own alternative subject heading classification system to the LC. Within a few months of Sandy's first letter and several of support from me and others, the LC created the heading. In May 2005 Sandy submitted a proposal for "West Virginia Mine Wars," after the landmark book, *When Miners March* by William C. Blizzard. We held another campaign and in June 2005 the LC created the subject heading "Blair Mountain, Battle of, W. Va., 1921." This battle is the largest armed-labor conflict in American history. These subject headings have energized the West Virginia Labor History Association which is trying to save Blair Mountain from being demolished by mountaintop removal mining. Other new subject headings include "Plutocracy," "American Dream" and soon, "Vietnam War, 1961–1975" to replace "Vietnamese Conflict, 1961–1975." Sandy also suggested new subject headings for "Zines," "Krumping" and several others. His most recent suggestions include replacing the outdated "Armenian Massacres, 1894–1896" with the preferred "Armenian Genocide, 1915–1923" and "Anti-Arabism." Sandy's Web site, www.sanfordberman.org, lists many of the subject headings he proposed before 1974. Today, the LC has a Web site where you can recommend new subject headings.

Selective Dissemination of Information

Both Sandy and I are known by friends, family, and colleagues for being obsessive info sharers. Sandy has his own key to the local photocopying and shipping store in Minnesota. I have the Web. As Chris Dodge famously wrote in *Everything You Always Wanted to Know About Sandy Berman but Were Afraid to Ask*, "Sandy cannot have information that he thinks you could use without sharing it with you." I have independently been the same way all of my life. As one relative asked one once, "Steve, isn't it enough that *you know something?*" I used to spend a lot of time photocopying and mailing as Sandy still does—about 100 envelopes per week. Sandy was able to professionally distribute this information for 20 years in his essential series, Alternative Library Literature. I am famous for my vast number of e-mails despite being threatened professionally and personally many times. Both Sandy and I are born librarians and all librarians should have a similar compulsion. I often search the Web for Sandy, especially doing Google searches in support of his newly proposed subject headings for the LC. I was taught in library school that this is an essential function of the good reference librarian. Sandy and I share information weekly and sometimes daily, sending our respective friends some of the information we uncover. We specialize in different areas— Sandy in the areas of zines, homelessness, subject headings, library activism, and labor issues and myself in films, current library news, online information, cosmology, and other areas. I have written a monthly column on film for *Graffiti* magazine since 1984, throwing in some info on libraries, books and even new subject headings. I have contributed more than 100 stories to lisnews.com.

Homeless People and Libraries

Sandy is the founder of the Homelessness and Poverty (HHP) Task Force, one of several task forces within the Social Responsibilities Round Table (SSRT) of the American Library Association (ALA). In this role he convinced the ALA Council to pass a resolution requiring that all public library services be evaluated from the viewpoint of a homeless patron. He wrote the introduction to the only book on libraries and the homeless, *Poor People and Library Services*, edited by Karen M. Venturella. I finally found a way to become active in this area when a high school junior in West Virginia, Francesca Karle, created a feature film about the homeless in Huntington called *On the River's Edge*. I reviewed the film locally and nationally for *Counterpoise*, screened it at the fall 2005 state library conference, and presented it at my 2006 West Virginia film series in South Charleston. I also wrote the article "Can Public Libraries Help the Homeless?" for *WV Libraries* magazine. This led John Gehner, the current chair of the task force, to ask me to create two filmographies— one on the homeless and one on films on poverty. Coincidently, one library director asked me to do research on parking and libraries. Several new shelters for the homeless and poor have moved in near her library, taking away scarce parking spaces. By doing research on this, I discovered that many American public libraries are facing several problems linked to nearby homeless shelters. Amazingly, the state fall library conference had three separate events about the homeless and libraries, after not ever sponsoring *any* such events in more than 70 years. The public library directors of the state have become interested in this reality on their own, but the new local film has helped keep their interest going. Likewise, my own interest in the area has dramatically increased.

Cuban Librarians

Besides founding the HHP Task Force, Sandy has been a longtime activist inside the SRRT. When I joined ALA several years ago, I also joined the SRRT. Soon I became active in the attempt to convince the ALA to pass a resolution against the imprisonment of independent Cuban librarians. During the last several years, this issue has become very polarizing in the SRRT community. I became a member of Friends of Cuban Libraries, a group founded by Robert Kent and others. I made a button in honor of First Library Workers Day 2004, with a picture of Nat Hentoff and the saying, "Remember Imprisoned Cuban Librarians." A picture of this button was published in *American Libraries* (AL) and copies were made for various people, including Nat Hentoff's children. Both Sandy and I have taken a stand with virtually every other human rights group in the world, demanding that Fidel Castro release all of his political prisoners. We have also fought inside the American library community to make ALA join these groups. Celebrity writers, including Ray Bradbury and Andrei Codrescu, have spoken at national ALA conferences, asking ALA to reconsider their failure to join the rest of the world. Sandy and I have both written and spoken on this issue. Sandy has been quoted by Hentoff in the *Voice*. A recent AL instant poll showed that 75 percent of its members are against ALA's stand on this issue. Hopefully, sanity will finally gain control and ALA will fight Castro as it fights negative internal influences like the Patriot Act.

Still Eager to Learn

Outreach for Seniors

Rhonda Harris Taylor *and* Nancy Larson Bluemel

For four years, as a former academic librarian/current graduate library and information studies program faculty member and as a former school library media specialist and adjunct faculty/current independent scholar and vendor, we have collaborated on a yearly gift to ourselves: We volunteer for Mornings with the Professor.

Mornings with the Professor

Each week during the fall and spring semesters, faculty at the University of Oklahoma (OU) volunteer presentations in areas of their own expertise/interests for seniors in the community (http://outreach.ou.edu). From the pool of proposed presentations, each semester's offerings are selected by program development specialist staff within the College of Continuing Education. Presentations must fit within an hour and a half slot, including questions and answers. As part of a number of programs offered by the Osher Lifelong Learning Institute at OU, the Mornings with the Professor series brings together individuals who are continuing their lifelong learning and faculty members willing to share their research and ideas.

For us, one of the personal rewards of the program is the interaction with the diverse participants, who bring a wide-ranging variety of professional/work experiences and personal interests to the dialogue. And, these sessions are a dialogue between participants and between participants and presenters! Without exception, audiences are engaged, eager to learn and to share, and we always learn as much or more from them than they do from us.

Why Do We Do This?

The Mornings series has given us the following opportunities:

- The chance to share with a group of lifelong learners outside of the boundaries of a particular library setting or the traditional classroom.

- The chance to draw simultaneously on both our professional expertise and our personal interests in designing topics for the presentations.
- The chance to encourage an audience of lifelong learners to visit their local libraries for further reading and/or reference.
- The chance to present another face of librarianship, appearing in the role of faculty as well as experienced library practitioners.
- The chance to preview conference and/or publication ideas/approaches with yet another audience. We have found this audience to be very interested in scholarly publications in progress and already published.

What Do We Talk About?

The seniors who participate in the program are voluntarily building time into their busy lives for this experience for their own edification (no grades here!). A quick review of past and present topics reinforced for us the fundamental principle that our presentation must be both rich in content and yet appealing to a lay audience. It was also clear to us that librarians, including the two of us, would have a plethora of topics from which to draw! Nor are we the only librarians who have presented to this particular audience. To date, we have presented on various aspects of pop-up books (which we both collect and about which we write) and mysteries (which we both read) and celebrity-authored children's books (another mutual professional interest).

No, We Don't Lecture!

We have found that using a miniversion of a workshop format works best for us in this series. We also incorporate basic principles of reader's advisory (guidance for leisure reading, both fiction and nonfiction). Here are the rules that we've devised for ourselves:

1. Don't bore ourselves! We've found that if our presentation is interesting to us, other adults will find it interesting too.
2. Allow as much opportunity for interaction as possible. This means that besides the requisite question-and-answer session for a finale, we provide built-in points for interaction with the audience.
3. Allow for multiple learning styles. We include visual, auditory, and text delivery in each presentation.
4. Provide information for continuing learning beyond the presentation.
5. Use of a larger print font size for handouts.
6. Incorporate fun into the content, which should be substantive and informative.
7. Plan plenty of content to fill the time frame, but be prepared if you are not able to present all the material.

Here's What We Do

We unabashedly love books, and we believe that other people do, too. We also believe that readers love to browse. Therefore, we always have a minibook exhibit of items that we discuss. Because of the topics, the exhibits are mostly of our own books, but we also use library books to supplement our collections (especially for reference and critical works) and to reinforce the concept of library use. We encourage the participants to take a look at our books.

As conference and workshop attendees, we love handouts! We personally like to have something in hand for reference, and we provide that extra resource for participants. Participants find that they don't need to take notes, and it's a method for providing resources that there's not time to cover in the presentation. It's also an easy way to provide an overview of the organization of the session, for both presenters and participants.

Handouts are good but so is media! A brief video clip can be a clear illustration of an idea, and it always captures attention.

We like providing opportunities for participants to draw on their own expertise. For instance, a very short pretest (no more than five questions) of interesting facts and firsts makes for a quick icebreaker and provides an interesting conclusion when we give the answers that were buried in the presentation. Just remember to bring along some pencils! A fast brainstorming session that captures ideas on a flip chart or white board or ELMO is another easy way to draw participants into the topic.

We enjoy providing opportunities for participants to have hands-on experiences. For instance, we found them to be very receptive to making simple pop-up cards during a discussion of how paper engineers create their works.

Even auditory experiences can be made more interesting. Doing a variation of reader's theater for a reading from a mystery novel was fun for us and the participants! Having audience members read aloud brief reviews (that we provide) of books by celebrity authors was a participative way to keep interest in the flow of ideas.

We allow plenty of time for questions and answers, but we don't just rely on questions provided by the audience members. We like to ask them questions, too, in order to open the conversation. Our questions are planned and spontaneous.

What Have We Learned?

Our experiences have taught us quite a bit about outreach for seniors. Perhaps the most important thing that we learned is to recognize success in such occurrences as:

- familiar faces returning for our presentation the next year
- participants asking questions that we did not anticipate
- participants telling us how they followed up on a presentation topic, such as reading a new author, purchasing a book or being alerted to further examples of ideas presented
- audience enthusiasm for the topic

Little wonder that this outreach service is our gift to us!

Training Cyberlibrarians

The New Skill Requirements

John H. Heinrichs *and* Nancy Czech

The library and information science (LIS) profession must undergo a major transformation in the wake of the emerging library that melds the functions of a traditional library with the vision of a cyberlibrary.[1] The emerging library expands upon the free Internet access already being provided and is a training center. Expert librarians predict the expansion of the librarian's role in these emerging libraries to include instructional and training responsibilities.[2] Therefore, the librarians in these emerging libraries will frequently design and deliver training programs that help customers maximize their use of software productivity tools designed for information access and knowledge creation. So, achieving this transformation involves understanding both the future role and requisite skill requirements of cyberlibrarians.

Library directors are already looking for librarian candidates who possess technology skills. In a recent survey, public library directors not only felt that productivity skills were beneficial, but that evidence of these skills could also influence hiring decisions. Library directors are interested in seeing concrete evidence of the candidate's skill proficiency, which could include software certifications.[3] In fact, in another survey, software productivity tools (word processing, presentation, spreadsheet, and database) skills were the second-most highly ranked skills requirement.[4] The software productivity tool skills have become essential for cyberlibrarians as library directors are looking for individuals comfortable and confident with their information technology skills and abilities.[5] Further, these library directors want individuals who can help customers solve computer problems, use software productivity tools, act as learning facilitators, and apply technological expertise.[6]

The cyberlibrarian's role of information adviser and trainer necessitates proficiency in software productivity tool skills and teaching abilities. Further, the required information technology literacy skills encompass those skills that enable the librarian to use computer technologies as well as to use and to explain software productivity tools. Now that the requirement for them is clearly understood, LIS program curricula can be enhanced to ensure that cyberlibrarians acquire these new skills.

Software Productivity Tool Course

The Library and Information Science Program (LISP) at Wayne State University (WSU) (www.lisp.wayne.edu) in Detroit, Michigan, offers a Software Productivity Tools course where students have the opportunity to develop and enhance their technical skills in various software productivity tool applications. In this course, the students utilize the Microsoft Office 2003 suite of productivity tools as well as OneNote 2007 and MapPoint 2006. The various productivity tools utilized in this course focus the student on creating and using Web centric forms, enhancing analytical skills, understanding relational database development and management techniques, and team collaboration and document sharing. One of the goals of this course is to help the students achieve master level certification in these software productivity tools thus demonstrating that they have the skills and knowledge to assist customers in a public library setting. Master level certification implies that the student has passed rigorous tests in Microsoft Word, Excel, PowerPoint, Access and Outlook. Starting in the winter 2008 semester, students in this course will be required to pass Windows Vista/Office 2007 certification exams and thus become application specialist certified (www.microsoft.com/learning/mcp/msbc/default.mspx). In addition, the Software Productivity Tools course is offered as a distance learning course and provides students the opportunity to watch/rewatch the lectures. It is offered annually with a current demand of 45 to 65 students.

In the course, the student approaches each software productivity tool using multiple learning methods. For each tool, students are required to complete 12 comprehensive projects which cover the required competencies needed to pass the certification examination. Other practice opportunities are also introduced to the students. Students are encouraged to answer questions posted for each lecture, take online practice exams, use supplemental written materials, and consult the Microsoft (www.microsoft.com/learning/default.mspx) and Certiport (www.certiport.com) Web sites. The books used in the course also provide additional practice exercises beyond the basic required assignments. Additional staff members are available to assist students with answering application questions, developing test strategies and completing course projects. During the semester, the instructor uses the live question-and-answer session capability as well as an online discussion board to respond to the students' questions.

When the students feel that they are fully prepared, they take the certification exams in the LISP testing center. These various certification exams, which were developed and validated by industry experts, simulate real-world problems and ask students to fulfill various tasks using their newly acquired skill set. Each question on the certification exam requires the student to perform multiple tasks and calls on the student to use the various features of the software productivity tool. For example, the Word expert exam covers the skills associated with collaborating with others, customizing the Word application, formatting content, formatting the document, and organizing the content in the document (see table 1 for the Word proficiency requirements or www.microsoft.com/learning/mcp/office-specialist/requirements.mspx for all exam requirements).

Table 1: Microsoft Word Proficiency Requirements

Word Skill Category	Productivity Tool Proficiency Requirements
Collaborating	Attach digital signatures to documents Manage document versions Modify track changes options Protect and restrict forms and documents Publish and edit Web documents
Customizing Word	Modify Microsoft Word default settings Create, edit, and run macros Customize menus and toolbars
Formatting Content	Create custom styles for text, tables and lists Create and modify diagrams and charts using data from other sources Control pagination Format, position and resize graphics using advanced layout features Insert and modify objects
Formatting Documents	Create and manage master documents and subdocuments Create and modify forms, document background, and document indexes and tables Insert and modify endnotes, footnotes, captions, and cross-references
Organizing Content	Merge letters and labels with other data sources Modify table formats Perform calculations in tables Sort content in lists and tables Structure documents using XML Summarize and navigate document content using automated tools

Conclusion

The Software Productivity Tools course helps to prepare librarians for their future role and begins to provide them with the skills required of cyberlibrarians. These librarians will be expected to be advisers, consultants, and tutors, providing technology instruction including software productivity tool instruction. For example, when one library offered software productivity tools for use by their patrons, it was determined that 20 percent of the total questions asked of its reference desk personnel were related to the usage of those tools.[7] These librarians thus became teachers of the various software productivity tools and were required to be the first level of technical support for questions and issues.[8] The LISP Software Productivity Tools course prepares students to enter the workforce ready to instruct customers as they access information and prepare documents, spreadsheets, presentations, and databases.

Notes

1. Baruchson-Arbib, S. and Bronstein, J. (2002). A View to the Future of the Library and Information Science Profession: A Delphi Study. Journal of the American Society for Information Science and Technology 53(5), 397–408.

2. Ibid.

3. Messmer, M. (2003). Five Things to Look for in Job Candidates. Strategic Finance 85(3) 15.

4. Moody, J.B. and Steward, C.B. (2002). Showing the Skilled Business Graduate: Expanding the Toolkit. Business Communications Quarterly 65(1) 21–36.

5. Adkins, D. and Esser, L. (2004). Literature and Technology Skills for Entry-Level Children's Librarians: What Employers Want. Children and Libraries 2(3) 14–21.

6. Materska, K. (2004). Librarians in the Knowledge Age. New Library World 105(3/4) 142–148.

7. Graham, K. (2003). When the Library Becomes the Largest Computer Lab on Campus: Supporting Productivity Software in an Academic Environment. C&RL News 64(7) 462–468.

8. Hein, K. (2006). Information Uncommon: Public Computing in the Life of Reference. Reference Services Review 34(1) 33–42.

About the Contributors

Editor

Carol Smallwood, a public library consultant, school librarian, and teacher for more than 20 years, has written 18 books, including *Educators as Writers* (Peter Lang, 2006). Her poems and short stories have appeared in literary magazines, such as *English Journal, Iris,* and *Poesia.* Her columns have appeared in magazines and newspapers, including the *Detroit News.*

Forewordist

Joy M. Greiner, professor emeritus of library and information science at the University of Southern Mississippi, has published two books, numerous book chapters and articles in *Library Trends, The Acquisitions Librarian, Public Libraries* and the *Australasian Public Libraries and Information Services.* She conducted research in public libraries in England, Scotland and the United States for *Exemplary Public Libraries* (Libraries Unlimited, 2004). She was the director of the School of Library and Information Science for eight of twenty years at the University of Southern Mississippi.

Contributors

Melissa Aho is the campus, acquisitions, and business resources librarian at the Minnesota School of Business in Brooklyn Center, Minnesota and is a reference librarian at Metropolitan State University Library in St. Paul, Minnesota. She has a MLIS and a MS, and has had articles and book reviews published both in print and online. Aho also contributes to professional blogs.

Sara Albert graduated from the School of Information at the University of Texas at Austin in 2005. She has worked as adjunct reference librarian at Austin (Texas) Community College and as the assistant to the ALA president.

Melissa Allen is the current head media specialist at Glynn Academy in Brunswick, Georgia. She is certified in secondary science, elementary education, reading, and educational leadership. She is a teacher support specialist, national board certified, and is working on her doctorate in curriculum studies. Allen has been published in *Library Media Connections.*

Ruth B. Allen, youth librarian at Multnomah County Library in Portland, Oregon, is involved in the Oregon Young Adult Network, a division of the Oregon Library Association, and has been active in the Young Adult Library Services Association of ALA, serving on the Michael L. Printz

Award, the Margaret A. Edwards Award, and other committees.

Kathy Barco is coauthor of *Breakfast Santa Fe Style* (Sunstone Press, 2006). Currently children's librarian with the Albuquerque/Bernalillo County Public Library, she formerly served as youth services coordinator at the New Mexico State Library. A recipient of the New Mexico Library Association's Leadership Award in 2006, she is also the author of *READiscover New Mexico: A Tri-Lingual Adventure in Literacy* (Sunstone Press, 2007).

Ruth A. Barefoot has provided 30 years of service in four states. She is currently working on changes in library management, especially staffing issues, training, and building design, that will assist implementation of the San José Way service model throughout San José Public Library in San Jose, California.

Robin Bartoletti's background includes over 15 years coordinating, planning, developing, and conducting library, information, and technology teaching and training. Several of her works have been published by Highsmith Press, Scarecrow, and Neal-Schuman. She currently teaches graduate courses in library media and information technology at Northeastern State University in Broken Arrow, Oklahoma.

Erika Bennett has a MLIS and is a reference librarian and liaison to the schools of human services and psychology at Capella University. Previously, she was librarian at the Institute of Production and Recording in Minneapolis, Minnesota. Bennett has had articles and book reviews published, contributes to professional blogs and was the first chair of Career College Libraries of Minnesota.

Sommer Berg-Nebel has an MLIS and is currently the reference librarian–liaison to undergraduate studies at Capella University. Previously, Berg-Nebel was the campus and distance education librarian at the Minnesota School of Business St. Cloud Campus, where she marketed the enhanced distance education library services, which included a new library instruction policy for online students.

Bob Blanchard is an adult services librarian at Des Plaines, Illinois, Public Library. Among his passions are assistive technology services for people with disabilities and programming for older people. He has presented at the state library association and paraprofessional conferences and executed a successful grant project to raise awareness about help for people with visual disabilities.

Nancy Larson Bluemel, school library media specialist and former school district library coordinator, is now an adjunct instructor in graduate library education at Texas Woman's University in Denton, Texas, and an independent consultant. An advocate of promoting literacy and learning, she has presented at many state, national, and international library conferences.

Sian Brannon, a graduate of the University of North Texas, is an adult services librarian at Denton Public Library in Denton, Texas. A self-described "policy fiend," Brannon enjoys writing and enforcing policies. Her true library-related passions lie in collection development, statistics, and weeding. She has written articles for *Public Libraries*, *Texas Library Journal*, and *Library Worklife*.

Perry Bratcher began his professional career as a cataloger at Northern Kentucky University in 1983 and currently holds the position of library systems manager. He coauthored *Music Subject Headings* with Jennifer Smith, and has authored or given presentations on a variety topics ranging from merit guidelines for faculty to biometrics.

Anne Marie Candido is assistant to the dean, library editor, and subject librarian for literature and foreign languages at the University of Arkansas Libraries. Her publications include "Fabricating and Pre-Fabricating Language: Troubling Trends in Libraries," in the *Journal of Aca-*

demic Librarianship. She earned her PhD from Indiana University.

Sharon Carlson is the director of the Western Michigan University archives and regional history collections in Kalamazoo, Michigan. Her MLIS is from Wayne State University, and she holds a PhD in American history from Western Michigan University. She teaches courses on archival administration and research methods in archives and special collections.

Cathy Carpenter is assistant head of information services, maps and special formats and public policy librarian at Georgia Institute of Technology in Atlanta, Georgia. She spoke about her experiences organizing a campus voter registration drive at the 2005 American Library Association Conference program "Fostering Civic Engagement."

Jill S. Carpenter received her MLS at the University of Tennessee in Knoxville. Currently, she is the coordinator for Teen Services at Pikes Peak Library District, Colorado Springs, Colorado. She oversees the design/construction of the new East Teen Center as well as book talks, plans teen programming, and helps teens with homework projects.

Christen A. Caton, teen specialist for the Monument Branch of Pikes Peak Library District, Colorado Springs, Colorado, enjoys doing readers' advisory, introducing patrons to electronic resources, and considers booktalking her favorite part of her job. Caton also plans teen programming for her branch and is currently organizing a youth advisory council for the northern library branches.

Mary Beth Chambers is catalog/archives librarian and associate professor at the Kraemer Family Library at the University of Colorado at Colorado Springs. She has coauthored journal articles for *Serials Review, Library Hi Tech,* and *Colorado Libraries.*

Tamela N. Chambers is a children's librarian at the West Englewood Branch of the Chicago Public Library. Chambers holds dual master's degrees in early childhood education and library science and has worked with children and young adults in a variety of capacities for ten years. She lives in Chicago with her husband and three children.

Diane Colson is a youth services manager at the Alachua County Library District in Gainesville, Florida. She has reviewed books for *Voice of Youth Advocates* since 1999. Colson has served on YALSA's outstanding books for the college bound and popular paperbacks for young adults and is currently serving on the Alex Award committee.

Nancy Czech is a graduate student in the Wayne State University Library and Information Science Program in Detroit, Michigan. She is focusing on enhancing her information technology skills to prepare for the cyberlibrarian role and has been the research assistant for John. H. Heinrichs, assistant professor at Wayne State University.

Carolyn Davis is a specialist in development issues. The first Internet reference librarian at the Providence Athenaeum; past chair of the Resource Center, Peace Corps headquarters, Jamaica, as well as a facilitator of the Jamaica Coalition on Disability, Davis has 17 publications and presentations in the United States, Britain, Jamaica and Turkey.

Marcia B. Dinneen is an associate librarian at Bridgewater State College, in Bridgewater, Massachusetts. She is head of Reference Services and also teaches English classes at the college. Dinneen has a PhD in English literature and has published a number of articles for both scholarly journals and reference books.

Nicole C. Engard is Web manager at Jenkins Law Library in Philadelphia, Pennsylvania. In her position, she directs the development of the library Web site (www.jenkinslaw.org), intranet, and database systems. Nicole also writes about library-related technologies on her blog, what I Learned Today, at www.web2learning.net. In 2007, Nicole was named one of *Library Journal's*

Movers and Shakers.

Stephen Fesenmaier is a state data coordinator at the West Virginia Library Commission and a film columnist. He was awarded the West Virginia International Film Festival Lifetime Achievement Award in 1985. He was also a researcher for the films *Save and Burn* (2005), *Matewan* (1987), and *In Heaven There Is No Beer?* (1984).

Lisa A. Forrest is a senior assistant librarian for Buffalo State College in Buffalo, New York, and the founding member of the school's Rooftop Poetry Club. Lisa's work has appeared in a variety of publications, including *American Libraries, Buffalo News, eco-poetics,* and *WordWrights.* Her essays have been featured on *WBFO,* Buffalo's local National Public Radio station.

Travis Fristoe is a librarian with the Alachua County Library District in Gainesville, Florida, a book reviewer for *Library Journal* and *Maximum RocknRoll,* and a volunteer with the local Books to Prisoners program. In his spare time, he reads, gardens, fixes bicycles and studies the Choy Lay Fut style of martial arts.

Gwen Gregory is head of bibliographic services at the Tutt Library of Colorado College in Colorado Springs, Colorado. Her work has been published in journals, including *Information Today, American Libraries, Public Libraries,* and *Technical Services Quarterly.* She compiled and edited the book *The Successful Academic Librarian.*

Pamela Hayes-Bohanan is head of Library Instruction Services and a Spanish instructor at Bridgewater State College (BSC) in Bridgewater, Massachusetts, where she serves on the college's Core Curriculum Steering Committee. Prior to coming to BSC in 1997, Hayes-Bohanan was head of reference at the McAllen Memorial Library in McAllen, Texas.

John H. Heinrichs is an assistant professor at Wayne State University in the Library and Information Science Program in Detroit, Michigan. He received his PhD in manufacturing management from the Colleges of Business Administration and Engineering at the University of Toledo. His interests include utilization of systems for competitive advantage and data mining.

Merinda Kaye Hensley is the instructional services librarian at the University of Illinois at Urbana-Champaign. Her passion for cookbooks led her to create the online exhibit Communal Cuisine: Community Cookbooks 1870–1960, in order to reach interested culinary foodies across the country.

Robert P. Holley is a professor in the Library and Information Science Program at Wayne State University in Detroit, Michigan. An academic librarian for over 20 years, he teaches library management, collection development, grant proposal writing, and academic libraries. His current research interests are intellectual freedom, subject access to information, and the out-of-print book market.

Lee Johnson is a middle/high school librarian at San Antonio Christian Schools. She holds a master's degree in library and information science, specializing in youth librarianship from the University of North Texas at Denton. In addition to hosting the coffeehouse, she is passionate about encouraging kids to discover the joy of reading.

Jennifer Johnston received her MLIS from the University of North Texas. She has published numerous articles and reviews in publications such as *Library Journal* and *Multicultural Review* and is currently a librarian at Arrowstreet, an architectural firm in the Boston area. You can find publications, projects, and more on her Web site, www.jenjohnston.com.

Connie Lamb is the anthropology, ME studies, and women's studies librarian at the Lee Library, Brigham Young University. Connie was president of the Utah Library Association and received its Distinguished Service Award. She is active in several professional associations and has coedited two book-length bibliographies on Middle East women and Jewish fiction writers.

Jaina Lewis is the teen services coordinator at the Westport Public Library in Westport, Connecticut. When she told her Dad that she wanted to be a librarian, he asked, "Aren't you too loud?" She has learned to embrace this dichotomy. Outside of librarianship, Lewis enjoys bad karaoke, loud music, and vegetarian cooking.

Margaret Lincoln is a library media specialist at Lakeview High School in Battle Creek, Michigan. She is also a database trainer for the Library of Michigan and a contributor to professional publications. Lincoln is a Library of Congress American Memory Fellow and U.S. Holocaust Memorial Museum Teacher Fellow. She earned a doctorate in information sciences from the University of North Texas in 2006.

Mardi Mahaffy holds a master's of library science degree from Indiana University and serves as the humanities librarian at New Mexico State University in Las Cruces, New Mexico. Her research interests include the formation of collaborative partnerships between libraries and other university faculty or services. She has joined with coworkers in planning and executing successful library events.

Elizabeth Chadbourn McKee is assistant head of reference at the University of Arkansas Libraries and education reference librarian. She received her master's in library science from the University of Oklahoma. She has published in the field of information literacy and is interested in professor/librarian collaboration, general reference, and regional periodical indexing.

Susan Metcalf is currently the social sciences reference librarian at Western Carolina University. Previously she held a similar post at New Mexico State University and was involved in promoting *el Día de los Niños/Libros* there. She has also held positions in public and corporate libraries and has authored book chapters and articles.

Ivy Miller is a librarian at Wyoming Seminary Upper School in Kingston, Pennsylvania. Her specialties are young adult programming and young adult collection development. Miller has written and won dozens of grants to enhance young adult library services. She is also a reviewer of young adult books for *School Library Journal.*

Gabriel Morley is director of the five-branch Washington Parish Library System headquartered in Franklinton, Louisiana. Prior to earning his MLIS at the University of Southern Mississippi, Morley was a daily newspaper reporter and editor for seven years in Louisiana and Mississippi. He has published essays and reviews most recently in *Library Journal* and *Louisiana Libraries.*

Anita Rao Mysore is curriculum developer at the University of Arkansas Libraries. She received her PhD in curriculum and instruction from the University of Arkansas at Fayetteville. Her dissertation is titled, "Attitudes of Preservice Teachers Toward Issues in Multicultural Education." She is interested in preparing teachers for cultural and linguistic diversity.

Sarah Nelsen received her MLIS from San Jose State University and has worked at public libraries in San Jose and San Francisco, California, and assisted at the Fine Arts Museums of San Francisco library. She is a school corps librarian at Multnomah County Library in Portland, Oregon, and reference and instruction librarian at Portland Community College.

Pam Nutt is a media specialist at Moore Elementary School in Griffin, Georgia. She is also in her 12th year an elected school board member for Henry County. Nutt is currently working on her PhD in educational leadership and she completed her national boards in 2004.

Eileen O'Connell has been writing poems for more than 20 years. Her poetry has appeared in the *Rockhurst Review*, the *Sunday Suitor*, and *Other Voices*, and she was twice featured in the Albuquerque Tribune Poetry Contest. She is the general services librarian at the Taylor Ranch Library in Albuquerque, New Mexico.

Darby Orcutt, senior collection manager for humanities and social sciences, leads collections programs for North Carolina State University Libraries. A frequent reviewer for *CHOICE* and other publications, he regularly teaches religious studies, interdisciplinary honors, and library science. He holds an MS in library science and an MA in communication studies.

Victoria Lynn Packard is an assistant professor and government information/map/research and instruction librarian at Texas A&M University–Kingsville. She currently team teaches WebCT classes in world geography, GIS, and remote sensing. Presentations include international, federal, national and state conferences in the areas of geography, GIS, remote sensing, information technology, business, grants, and federal and state government information.

Kathy Piehl, a reference librarian at Minnesota State University, Mankato, manages the library's juvenile book collection and directs the Center for Children's and Young Adult Books. Kathy's reviews and articles have appeared in a variety of publications. She has served on the Minnesota Book Awards Advisory Committee and the Children's Literature Association's Phoenix Award Committee.

Ann Marlow Riedling, an associate professor at Mansfield University in Pennsylvania, has received two Fulbright Scholarships, serving in Bahrain, Yemen, Egypt and Oman. She has published ten textbooks and one trade book, has contributed to textbooks, and has written numerous articles, case studies, and columns. Riedling has presented locally, nationally and internationally regarding a number of library-related topics.

Sandra E. Riggs is an electronic resources librarian at Campbellsville University in Campbellsville, Kentucky. She is in the process of planning an information mastery course at Campbellsville University. In October 2006 she presented a session on "Pedagogical Planning for Information Mastery" at the Appalachian College Association Summit IX in Abingdon, Virginia.

Loriene Roy is a professor in the School of Information at the University of Texas at Austin. She is founder of If I Can Read, I Can Do Anything, a national reading club for Native Children and Honoring Generations, a graduate scholarship program for indigenous students. She is president (2007–2008) of the American Library Association.

Sara Ryan is a teen services specialist at Multnomah County Library in Portland, Oregon. Working with school librarians and other community partners is one of her favorite parts of her job. She is also the author of the young adult novels *Empress of the World* and *The Rules for Hearts*, both published by Viking.

Diane L. Schrecker, curriculum librarian and director of the Instructional Resource Center at Ashland University Library, Ashland, Ohio, is library and IRC Web master, authors two IRC blogs and coauthors Library Cloud, an academic library blog. A graduate of the University of Pittsburgh, Schrecker is an active member of ALAO, ACRL, and EBSS.

Irene Shown works at New Mexico State University Library in Las Cruces, New Mexico. She started in 1984 as a library assistant and is now a library specialist in Reference and Research Services. Her interests are library instruction and outreach, and she has a deep appreciation of issues facing non–English speaking users.

McKinley Sielaff is the government documents librarian at Colorado College. She has earned both an MLS and a master's in public administration, aiding her work in a variety of public, special, and academic libraries. After receiving tenure, she continues to share her knowledge in articles and presentations. An active reader, she participates in reading programs.

Judith A. Siess is the editor/publisher of the *One-Person Library* newsletter and was the first chair of the SOLO Librarians Division of the Special Libraries Association. She has written seven books, including *Out Front with Stephen Abram: A Guide for Information Leaders,* and *The New OPL Sourcebook: A Guide for Solo and Small Libraries.*

Paula M. Storm, a science and technology librarian at Eastern Michigan University in Ypsilanti, Michigan, has appeared in *Science & Technology Libraries, Journal of Educational Media and Library Sciences, Magazines for Libraries,* and *Choice.* She's interested in digitization of herbarium specimens, science information literacy, and engineering education.

Diana Brawley Sussman is the director of the Southern Illinois Talking Book Center in Carterville, Illinois, part of the Library of Congress's National Library Service for the Blind and Physically Handicapped. She has authored or coauthored articles in *Computers in Libraries, Library Hi Tech News* and the anthology *Revolting Librarians Redux,* among others.

Rhonda Harris Taylor, associate professor in the School of Library and Information Studies at the University of Oklahoma, began her career in librarianship as a paraprofessional in an urban public library. Other paraprofessional experiences were in academic library settings. She served for a decade as director of a small liberal arts, denominational library.

Russ Taylor has been supervisor of reference services at the L. Tom Perry Special Collections of Brigham Young University's Lee Library since 1999. Before that he spent 15 years as a corporate speechwriter. He has published articles, is working on a bibliographic book about Yellowstone Park, and is active in archival and library organizations.

Stephanie A. Thomas is a district/high school librarian for the Parkrose School District in Portland, Oregon, and she has been a high school and elementary librarian in Michigan and Oregon. Thomas is active in school library associations, presents workshops and contributes articles on the topics of emerging technologies and collaboration.

Elizabeth M. Timmins is the library director and children's programmer at the Muehl Public Library in Seymour, Wisconsin. She is a model in the Desperate Librarians calendar. She received the Advocate for all Children Award from the National At-Risk Education Network. She arranged for at-risk high school students to teach computers to elders at the library.

Alexandra (Alex) Tyle is the adult services director at the Homer Township Public Library located in Homer Glen, Illinois. She has spoken at various meetings and conference on topics such as teens, technology, and gaming. Tyle believes in the importance of encouraging teens to read, learn, and build new skill sets.

Susan Wakefield has a MLIS and has worked for academic and school libraries. She has 12 years of publishing experience with university presses in Minnesota, Utah and Ohio, as well as with a literary press. Her articles have appeared in *Library Journal* (online), *Information Outlook,* and *New Books for Young Readers.*

Mary A. Walker is head of the monographs cataloging and acquisitions unit at the University of Arkansas Libraries. She received her master's of science in information science from the University of North Texas. She has published on cataloging issues and has expertise in MARC record mapping and loading as well as acquisitions and cataloging management.

Rick Walter is an adult services librarian in Albuquerque, New Mexico, and vice president of the North American Jules Verne Society. He cotranslated and coedited (with Walter James Miller) the first English edition of Verne's *The Meteor Hunt* and scholarly editions of Verne's *20,000 Leagues under the Sea* and *The Mighty Orinoco*.

Lori Widzinski has an MLS and an MS and is head of computing and multimedia services at the Health Sciences Library, State University of New York at Buffalo. She is founder and editor of Educational Media Reviews Online (http://libweb.lib.buffalo.edu/emro/search.asp), as well as *MC Journal: The Journal of Academic Media Librarianship* and has authored numerous articles and reviews.

Thayla Wright has been employed at the Arthur Johnson Memorial Library in Raton, New Mexico, since 1993. In 1998 she became the library director. She has been published in *Today's Librarian* and served on the New Mexico State Library Board in 2002.

Kathryn Yelinek works as government documents coordinator at Bloomsburg University of Pennsylvania. Her essays have appeared in *Sacred Journey*, *flashquake*, and *Thereby Hangs a Tale*. Within library science, she has written for *College and Research Library News* and *PaLA Bulletin*. Her book, *The History of South Mountain Restoration Center*, was published in 2001.

Index